D0915625

Publications of the
MINNESOTA HISTORICAL SOCIETY

RUSSELL W. FRIDLEY
Editor and Director

JUNE DRENNING HOLMQUIST
Managing Editor

On Stone by W.L. Walton.

Hullmandel & Walton lithographers.

THE PILOT KNOB.

London: Richard Bentley, 1846.

A CANOE VOYAGE

UP THE

MINNAY SOTOR

WITH AN ACCOUNT OF
THE LEAD AND COPPER DEPOSITS IN WISCONSIN;
OF THE GOLD REGION IN THE CHEROKEE COUNTRY;
AND SKETCHES OF POPULAR MANNERS

By George W. Featherstonhaugh

Volume 2
REPRINT EDITION
MINNESOTA HISTORICAL SOCIETY   ST. PAUL
1970

THIS WORK WAS FIRST PUBLISHED BY RICHARD BENTLEY
OF LONDON, ENGLAND, IN 1847.

Library of Congress Catalog Card Number: 71-111618
Standard Book Number: 87351-057-7

A CANOE VOYAGE

UP THE

MINNAY SOTOR

WITH AN ACCOUNT OF
THE LEAD AND COPPER DEPOSITS IN WISCONSIN;
OF THE GOLD REGION IN THE CHEROKEE COUNTRY;
AND SKETCHES OF POPULAR MANNERS

By George W. Featherstonhaugh

Volume 2
REPRINT EDITION
MINNESOTA HISTORICAL SOCIETY   ST. PAUL
1970

THIS WORK WAS FIRST PUBLISHED BY RICHARD BENTLEY
OF LONDON, ENGLAND, IN 1847.

Library of Congress Catalog Card Number: 71-111618
Standard Book Number: 87351-057-7

CONTENTS - SECOND VOLUME

ILLUSTRATIONS

MAPS

A CANOE VOYAGE
UP THE
MINNAY SOTOR

A CANOE VOYAGE

TO THE

SOURCES OF THE MINNAY SOTOR.

CHAPTER XXXVII.

REACH FORT SNELLING.—HOSPITABLY RECEIVED BY THE COMMANDANT AND HIS LADY. — IMPORTANCE OF SOME KNOWLEDGE OF INDIAN TONGUES AND CUSTOMS TO A TRAVELLER.—OVERTAKEN BY WINTER.

October 13.—Anxious to reach Fort Snelling before the impending change should bring us snow, I had the camp struck at break of day, in the midst of the rain; and vigorously pursuing our way, we only stopped half an hour to breakfast, and getting our paddles in motion again passed the *Makato* about half an hour after noon: we found the water diminished in quantity, and the current comparatively gentle to what we experienced on our ascent of the St. Peter's; neither was the river, after passing the junction, much discoloured; tending, I think, to prove that its muddiness at other times commences near its sources, which, like those of all other streams, at this moment were very low. The afternoon was rather stormy, but we stuck to our paddles—except landing for five minutes to kill a couple of racoons

—and made a capital day's work of it, encamping
at sunset on a tolerably good place upon a narrow
willow ridge, with room only for my tent and one
fire, so that I was near enough to hear the conversation of the men, which amused me exceedingly.
The racoons they had killed were an old one and a
young one, and the old one was offered to me, because, I suppose, it was the largest; but old dog racoons being outrageously strong, I declined it. Had
they offered me the young one, I do not know but
I should have accepted it, as they are generally fat
and sweet; but as they did not think of doing so,
nothing was left to me but to examine their method
of cooking these animals. They first partially
eviscerated them, then singed the hair still more
imperfectly by drawing them a few times across the
fire. This done, they consigned them neck and
heels to their *pot au feu*, where pork was boiling
with three or four grouse, and as many wild ducks.
Such a mess I certainly never saw prepared before.
When all was ready, they began first with the soup,
for soup they will have if made with nothing but
salt pork : the pork, with some potatoes, were then
taken out, and soon devoured; last came the racoons, with the stiffest part of their fur on their
skin. Beaupré, who did the honours of the feast,
took the youngest and divided it betwixt Milor and
himself, leaving the dog for l'Amirant and the rest
of the men. Besides being intolerably strong, it
appeared, to judge from their grimaces, to be as
tough as a bull's hide; at every mouthful I heard
l'Amirant exclaim, " Sacre crapaud, comme il est
dur !" whilst Milor, who had a good share of dry

humour, said to him, " Tu ne devrais pas dénigrer ce pauvre animal, il doit être assez bon pour toi, puisque tu as voulu en régaler le Bourgeois avec." I then told them the story of a Yankee and an Indian, who had been hunting together, and at the close of the day had got nothing but a wild turkey and a carrion turkey-buzzard.* Having, when they separated at night, to go in different directions, the Yankee said to the Indian, " Well, we'll divide our sport ; you may take the turkey-buzzard, and I will take the turkey." Upon which the Indian said, " Kaween " (no), and gave a grunt of dissatisfaction. " Well then," continued Jonathan, "we'll take it t'other way ; I'll take the turkey, and you may take the turkey-buzzard." They all laughed at this, and said, " Les Bastonnois† sont fins comme le diable," which induced Milor to say, " Ils ne sont pas plus fins que vous autres, qui aviez bien soin de ne pas offrir le jeune chat à Monsieur."

October 14.—We had a stormy night, with loud thunder, vivid lightning, and heavy rains ; I sometimes thought the high wind would carry my tent away, and did not get much sleep. Being convinced that our late fine weather was exhausted, and that we had nothing to look to but frost and snow, I had the encampment struck before sunrise, and in an hour we reached Traverse de Sioux, where I found the baggage we had sent from Lac qui parle in the *charette.* M. Le Blanc's squaw made me a present of

---

* This bird, which resembles a turkey, is a vulture, and feeding upon the most offensive carrion, is, of course, not eatable.

† The Canadians call the Americans " Bastonnois," Boston being in old times more known to them than the other colonies.

a fawn-coloured musk-rat's skin, which is considered a rarity, and having bartered some things she was in want of for pipes and Indian embroidery, and made a hasty breakfast, we pushed on, and at 10 a.m. passed the Chagnkeuta or Bois Franc river, and paddling the whole day amidst a steady and penetrating rain, reached one of our encampments half an hour before sunset, where building a couple of stout fires, I hastened to put dry clothes on, and having made a comfortable meal, lay down to rest.

October 15.—Every thing was in the canoe before sunrise, and we resumed our paddles on a cloudy, damp morning, but warm : plying them at the rate of about two leagues an hour, I could calculate almost exactly at what time we should pass any particular places I had noticed on coming up : and this I did in reference to the encampment, where we had left our tea-kettle, &c. on the 19th of the preceding month. We found them all there waiting for us, as many other things which we left in this vast wilderness are no doubt doing to this day. We stopped to breakfast at Le Grand Grés, which we had done on the 18th ult., and starting again in an hour and driving our paddles vigorously to reach Fort Snelling at night, we passed in succession Carver's River, the village of Sixes, and other localities which have been noted, but the rain began to fall in such torrents, and the night set in so dark and stormy, that it became at length impossible to see any thing before us, and regretting now that we had not encamped before sunset, we put ashore at random, a little below Penichon's village, and having succeeded with the greatest difficulty in getting the tent up, we found ourselves at length checkmated. The night was as black as pitch, not a bit of wood was to be had, and the wind was so high that it was not at all an unlikely thing for the tent, which was not very well secured, to be blown away. As we could have no fire, either to cook or dry our clothes, I laid myself down on some skins, contenting myself with dry biscuit. What the men did I knew not, for I never pretended to look out of the tent; I could sometimes hear their voices, laid down to leeward of it, munching biscuits I dare say half the night, and smoking at the same time. It was out of the question taking them into the tent; they would have been wretched without their pipes, and their pipes would have made me equally so, so that we had nothing to do but exercise our patience, and be thankful that matters were no worse.

October 16.—The storm lasted almost the whole night, and having got very little sleep, I was glad to embark again as soon as ever we could see our way on the river; keeping ourselves warm with vigorous paddling, in an hour and a half we came in sight of Fort Snelling, and soon after reached the landing-place. Sending my luggage up to the Commandant's, I left the tent for the men, that they might make themselves comfortable after being wet so long, and walked up the hill to the garrison, where I was cordially received by Major Bliss and his lady, who presented me immediately with the most refreshing of all imaginable comforts, agreeable letters from my family. I was soon installed in a pleasant and commodious room, and having made

my toilette, partook of an excellent breakfast. I
had been absent exactly a month, having left the
fort on the 17th September. The remainder of the
day I asked permission to have to myself; so, having
bundled off my linen to one of the soldiers' wives to
be washed, I sat down by a comfortable wood fire,
and after transcribing my notes, writing letters, and
packing up my shells, minerals, &c., I sent for Milor,
and went over my Nahcotah vocabulary and phrases
with him, correcting what I had not exactly compre-
hended, and noting, according to my own system of
accentuation for Indian languages, the proper pronunciation, that I might be at no loss to remember
it when I had left the country; for vocabularies,
without the true pronunciation, are very imperfect
guides in comparing one Indian language with
another, and often mislead those philologists who
engage in the delicate task of establishing the just
affinity between Indian dialects. Travellers who are
careless in fixing the true pronunciation, often put
down words in such a form that the true roots from
whence words are derived are frequently lost sight
of.

During the time that Milor had remained with me,
I had compiled an immense number of phrases
which he translated into the Nahcotah, relating to
every possible situation in which a traveller would
find himself, consisting of a particular question, with
the answers that might be given to it. These questions Milor taught me to pronounce perfectly, so that
he often said, "Monsieur, vous parlez Sioux tout
aussi bien que moi." " Yes Milor," I used to answer,
" but I only know what you have taught me, and if

you were to ask me questions that are not down in my book, I should often not be able to answer them." I now told him to come to me at the fort twice a day, once in the morning and once in the evening, to teach me other phrases, which I would write down. Upon this, he replied, with an air of an ancien emigré, " Monsieur, on me dit que vous allez mettre tout cela dans un livre, et tout ce que je desire est que vous me ferez l'honneur de mettre le nom de Milor dedans." And this I certainly did promise him, if ever I should publish a narrative of this excursion.

This plan of having a list of questions and answers I had found very useful, and would recommend it to all travellers in Indian countries. Frequently, when in advance of my party—which I often was when on horseback—I met families on the prairies, which gave me favourable opportunities of trying Milor's lessons. Once I fell in with a party, with their wives and horses, trailing the wigwam poles, with several young children tied upon them, and, assuming the confidence of an old trader, I rode up to them and said, " *Tuchtáy chankoo mindáy eatáhtĕnkah*" (which is the way to Big Stone Lake?) Immediately all the women broke out with different questions, many of which I did not comprehend ; some asking me if I was going to the *weetah,* or island, others if I was going to another part of the lake. The fact was, that I did not want to know the way to any particular part of the lake; I only wished to know if they understood me, and was exceedingly pleased to find I had got an intelligible pronunciation. The question, however, would not

have been an intelligent one in the Indian sense, if
I had been in want of geographical information. Big
Stone Lake is not far short of forty miles long, and
the Indians frequent particular parts of it, either
because they have settlements there—as upon the
islands—or for particular purposes. The questions
they expect therefore to be asked, are purely topical
ones, as they suppose you have some reason for going
to one of the places they frequent. To ask the way to
a great lake, when you are in its neighbourhood, is
somewhat to stultify yourself in the eyes of the
Indian, and is something like a traveller in England
asking the road to a county, and not to some village or town within it. I found these things out
gradually.

Upon another occasion I asked some natives how
far it was to any water, when they immediately
answered, that I should meet with *minnay* or water
when the sun would be in that part of the sky to
which they pointed. This I understood perfectly,
but as I was coming away, one of them made me a
speech which broke me down completely, repeating
two or three times over the word *kahkindoozah*, of
the meaning of which I was quite ignorant. As soon
as I met Milor I asked him what that word meant,
and he said they used it with *minnay*, to signify
" running-water," in contradistinction to stagnant
water. And no doubt the fact was that these Indians
hearing me ask for water, without saying what I
wanted it for, had directed me to a swamp where
there was a stagnant pond, but lest I might want it
to drink, had obligingly told me there was *minnay
kahkindoozah*, or running-water, in another place.

To converse intelligently with these untutored
people, it is evidently necessary to understand something of their manners and customs.   As to the
vocabularies which are current out of the Indian
country, they are mere playthings for etymologists,
and have been of very little use to me in my Indian
wanderings.

In the evening I joined the cheerful meal of
Mrs. B., which was very good and nice.   The only
child of these excellent people, was, as has been
stated, a fine boy, now growing too old to remain at
this garrison, where there was not much improvement to be had.   In the evening I strongly advised
the major to send him to some respectable school in
the United States, a movement he told me he had
long seen the necessity of, but that the trial would
be a great one, both to him and his wife.   It was
evident that the moment of separation would be a
particularly cruel one to her, for she had little or no
society in the garrison, the pious preaching L.
having broken up the very limited social circle there
with his stupid fanatical practices.   This evening
I had the luxury of a bed for the first time
since I left Navarino, the 21st of August, and a
very nice one it was, owing to the great kindness of
Mrs. B.

October 17.—After an excellent night's rest, and
very pleasant breakfast, I went with two officers of
the fort to visit some Nahcotah lodges, at a short
distance, where we found some young Indian women
working very neatly on deer-skins; from thence I paid
a visit to a Mr. Baker, an intelligent trader, who
resided several years in the Indian country.   Mr.

and Mrs. Tagliaferro having invited me to dinner,
I availed myself of their kindness, and in the evening was taken to the house of a Mr. and Mrs. Mirie,
who kept a kind of suttler's store for the garrison.
I had now made the tour of all the society of the
place, except the religious party. I found they did
not mix with the others, and that, instead of loving
their neighbours and fellow-creatures in this remote
situation, they lived as if their doctrines and practices had taught them to hate and avoid all who
were not as extravagant as themselves. The leading
person of the party was the Major L. I have before
alluded to, a weak man in his intellect, and shabby,
penurious, and covetous in his actions, using fanati-
cism as a cover to his want of ordinary merit. He
had not even the decency to call upon me.

October 18.—The next day, after breakfasting with
the Commandant and his lady, I rode out to a pretty
sheet of water called Lake Calhoun, about eight
miles across the prairie, and four miles from the
Falls of St. Anthony. This very pellucid body of
water is about three miles in circumference, and is
named after that distinguished statesman, Mr. Calhoun, of South Carolina. There is an Indian village
near it, consisting of numerous Indians belonging to
various bands. Two brothers named Pond, who
were Connecticut farmers, had travelled to this distant part of the continent, with the philanthropic intention of being useful to the Indians, and especially
of teaching them to raise maize and pulse. To this
benevolent work they had voluntarily devoted themselves, and carrying out their intentions at their own
expense, had neither sought nor received assistance

from any religious societies or individuals whatever.
From about thirty acres of land they had harvested
about 800 bushels of maize the present season, all of
which they had put into *caches*. When I visited
the place the Indians were out trapping musk-rats,
and the elder Pond had accompanied them with the
view to learn their language and customs more
effectually. The spectacle this establishment afforded
me gave me a great deal of pleasure, and I was
happy to express to the brother I found there,
my sincere admiration of their rare benevolence,
and of the ability they had evinced in their generous
enterprise.

From Lake Calhoun, I ride to another pretty
sheet of water almost circular, called Lake Harriet,
equally pellucid with the other. Its shores were
perfectly surrounded by woods; and a missionary
named Stevens had erected a small house in a beautiful grove near to the lake.   The situation was
chosen with great judgment, and I could not but
admire the taste of this gentleman, who had not
only built a pretty tenement near a pretty lake, but
had also put a very handsome young wife in it, and
a very attractive niece only sixteen years old.
Several healthy young children were running about
of all sizes, and the pretty mama had a baby only
three weeks old in her arms.   He told me that he
proposed to " *christianize*" all the Indians, and to
establish a village of them near to his house, and I
learnt afterwards that his handsome niece was in
the way of christianizing one of the officers of the
garrison.   Having passed a very pleasant day, I
returned to take my evening meal at the Comman-

dant's, with whom, after supper, I had a long conversation, the result of which was, that his son John should accompany me back to the United States for the purpose of receiving a proper education.

October 19.—This was a very rainy day, and I kept the house, packing all my shells and minerals into boxes, preparatory to my departure. Milor came and passed a great part of the day with me, expressing great sorrow that he was to separate from me. I felt also regret at the prospect of parting with this worthy man. Poor Mrs. B. prepared with an aching heart for the sad separation from her dear boy. I had announced my departure for the succeeding day, if the weather should clear up, and there was a good deal of bustle amongst us all.

October 20.—On rising this morning, expecting to start, I found, on looking out of the window, that it had been snowing all night; soon after, one of the men came to inform me that it was a hard frost, and that ice had formed on the edge of the river. Winter then had overtaken us, for on going out I found it bitterly cold and inclement, too much so to depart. This was joyful news to the Commandant's family; so leaving them to enjoy the society of their son, I ordered out the canoe and crossed the St. Peter's, to Mr. Sibley's, to ask him if he had any commissions for me to execute at Prairie du Chien. Milor returned with me to the fort, where, after our usual conversations about the Nahcotahs and their language, we walked over to Mr. Baker's, to converse with a person named Slit, whom Milor said knew the Indian country perfectly well. Mr. Slit informed me, that he had been many years in the Hudson's Bay Company's service, and had traversed a great part of the country which I had visited. He informed me, that where the Côteau de Prairie terminates near the Shayanne, the country becomes flat to Turtle River, near to which the Pembinaw hills—which may be considered a continuation of the Côteau—begin. These continue beyond the Assiniboin River, and die away about Flat Lake, which is about seventy miles from Lake Winnepeg. Coal is said to be found a little south of Pembinaw, according to the report of several persons who had seen it; shale and fire-clay, resembling those of the coal district near Glasgow—with which he was acquainted—he had seen himself. Mr. Moore had previously informed me that he had found coal in the neighbourhood of Lake Travers, but I had thought it probable that this was lignite, great quantities of which are found in some parts of the banks of the Missouri. Still, as there are salt springs east of the Pembinaw Hills, and many of the small lakes in that part of the country are briny, it may be that coal exists, for salt and coal are very frequently associated in North America. Mr. Slit also said, that the charrettes went from the Grizzly Bears' Den to *Minday Wakon*—which the voyageurs have chosen to call Lac du Diable, instead of Great Spirit Lake—in five days of thirty miles each. As to the extent of the Côteau de Prairie to the south, all the persons who have seen that part of the country, and with whom I have conversed, agree that it terminates near the sources of the Makato, the south-west branches of which river rise near

those of the De Moine, the land in that neighbourhood being all well wooded and fertile.

October 21.—The snow-storm continued, with
very inclement weather. A fortnight ago I was on
the Côteau deliberating whether to advance or retreat.
No doubt the winter had set in there, and, considering all the chances, I did not regret the determination I took to return. Milor came and gave me his
last lesson in Nahcotah, and, besides very liberal
wages for his services, I gratified him with several
things that were valuable to him in that distant
part of the world. Having determined to depart
to-morrow, I took leave of my acquaintances here,
and after the usual evening's repast with the worthy
Major and his lady, retired to my room.

CHAPTER XXXVIII.

LEAVE THE FORT. — THERMOMETER AT ZERO. — NUMEROUS SWANS ON
LAKE PEPIN. — REACH PRAIRIE DU CHIEN. — A TOBACCO VOLCANO. —
MASSACRE OF PEEAY MOSHKY AND HIS BAND. — PLEASING STORY OF
AN OJIBWAY AND HIS CHILD.

October 22.—This morning when I rose, the thermometer was down to zero of Fahrenheit, the whole
country covered with a deep snow, and the weather
bitterly cold. Having sent a messenger to the men
to have the canoe in readiness for my embarkation in
an hour, I went to a rather melancholy breakfast.
The moment had at length arrived when my kind
friends were about to lose the society of their only
child, whom they loved so much. He was an affectionate and amiable youth, and they looked forward
with dismay to the dreary winter they would have
to pass without their dear child. To soothe the
unhappy mother, I promised her repeatedly to be
careful of her boy, and to take a strong interest in
his welfare, but she appeared sensible to nothing but
the agony of the moment. The Major concealed
his emotions better, but was very much affected.
At length the sad moment for the last embrace
came, and, taking the little boy from them, I shook
hands most cordially with each, expressing the strong
sense I should always entertain of their kind hospitality. I also insisted upon the Major's remaining
with his wife, but as she preferred that he should

go down to the canoe to see their son depart, we
left the house, all the officers of the garrison accom-
panying us down the hill. The canoe was ready,
and giving the little boy a comfortable berth in it
close to myself, and wrapping him well up, I made
my last bow to the company, and pushed off from
Fort Snelling about a quarter before 10 a. m.

Passing round by the Cut, I called upon Mr.
Sibley, and thanked him for his many attentions,
especially for having selected Milor to accompany
me. Poor old Milor was sorry to lose me. I had
been kind to him, and had made him rather a man
of consequence. He was the last person I shook
hands with, and as the canoe was leaving the bank,
he said with earnestness, " Je suis sûr que Monsieur
mettra mon nom dans son livre !"

Once more launched upon *la bonne aventure*, we
paddled along with vigour, and about noon reached
the village of Le Petit Corbeau, and at half-past
three passed the mouth of the Ste. Croix. By this
time the weather had become piercing cold, and my
feet were so benumbed as to be insensible; it was
a very difficult thing to keep my young charge
warm; the poor little fellow chattered with cold,
and, afraid of injuring him, I stopped rather earlier
than usual to encamp, at a well-wooded place about
forty miles from the fort, the current having helped
us along excellently well. A good fire and a warm
cup of tea soon restored us all, and, taking possession once more of my comfortable tent, I covered
the young lad well up with blankets and bear-skins,
of which I had a great quantity. He was highly

delighted at the idea of sleeping on the ground in a tent, in that wild sort of way.

October 23.—The intense cold prevented my sleeping, for I found it impossible to keep my feet warm. When daylight broke, I found the boy, however, had made but one nap of it, such is the advantage of a young circulation of the blood. Rousing him, I gave him, I rather think, the first lesson he ever received in the important art of taking care of and providing for himself, telling him to take a tin basin and follow me to the river's side to wash himself. When it was over I asked him if it were not pleasanter and better to help himself than to depend upon others. " If you had waited until one of the men had brought you water," I remarked, " he would very probably have brought you dirty water, for he would have dipped the basin into the first mud-hole he found : whereas, when you go to the river side, as you have now done, you can select a clean place, and dip it up in a cup, and fill your basin, as you have done." The boy was pleased with having been of some use to himself, and said he would inform his mother of it when he wrote. " Yes, my lad," I said, " but I will teach you to make your own breakfast, and you can tell her that also." Accordingly, I shewed him how to fry ham and potatoes, when we stopped to breakfast, and he was perfectly delighted.

I had long known that to get through the world comfortably, it was important—although not always necessary—to be able and willing to do every thing for one's self: but in North America, to a traveller in Indian districts, where he is often abandoned to

his own resources, it is indispensably necessary to
know how to do every thing that is useful, and I
thought I might be rendering this fine boy a service
in giving him a few useful lessons of this kind.

Having got under weigh, we passed the mouth of
Cannon River, in the neighbourhood of which were
several lodges with some Indians, one of whom
called us to the shore under pretence of having some
venison; but when we reached it, he asked me for
some pork and biscuit, and said they had no venison.
I told him that good Indians did not want to tell
lies; that if he wanted food, and had asked me
for it, I would have given him some; but as he had
begun by telling me he had venison, he might eat
that until he procured something else. This was a
small band of those needy Indians that are always
to be found in the vicinity of white people.

We landed to breakfast opposite Red Wing's
village, and all did justice to our repast, especially
young Bliss, who seemed to be very much taken
with his own cooking, and was sharp enough after
making twenty miles before breakfast, with the
thermometer at zero. We re-embarked soon after
eleven a.m., and passed Le Grange, an outlier on
the right bank of the Mississippi, about three hundred
feet high, which presented a good section of the
sandstone and limestone.

About a quarter past twelve we suddenly came
upon Lake Pepin, and the weather having improved
into a fine sunny morning, the spectacle which
presented itself was as rare and beautiful as any
I had seen the whole summer. Upon the smooth
and glassy surface of the lake hundreds upon hun-

dreds of noble swans were floating with their cygnets, looking at a distance like boats under sail.
The cygnets were still of a dull yellow colour, and all
the birds were very shy. It made a beautiful picture,
and, after contemplating it awhile, we again plied
our paddles, and half an hour before sunset stopped
on the left bank of the lake, about eight miles from
its mouth, and encamped for the night on the beach.
We found the ground but slightly covered with
snow here, whence I concluded that we should soon
leave it behind us.

October 24.—During the night we were continually
serenaded by gangs of wolves, howling about our
neighbourhood, attracted, no doubt, by the smell of
the food in our camp. It was a cloudy and harsh
morning, with an east wind ; and, after a couple of
hours' work, we got out of the lake, passing Wáh-
jústahcháy's house, and stopped to breakfast in some
high grass on the right bank. Starting again, we
passed Rivière au Bœuf, on the left bank, its mouth
being indicated by a wide chasm in the line of the
shore. About twelve, we landed at the Cedar
Prairie, where Carver's fortifications are, which I
had examined on the 8th of September. Being
curious to examine them a little further, I walked
round them, a circuit of about four miles, and ascertained that they do not come to the river, some
bottom land intercepting them. The two excavations at the north end are the most regular and
artificial-looking. The ground at the south is much
thrown up, and grown over with short trees ; the
high mounds are all hollow inside. But every thing
connected with them is so complicated and irregular,

in consequence of the sand blown upon them, that it is evident that the whole has been greatly modified by the wind, if not entirely caused by it. If the work has been done by man, it may be asked why so sandy a soil has been chosen, when it must have been evident to those who constructed them, that the mounds were liable to be shifted about by the wind. On the other hand, it may be asked of those who attribute them to the wind, why this part of the prairie only has been disturbed? If they are nothing but sand-hills, why do not we find others making at this time in the same neighbourhood? There is much to be said on both sides of the question. Leaving this place, we proceeded on our course, passing those curious castellated-looking bluffs, separated from each other by the well-wooded coulées which I had observed when coming up, and which are so characteristic of this river. A little before sunset we reached an island opposite to Wabeshaw's Prairie, and here we encamped for the night, making a couple of rousing fires and a hearty meal to close the day.

October 25.—We got off in the grey of the morning, with a raw east wind, and in a short time passed *Minnay-chonkah*, or Trombalo, and stopped to breakfast on a clean sand island, where, having warmed ourselves with a comfortable meal, we resumed our voyage; and, passing Prairie la Crosse and Bad-axe River, as we thought, at three p.m., the men, cheered with the prospect of soon meeting their acquaintances at Prairie du Chien— the distance being only eighteen leagues—got into a lively singing humour, marking the time well with

their paddles: in the evening we came up with a
nice clean little island, and, seeing that it would
afford us a comfortable bivouac, I made the signal,
and, taking possession, we proceeded to establish
our encampment.

October 26.—After a tolerable night's rèst, I
roused the men as soon as any thing was visible, and
embarking in a thick fog, we went cautiously along,
on account of the great number of small islands;
when, to our surprise, we found ourselves abreast of
the mouth of Bad-axe, which we supposed ourselves
to have passed yesterday, having again mistaken its
position, owing, no doubt, to the intricacy of the
channel amongst the islands.   We landed about
nine at one of these, from whence we saw some
smoke proceeding, and found a family of *Howchungerahs* there.   These Winnebagoes, notwithstanding the numerous affinities of their dialect
with that of the Nahcotahs, are very different from
them, both in their dress and manners.   Although
of the same stock, they probably have been separated
from them a long time.   They did not understand
me when I spoke Sioux to them, and their strong
guttural and nasal twang was as unintelligible to
myself.   I felt some regret at having got out of the
district of the Nahcotahs; it had been a great
amusement to me to converse with them, and the
chance of making further progress in their language
was now at an end.

On leaving this place we soon got into the main
channel of the river, which crossed the valley in a
diagonal line about three miles long, to the right
bank of the Mississippi.   About one p.m. the sun

broke out beautifully for the first time in three days. We soon passed those rocks where rude figures of animals have been painted by the Indians. About three, the fog made a singularly curious appearance on the river, the heat of the sun having so attenuated it that it was as thin as gauze, waving about and assuming all sorts of forms, as if it was struggling between two forces, the attraction of the water and that of the sun. An immense number of water-spiders, suspended from their gossamer textures, were floating about in this airy fog. We reached Prairie du Chien at four p.m., and brought up the canoe opposite to Monsieur Rolette's, who had engaged me to be his guest on my return. Here a tolerable room was assigned to me, of which I was to have the exclusive possession—a most invaluable privilege—and having removed my luggage there, I hastened to the post-office, where I had the satisfaction of finding agreeable letters from my family.

My troubles began as soon as I had reached the verge of civilization, and before I went to sleep I had occasion to regret that I had accepted M. Rolette's invitation; a more vivacious and good-tempered person than himself I never had certainly met with, but I soon discovered that I should not enjoy a moment's comfort whilst I remained under his roof. It is rather a remarkable thing, that although I have been in the habit of making long voyages at sea from my youth upwards, and have resided more or less for forty years in countries where the pure atmosphere of nature is incessantly tormented by tobacco-smokers, I am never an instant at sea without being sea-sick, nor

capable of passing a man with a pipe or cigar in his
mouth without wishing him, for the moment, at the
bottom of Mongibello, to try how he likes to be
annoyed in the same manner with an atmosphere of
sulphur, which it would be my consolation to prefer
—in an extreme case—to an atmosphere of tobacco.
Nothing would frighten me more than to apprehend
an eternity of tobacco-smoke.

I had observed, when I first knew M. Rolette,
that he never was without a cigar in his mouth, but
I had forgotten this habit of his when I arrived.
On returning with my letters, I at once became
aware of the dilemma I was in. As soon as his
daughter—a tolerably well educated half-breed—
had given me a cup of tea, he commenced his vol-
canic operations, telling me at the same time an
endless number of old Indian stories. He smoked
at least twenty cigars in the course of the evening,
and at length, having become perfectly desolated with
a headache, I told him I was unwell, and would go to
bed. Taking a candle, I went to my room, and was
preparing to get into bed, when in he walked, with
a fresh cigar in his mouth, saying " Je ne dis pas
excusez mon tabac, parce que vous êtes, comme moi,
ancien voyageur, mais prenez ce cigar et fumez, et
croyez moi qu'il n'y a rien qui chassera votre mi-
graine comme cela." Then down he sat on the bed,
and began a story about the Assiniboins. Driven
to despair, I got into bed, and extinguishing the
light, begged his pardon for leaving him in the dark,
adding that I could not fall asleep if there was a
light in the room. He now groped his way down
stairs, and glad I was to get rid of him.

I had succeeded in getting asleep, when a tremendous thunderstorm, with heavy rain, awoke me, and I discovered that the rain came pouring through the ceiling into my bed, which was in a corner, and that the pillow and the bed-clothes were very wet. How I regretted the want of my comfortable tent! I had now to drag the bed in the dark to the middle of the room, and place a bear-skin under me, to prevent my catching cold.

October 27.—Fortunately I got asleep again, and awaking early in the morning, went down stairs, found some fire-wood, and returning to my room, lighted a fire and dried my clothes and papers upon which the rain had fallen. At breakfast, the good-natured Rolette expressed a great deal of sorrow at the inconvenience I had suffered during the night, always consoling me by saying, that as I was an " ancien voyageur," I of course did not mind it. I had the pleasure of dining to-day with the estimable Colonel Taylor, the commandant, whose amiable character has been before mentioned. He had seen a great deal of frontier service, and his conversation was very interesting. On reaching my quarters late in the evening, I found Rolette waiting for me with another batch of stories and cigars, and unable to escape, I was seized with another raging headache, and at length got away from him, every thing around stinking with the poisonous plant which I never was and never shall be able to endure.

October 28.—I rose unrefreshed and perplexed what to do, whether to stay and nose the tobacco until I was ready to depart, or leave Rolette's. Know-

ing that if I were to do so, it would give him a great
deal of vexation, I determined to bear with it awhile,
and implore Miss Rolette to interfere in my favour
with her father, which she afterwards did, so as to
secure me an immunity from it in my bedroom.
Here then I intrenched myself, brought up my notes
and worked a little at my sketches. The day was
very rainy, but I found a dry corner in the room,
and both father and daughter vied with each other
in providing me with every thing I was in want of.
It is really wonderful how some people who are
naturally amiable can resolve to make themselves
so disagreeable. Mr. Douceman was kind enough to
recommend a clever squaw to me for the purpose of
garnishing a handsome white skin dress I had
brought from the upper country, the companion of
a handsome suit I had before caused to be made by
a very distinguished Indian female, for a charming
lady friend in Sussex. That was finished in the
Nahcotah fashion, this was to be executed in the
Menominny style.

To-day I dined with Rolette and his daughter; he
produced some very fair claret and champagne, and
was kind enough to abstain from smoking, but, said
he, "Puisqu'il ne faut pas fumer, il faut boire."
Observing that I did not empty my glass as rapidly
as he did his own, he would say "Mais comment, un
ancien voyageur comme vous!" So that to keep the
tobacco out of the room, I was obliged to encourage
the circulation of the wine. We had a long crack
of it, and some of his Indian adventures were very
curious.

There had been a furious massacre in the neigh-

bourhood some time ago of some Sauks, one of
whom, named *Peeaymóshky*, the " man who shifts
his camp," was a great friend of Rolette's. *Shúnkahskah*, the " white dog," surprised him and his friends,
and murdered them whilst the treaty of Prairie du
Chien was in progress in 1830. Rolette being asleep
in his house, in a room on the ground-floor, was
awaked by a noise at the window; jumping up he
threw it open, and had scarce time to ask what was
the matter, when something wet and soft was drawn
across his face with a smart slap, and he heard
Shúnkahskah's voice say, " There's your friend
Peeaymóshky." It was in fact the bloody scalp of that
chief, which, after murdering him in a small island
where the Sauks thought themselves secure, they had
torn from his skull, and then hastened to Prairie du
Chien to pay Rolette that extraordinary visit.
Rolette afterwards met *Shúnkahskah*, and purchased
of him the war-club with which he had despatched
the chief, and having it by him at the time of my
visit made me a present of it.   *Peeaymóshky*
was a warrior of established reputation for bravery,
and *Shúnkahskah* paid him the greatest compli-
ment he could, after killing him, *by boiling his heart
and eating it.*

A more pleasing story than this was told me by
Rolette, of an Ojibway and his child. *Elazéepah*,
a *Musquawkée* or Fox Indian, being in ambush with
his party, crept to an Ojibway lodge at dusk, seized
a little girl of five years old, and escaped with her.
The mother, who was in the lodge, heard the child
cry, "Hinnah, hinnah! attáy, attáy! wandéktáydóh!"
(Mother, mother! father, father! they are carrying

me away !) The father arriving at his lodge at night, and learning the rape of his child, immediately pursued the party, tracking them by moonlight. Tracing their footsteps with unerring sagacity, he reached their lair when they were all fast asleep, and, stealing upon them, slew the whole party, four in number, and returned to his lodge with his child on his back, and the Indian's head in his hand that had carried her off.

CHAPTER XXXIX.

October 29.—This day was appointed for my departure, and whilst I despatched some persons to
collect my men, almost all of whom were the worse
for drinking, I called upon Colonel Taylor to bid
him adieu. I found him exceedingly distressed by
an account he had received the preceding night of
the death of his favourite daughter. She had been
much beloved by him, had married without his
consent, and he had not been reconciled to her since.
Her fault was now expiated and forgotten, and he
could think of nothing but his affection for her.
I shook hands with him silently and left him, much
affected myself by the situation of so respectable a
gentleman.

On reaching Rolette again, I found a friend
of his there, a M. Dubois, and his niece, waiting
to know if I would give them a passage in
my canoe to Du Buques. This was not very convenient; we had many heavy packages in it, and
they were apparently not very prepossessing people,
encumbered with some luggage. I told Rolette
we should be overladen, and some accident might
happen; but the party hung about the canoe, and
so much was said by Rolette and his daughter, that,
to avoid the appearance of being disobliging to those

who had been so hospitable to me, I told Beaupré
to see if it was possible to find room in the canoe.
They immediately took this as a permission, and
stepped into it; and as the matter had now gone too
far, I pushed off with the gunwale within two inches
of the water, and half of the crew stupidly drunk.
There was, however, but little wind, and we soon
became accustomed to our too-crowded situation.
M. Dubois, like all the rest of these people, was an
ancien voyageur; his niece was a married woman,
evidently with a dash of Indian blood in her veins,
very taciturn, and with no pretensions to any kind
of beauty but *la beauté du diable,* not being more
than eighteen years old.

We passed Turkey River between four and five
p.m., and landed on the beach for the night, a little
below Cassville, a new settlement lately established
on the left bank, at the foot of the Bluffs. We had
found very few islands in the Mississippi betwixt
Prairie du Chien and this place, the river, with few
exceptions, filling the whole valley, the cause of
which I have previously explained. The evening
closed in singularly cold, the thermometer stood at
14° Fahrenheit, and the air had a stinging quality
in it as if the temperature had been below zero.
The men built up rousing fires, and laid in a great
provision of wood for the night. Whilst supper
was preparing, I attempted to bring up my notes in
the tent, but it was too cold to write, so I took to
considering the way in which I should sleep my
guests, a rather puzzling affair, since it was impossible to let the young lady sleep out of doors upon

such a bitter night, and I had no other place to put her in but my own tent. M. Dubois, her uncle, like his friend Rolette, was unhappy when he had not a pipe in his mouth, and had done nothing but smoke ever since we landed. He would scarcely desist even when we took our evening meal, although I had told him twice what violent headaches it gave me. The moment we rose, not from table, but from the ground, he commenced smoking again at my fire, so that it was exceedingly unpleasant to me. To have had such a stinkabus in the tent with me all night was not to be thought of for a moment, so, determining to revenge myself in his person upon the whole Nicotian race, I decreed at once that he should sleep *al fresco.*

The question now was, what to do with Madame. Her uncle had brought no bed or mattress of any kind with him, only a single blanket for each of them, and it was very clear that I should have to provide her, at least, with covering of some sort to keep her alive all night. My young friend John was not of an age to turn his attention much to things of this kind, and very wisely laid himself down immediately after supper, and made himself as comfortable as he could. My mattress was then laid in the accustomed place, her blanket was spread near to it upon a piece of canvass, and two of my own, which, when doubled, were barely sufficient to keep me warm on such a very severe night, were opened and spread over the whole. It struck me that it looked very like an *affaire de ménage,* but really I thought of nothing but keeping the poor creature alive till morning, and that at the expense of my own comfort. Nothing makes a man more selfish than the necessity of preserving some warmth in himself during such bitter weather, even if others are to suffer; but when a woman is in the case, the sacrifice is less painful, and I certainly would have passed the night by the fire if the thermometer had not fallen to zero, and I had not been sure of finding M. Dubois' tobacco-smoke there.

Meantime, whilst these arrangements were making, Monsieur Dubois and the lady were standing near the fire, conjecturing, no doubt, as to how and where they were to pass the night, and seeing me leave the tent and approach them, looked anxiously for some announcement of the arrangements that were to be made. Monsieur was standing with his back to the fire, puffing away out of his little dirty pipe, about an inch and a half long, and she was bending over the edge of the fire. I told her that the fire would expire in a couple of hours if somebody did not sit up to replenish it from time to time, and that, under any circumstances, the weather was too severe for her to pass the night in the open air. I, therefore, offered her the protection of my tent, and told her that she could go to it now if she pleased, and "s'arranger le mieux qu'elle pourrait." Upon which, thanking me for my kindness, she withdrew into it, and having giving her a quarter of an hour, I bade Monsieur Dubois and his pipe " bon soir," a piece of politeness which seemed rather to surprise him. Having entered the tent, I fastened the entrance, that if he should follow me he might see clearly that I did not intend him to be there.

To be sure, it was altogether an amazing, droll affair, and I could not but see that if it were not for the boy's presence my conduct might seem rather " équivoque." I found Madame had taken me at my word to arrange herself " le mieux qu'elle pourrait," and had taken possession of my mattress. Nothing was left for me but to lie down upon her blanket, and draw part of our common cover over myself, improving our situation a little by laying some bear-skins over our feet. But a colder night I never passed ; my feet were like ice, and I was unable to sleep for the shortest period of time. Once I rose to peep out, and saw Monsieur Dubois smoking away, with his feet to the fire, that was almost extinguished ; perhaps he was asleep, for an *ancien voyageur* can sleep and smoke in any situation. What he thought of my hospitality, I never ascertained ; it was too cold for him to be seriously alarmed about his exclusion from the tent, and perhaps the presence of little John might inspire him with confidence. It is to be hoped it did, but alas ! little John slept like a top, and the drama of the Sabine Virgins might have been enacted for any attention he paid to what was passing.

October 30.—Long before the dawn, we heard the voices of the men and the crackling of the branches, and Madame, preferring them to my company, jumped up and took leave of me in not a very affectionate manner. When I joined them at the fire, she said, " La nuit avait été terrible," and Monsieur Dubois added, "qu'il avait pensé gêler vingt fois." I told them I was glad we had got through the night, and that I would give them a warm cup of tea whilst the men repaired the canoe, which had lost some gum in consequence of the intense frost; having accomplished which, we re-embarked at half-past seven, the river covered with a cold fog. The sun coming out betwixt nine and ten a. m., we stopped to breakfast, and having got our blood into a comfortable state of circulation, we took to our paddles again, the steamboat Warrior passing us on her way to Prairie du Chien.

Evidences of an advancing population increased upon us as we pursued our way, to my great regret. There was now an end to all the attractive simplicity and independence of the roving life I had been leading in the Indian country. I should soon be in the vortex of a white frontier population, must abandon my canoe, exchange the peaceful tent, pitched on the clean bank of an interesting river, for dirty accommodation at some filthy tavern, and make up my account to pay in money for every act of civility I might receive.

At one p. m. I put Monsieur Dubois and his niece ashore, on the left bank of the Mississippi, nearly opposite the lead-mining village of Dubuque, and after exchanging salutations with them, crossed the Mississippi, and landed at a small valley a little beyond the village, where there was a cupola furnace for smelting the sulphuret of lead.

After looking at the works, which were all very simple and unexpensive, and observing that the galena was brought up to the surface in loose masses, weighing from a quarter of a pound to ten pounds, consisting of aggregates of small cubes, dull at the surface, and of a rubbly appearance, I embarked again for Galena, a town distant about six miles, built upon a stream called Fever River, from a pestilential disease once fatal to many Indians there. The mouth of this stream, which empties into the Mississippi on the left bank, was said by my men to be very difficult to find, being what the Americans call a *slew;* indeed some of them were of opinion we had passed it. I accordingly landed, hoping to find some settler who could give me correct information, and after walking about two miles into the interior, found a log hut, with a squatter in it, who said the mouth of the stream was still two miles further south. On regaining the canoe, the sun was setting, and, considering the various disadvantages that would attend my reaching Galena in the dark,—such as my men getting drunk, exposing my things to be stolen by my white brethren, the great difficulty of getting lodgings, the probability that none were to be had, and that we should be trespassers if we attempted to encamp upon private property, to say nothing of the difficulty of obtaining wood for fuel,—I thought it advisable to defer until daylight the placing myself within the pale of what men have chosen to call civilization ; and, much in opposition to the wishes of my party, decided to give myself another night of comfort and independence, and encamped on the bank of the Mississippi for the last time.

October 31.—Taking an early start, we soon got into the mouth of Fever River, which is a fine, broad stream at its junction ; and after paddling vigorously for some time, reached Galena, a dirty, wooden, ill-arranged town, standing on a very sharp slope on the right bank. Here, after some difficulty, I succeeded in getting into a low den of a tavern, and procuring a dirty, shabby room in it for little John and myself. Our breakfast, however, was abundant, and better than I expected to find it. Having secured my effects and the canoe, I called upon a Mr. H., one of the principal lawyers of the place, whose brother I had formerly known in Virginia, and found him living in a neat, comfortable house. This gentleman was very attentive to me, and made me acquainted with some merchants of the place connected with the mining district, who appeared to be active and respectable men, and from whom I received some interesting information, which determined me to take another opportunity of visiting the lead-mines in the vicinity, and those of the adjoining Wisconsin district, the season being too far advanced to do it at present. During the day, I visited an air-furnace belonging to a Mr. Campbell, where they were pursuing an active business. From the returns of the smelting which I procured here, and the various accounts which were given me of the localities whence the sulphuret of lead is derived, I perceived that the deposit of galena in the western states was upon an immense scale, only inferior to that of the iron in the United States. I had traced it personally from White River in Arkansas beyond the *Makato* of the St. Peter's, near the sources of some of the tributaries of which stream masses of sulphuret in aggregate cubes are occasionally found. The geographical distance betwixt these points is equal to 2,000 miles, with an unknown breadth upon an irregular line east of north. The quantity of lead in this extraordinary area would seem to be enormous, especially in the part of it called the Wisconsin district; and having made a note of the principal localities where it is excavated, with the intention of hereafter visiting them, and various other lead establishments in the vicinity, I retired to my dirty chamber, which I found a miserable exchange for my clean tent.

November 1.—I had become perfectly ashamed of the companions of my long journey. They had been with me a great distance, and had been so useful to me, that I could not but feel anxious for their welfare, and was most desirous that they should get safe home to their families. My agreement with them was, that at whatever point I discharged them at the end of the season, the distance from their homes was to be estimated in leagues, and that I was to allow each of them one day's wages for every eight leagues. But they had been so drunk ever since my arrival, that it was not practicable to come to any settlement with them. I therefore rose with the dawn for the express purpose of collecting them together; and, having at length succeeded, brought them to the tavern, made an estimate of the distance they were from their homes, with which they were satisfied, gave them a breakfast, paid them their money, with a gratuity to each besides, shook hands with them all, and recommended to them to commence their journey immediately, which they promised to do. I now went to breakfast myself, and then sat down to write a letter.

On leaving the tavern to put my letter in the post-office, about an hour and a half after I had parted with the men, the first thing I saw was L'Amirant lying dead-drunk in the middle of the street, incapable of standing or speaking; and close by, near an obscure dram-shop, the rest of them, almost all at a white heat with drinking rum and whiskey. I reproached Beau Prè for terminating our journey in so disgraceful a manner ; but as I found they had been drinking my health, and sounding my praises, I thought it best to continue my acts of kindness to them. Canadian Frenchmen are, like their race in every part of the world, best managed by gentleness; so, asking them to oblige me for the last time, they assisted me in lifting L'Amirant and carrying him to a pump near at hand, and having first tried the projectile pitch of the spout, I had his head laid exactly within point blank shot, and taking the handle myself administered it most liberally to him. At first he did not mind the operation ; but we continued it until he began to grin and carry his hand to his head, and at length coming to his senses, we finally got him on his legs and able to walk. In about half an hour I had the satisfaction of seeing each of them march clear out of the town, with his *pacotille*, containing his blanket and provisions, well girded on his back, and his pipe in his mouth.

These thoughtless fellows had about 200 miles to walk before they would reach their homes, which, making allowances for weather, they would perhaps accomplish in ten days. Considering their habits and dispositions, they had behaved better than it was predicted to me they would do ; so I wrote to the merchant at Navarino who had engaged them, that upon the whole I was satisfied with their conduct. To manage men of this race, firmness and kindness are equally necessary; to keep them in good humour, they must have plenty of food—being immense gormandizers—and some tobacco : whilst things go on favourably they are cheerful and willing, but in adverse circumstances I had found they were not to be relied upon as Milor was. His Indian blood had tempered the volatile course of his Gallic descent, and the mixed reflecting animal thus produced was singularly contrasted, when sobriety and forethought were required, with the levity and insufficiency of these men. In engaging Canadian *voyageurs* for distant expeditions like the one I had just returned from, it is unwise to take any ardent spirits with you; for if they know you have any, they are always discontented if you do not share it with them, and whenever they can have free access to it they get beastly and dead-drunk in ten minutes, drinking until they can neither stand or speak.

CHAPTER XL.

MEET WITH AN OLD ACQUAINTANCE.—LEAVE GALENA FOR ST. LOUIS.—
CAVALRY DEPÔT AT DES MOINES RIVER.—BEAUTIFUL FOSSILS AND
MINERALS AT KEOKUL.—REACH ST. LOUIS.

I was now alone again in the world; I had first
lost Milor, and then the light-hearted companions
who had been so long with me, and had no longer
any one to interest myself about in this part of the
country, save little John, who seemed very happy
at finding himself in what was to him the great
world.   Thinking of these things, as I was standing
upon the bank of the stream, observing a steamer
that was advancing to Galena, I waited until it
came opposite to me, and there, to my great surprise and pleasure, who should I see standing
on the quarter-deck with a weather-worn white
hat on, but the Hon. C. A. M.   He had left Washington before myself on an excursion to the western
country, and I had learnt at St. Louis that he had
gone up the Missouri, but what regions he had
visited I knew not.   I was, however, heartily glad
to see a fellow-adventurer and a countryman of
Mr. M.'s acknowledged merit, and hastened to the
quay to shake hands with him.   It was a very
pleasant meeting; we had a long crack about our
mutual adventures.   Whilst I had been amongst the
Nahcotahs he had been passing a great part of the

summer with the Pawnees,* by his own account as
dirty a set of natives as are to be found on the
continent. The resolute manner in which he had
extricated himself and his companions from the encampment of these insolent vagabonds was a proof
that he possessed the highest qualifications necessary to a traveller in Indian countries. If we had
met in the wilderness, we should of course have
shared each other's comforts without any formality;
here I had no tent to share with him, and he had
no room to go to, so when night came he very
quietly folded up one of my grizzly bear skins for
a pillow, and wrapping himself up in some of my
buffalo robes, lay down to sleep in a corner of my
room.

Having made a hasty breakfast in the morning
and sent our luggage on board the Warrior
steamer, Mr. M. and myself embarked at 8 a. m.
for St. Louis, and found a great many passengers
on board. The day passed pleasantly; I received a
great deal of information of what was going on in
the world; the country was beautiful, and the Mississippi of a magnificent breadth. Our fare was
tolerably good, and what with the power of the
steamer and the favouring current, we made great
progress. Our fellow-passengers were either small
store-keepers from the new settlements, going to
St. Louis on their affairs, or speculators. We tried
to obtain some information from them, but generally in vain: collected in groups, their discussions
appeared to be carried on with great animation; but

* Mr. M. has since published a narrative of his travels.

when you approached to find out what interested
them so much, it invariably turned out to be the
price of building-lots in the settlements they had
made, of which they gave the most flaming accounts; nothing could be so good as the soil, so
healthy as the country, so good as the water, " so
amazing calkerlated to do a power of business."
It was evident enough, however, that this palmy state
of contentment which each of them professed to feel
for his own habitat, whether it was Van Burenberg,
or Jacksonville, or by whatever name it went, meant
only one thing, that the party was exceedingly desirous of selling his own particular paradise, and I
believe that any one so disposed might have purchased the whole of them before we sat down to
dinner.

November 3.—We reached Fort Armstrong, on
Rock River Island, distant about 100 miles from
Galena, about 10 a. m., and as we were to remain
there a few hours, I landed to examine the rocks,
which were non-fossiliferous, buff-coloured limestone.
Bituminous coal abounds in this part of the country,
but I could not learn that the lands had risen much
in price in consequence of containing that mineral;
that will probably only happen when the population
has been much increased. I took an opportunity of
calling upon the commandant, Colonel Davenport,
a gentlemanly person. On taking my departure,
his lady presented me with some flint (Indian) arrow-
heads, of a different form from any I had before
met with. Opposite to this place the Iowa River
empties into the Mississippi. This stream takes its

rise in the Nahcotah country, south of the St. Peter's, its sources interlocking with those of the *Makato,* and holds its course the whole distance through a fertile territory. Resuming our voyage, towards evening a steady rain came on, which prevented our remaining on deck. M. and myself took to our books, and the rest of the passengers got into knots in the large cabin, and became engaged in that noisy, low kind of gambling, which all the people of these western countries, with the fewest exceptions, seem devoted to.

November 4.—The succeeding day we had a continuation of the rain, and about noon reached the United States cavalry depôt, sixteen miles north of the Des Moines River. The small body of horse stationed here visits the Indian districts occasionally, for the purpose of keeping the natives in order. As we were to be detained here awhile, M. and myself called upon Colonel Kearney, the commanding officer, and his lady, and were asked to dine. In the meantime, the cargo of the steamer, which consisted principally of pigs of lead, was shifted into flat-bottomed barges, on account of the Des Moines Rapids, which we had now to pass over, and which extended twelve miles below this place, the rocks, in many places, coming to within two feet of the surface. The steamer being lightened, we re-embarked, and after a good many rude bumps at the bottom, got clear of these shallows, and reached a sorry settlement on the left bank, called *Keokuk,* after a celebrated Sauk chief, inhabited altogether by a set of desperadoes of this part of the Mississippi.

The cargo being to take on board again, I landed, and finding a very good section of beds equivalent to our mountain limestone, containing beautiful fossils, and beautiful geodes filled with the most interesting crystals, I went vigorously to work, and made a valuable collection of them.

These geodes tell a very interesting story of the ancient condition of these rocks, which are of the cavernous kind, abounding in cavities of various sizes, from a foot to an inch in diameter. The inner walls of the geodes are generally studded with brilliant crystals of quartz, that appear to have been formed from solutions of silicious matter, with which the cavities were once filled. Many of them are of a beautiful chalcedonic structure, like those from Iceland, where silicious matter is in so perfect a state of solution. Subsequent to the formation of the crystals of quartz, the geodes seem to have been filled with successive solutions of minerals, which have become solidified in turns, until the geodes were nearly filled. Thus a crust, studded with neat crystals of pearlspar and small brilliant cubes of galena, is often superinduced upon the crystals of quartz. Crystals of carbonate of lime are also found in great varieties, together with many other minerals. These interesting objects, so rare and beautiful, were exceedingly abundant; and I returned to the steamer loaded with my treasures. At Keokuk I found an old acquaintance in Mr. Catlin,* who joined us on board. He also was returning from a visit

* Now well known in Europe by his talents and his admirable collection of Indian arms and accoutrements.

amongst the Indians, having accompanied an expedition of American cavalry, under Colonel Dodge, amongst the tribes living betwixt the sources of the Canadian and the Rocky Mountains.

Mr. Catlin, who is a man of good feeling and great enterprise, was full of enthusiasm about the Indian races. Availing himself of his talent for portrait painting and sketching, he had brought from the Indian country a collection of portraits of the principal chiefs he had seen, as well as specimens of their arms, habiliments, and accoutrements. In short, a more determined virtuoso I never knew, for nothing escaped him, from a geode to a tomahawk. He communicated to me a project he had of devoting several years to the illustration of the manners and customs of the Indian tribes by these collections and by his art, and finding him admirably adapted, by inclination and experience, to accomplish such a task, I encouraged him to persevere, for he appeared to me to be the very man that was wanted to secure the information we were in want of respecting the aborigines, before they were extinct. Still it was an arduous task for an unassisted individual ; most of the objects would be perishable, and the collection would be a cumbrous one. I remarked to him, that if his enthusiasm should abate, and he could not dispose of it, it would become a great burthen to him, all which he admitted ; but observed, that its rarity could not fail to attract much attention in the large cities of America and Europe, which might indemnify him for his labours.* We also took a great

* On my return to Washington, I recommended strongly that

number of persons on board at this place, who were far from possessing Mr. Catlin's merit, and left it with a set of as thorough vagabonds as the town of St. Louis might reasonably expect us to bring.

November 5.—Our steamer had now become a Babel of noise and vulgarity; drinking, smoking, swearing, and gambling prevailed from morn to night, the captain of the steamer refusing to suppress any of these irregularities. We staid a couple of hours at Quincy, a new town rising from the right bank of the Mississippi, about 200 miles from St. Louis; having inquired for the quarry where the building-stone was procured, I went to it and procured some interesting fossils. The picturesque shores and bluffs in the neighbourhood of this place are very beautiful; indeed, all the upper part of the Mississippi, from the junction of the Ohio, possessing a thousand beauties that are wanting below that stream, where the flood is wide, without islands, and no sections of rock to be seen. We had a lovely moonlight night, and but for the horrible disorderly set on board, should have enjoyed the scenery very much.

A thick fog obliged us to come to an anchor in the night; but getting under weigh at daylight, we soon passed the mouth of the Illinois River, said to be forty-five miles from St. Louis: the limestone bluffs are very fine there. We stopped a short time at Alston, another thriving town on the left bank, in the state of Illinois; here are a great many well-con-

the government of the United States should authorize an investigation of all the Indian languages, and the purchase of Mr. Catlin's collections.

structed houses made of excellent limestone. All was
bustle and activity at this place, that sort of activity
which is only to be observed where slavery is not
tolerated. If this western country continues to
prosper in the fortunate manner it has done, and
slavery is excluded from it, it will only take one or
two generations to see towns built all the way to
St. Peter's. We soon passed the broad mouth of the
mighty Missouri, that, after a course of 2,000 miles,
mingles its turbid waters with the clearer stream of
the Mississippi. For some time the river had been
comparatively without islands, the explanation of
which I suppose to be found in the sedimentary
matter brought down by its head streams being
deposited in ancient times, before it reached the
clearer part of the stream.

At noon we reached St. Louis, and landing,
found that all the hotels were full, not a room
being to be had for love or money. This was not
very pleasant to a couple of Englishmen disgusted with the dirt and ribaldry of a western
steamer, and who were sighing to be alone. There
however seems to be a remedy for every evil in this
world, if you have patience and perseverance; so I
returned to the National Hotel, where I had lodged
when on my way to the Mexican frontier, in 1834,
and told the landlord that he must, upon some condition or other, give M. and myself a place to ourselves, as we could not remain in the streets all night.
He declared that he had not a room in the house;
that we must see he could not turn others out to
put us in their place; and that, if he were to die for
it, he had no other place but a small cellar, where

he kept his fire-wood. It immediately occurred to me, that if we could not turn his lodgers out of their rooms, we might take that liberty with his fire-wood; and as to its being a cellar, we were too much accustomed to lie down anyhow, provided we could do it in safety, to trouble ourselves about the name. I therefore instantly went to reconnoitre this same cellar, and found it to be a tolerably dry, small place, beneath the house, with an old window about a foot square, letting the light in from a yard. It was large enough for us to spread our buffalo-skins, and to contain our luggage, so, procuring some assistance, I turned the fire-wood out of the window, got the place well swept out and ventilated, and had our *matériel* brought there. When M. came to look at it, he laughed heartily, and made the sensible remark, that, indifferently as we were lodged, we should be better off than most of the people in the hotel, who occupied rooms containing five or six beds. Upon this occasion he related to me an adventure which happened to him at Dubuque some time before we met. Being obliged to pass the night at a low tavern, frequented by miners and gamblers, and knowing their habit of gambling until a late hour, he went as soon as he had supped to the only bed-room there was in the house, and out of a great number of beds, selected the one that appeared the most promising, a surgeon in the American army, with whom he was acquainted, taking the next adjoining.

This dormitory, like the hotel itself, had an entrance, but no door, or hinges to hang one by, so

that passengers could enter into both without noise,
at any hour of the night.   Towards morning M. was
awakened by a fellow turning down his bedclothes
to get into bed to him. Aware that no time was to be
lost, he gathered the clothes up, threw himself into a
boxing attitude, and told the fellow in a peremptory
tone that he should not get into his bed without
fighting for it to the last moment.   A little puzzled
at this unusual reception, and not fancying the
attitude M. had put himself into, he exclaimed,
" Stranger, you sartin don't kalkerlate upon keeping
all that are bed to yourself?"   " Yes I do," said
M., " and that you shall find."   " Well, then," replied the fellow, " if you are so almighty pertiklar,
I swar I'll be as pertiklar as you, and I'll turn
in to this ere gentleman."   But the doctor, finding
how things were going on, had got upon his haunches
too, and told the fellow to stand off, or he'd knock
him into his ninety-ninth year in no time.   Thus
rudely repulsed by these two specimens of civilization, this poor, ill-treated, social animal exclaimed, " If this don't beat all creation!" and, as
he related in the morning, " walked " into the next
bed, where three of his companions had turned in
before him.

The landlord's family, finding we were in earnest,
and that we put up with our humble lodgings, very
good-naturedly now took compassion upon us, which
they certainly would not have done if we had been
at all restive, and sent us a couple of chairs, an old
table, two small beds, and some linen ; so that we
really were better off than in the steamer, with all

its spitting and disorder.   When dinner was announced, we went to the *table d'hôte*, and indeed
found a very capital one.   There were two saddles of
delicious fat venison, exceedingly well roasted ; two
large wild turkeys, roasted ; and beef, mutton, and
pork in profusion.   Great was the onslaught made
by the guests upon this banquet, every individual
of whom, with the exception of M. and myself,
having bolted his ample share in less than ten
minutes, left us to survey the destruction that had
been made.   The landlord was full of attentions to
us, and as soon as we had dismissed our venison,
sent us a couple of fat, well-roasted wild ducks, to
which, and other good things that succeeded, we did
ample justice at our leisure.

In the evening we walked to the suburbs, to
examine those fine Indian mounds which had
attracted my attention so much in 1834.   As we
proposed remaining here a few days, I sought out
a lady, who was a friend of Mrs. Bliss, and being
fortunate enough to find her, I placed young John
under her care during my stay.

The succeeding morning we went, after breakfast,
to see the new Roman Catholic cathedral, which was
consecrated the day of my departure from this place
in 1834.   Learning from one of the priests that M.
Nicollet, a member of the Institute of France, was
at St. Louis, I called to see him.   I knew that he
had been engaged some time in effecting a series of
barometrical observations, to ascertain the elevation
of particular points in the United States above the
general level of the ocean, and was desirous of

learning how far he had succeeded, and what assistance he had been able to obtain to carry on so important an undertaking. Very vague and superficial notions seemed, as far as I could judge, to prevail in the United States about barometrical observations. Many had thought it sufficient to go from point to point with one of Englefield's imperfect and cumbrous instruments, and report the results they obtained, which could not fail to be erroneous. At any one point, the apparent elevation, under a particular state of the atmosphere, might be increased or diminished another day, under the same process, with a different state of the atmosphere, from one to five hundred feet.   The elevations I had seen recorded in books were found, upon examination, to be often absurd. Without numerous standard observations or fixed stations, where the true elevation has been obtained, and to which locomotive observations can be referred, no accurate results can be obtained.   I found M. Nicollet a most amiable and sociable person, full of intelligence and zeal. He had registered his observations for a long time, and had left a barometer at one or two particular points, for the purpose of reference ; but his instrument appeared to me to be a very unsatisfactory one, although I dare say his results would be less defective than those which had preceded his labours. M. Nicollet was said to be also a person of fine musical taste, and was kind enough to propose to take M. and myself to a private society, where we should hear some good music—a great treat to me, whose gratification in that line had for a long time been confined

to the Canadian boat-songs, and the scalp-dances at
Lac qui parle. In the evening we had an opportunity of looking over Mr. Catlin's portfolio of
drawings, consisting of Indians engaged in their
national dances, their pursuit and slaughter of the
buffalo, and some very good landscapes with sections
of the banks of the Missouri ; all full of life and
graphic force, especially his animals, many of which
merited the highest praise.

CHAPTER XLI.

PROFUSION OF GAME IN THE PUBLIC MARKET.—A FASHIONABLE SOIRÉE.
—GENERAL LAFAYETTE.—NEZ PERCÉS INDIANS AND THEIR PATRON
SIR WM. D. S.—LEAVE ST. LOUIS.

THE weather was now very fine, and on the morrow we walked out to pay a visit to General Ashley, a fur-trader, celebrated for his expeditions to the Rocky Mountains, and for the address and courage with which he had upon various occasions extricated himself from dangerous situations. He had now retired with a competency, had married an agreeable wife, and together they inhabited a quiet suburban house built upon one of those Indian mounds which have been before alluded to. I did not learn that he had ever been in the army, but it is not necessary to be a military man in the United States to be called general. We found him a modest, intelligent, and rather a superior man, full of interesting information of the Indian countries he had visited, especially of those valleys and coves found in the interior of that great belt called the Rocky Mountains, which in some directions has a breadth of about one hundred miles. In penetrating through this belt, he had often led a life of great jeopardy, followed and tracked by the Blackfeet and other Indians, whose inveterate hostility he had escaped by his prudence and courage. Our dinner to-day at the hotel was a most remarkable affair; such a quantity of well-roasted joints of fine venison, and other game, I had never before seen upon a table. The wild ducks I thought equal to the famous canvass-backs of the Susquehanna.

November 9.—This morning M. and myself rose early, and went to the Market as soon as it was opened, where we saw a surprising collection of good things. We counted eighty-seven fat deer with their skins on, at least two hundred large wild turkeys; the quantity of wild ducks, many of which were wood-ducks with their brilliant plumage, was enormous. We both agreed that we had never been in any place so well supplied by good things as St. Louis. Breakfast being over, I took up my hammer and chisels, and went with them to the limestone quarries, where I passed the rest of the day, returning home with a fine collection of good fossils. Having got through our usual banquet, we learnt that there was to be a ball at the hotel, in a long room exactly over our cellar, from which it was separated only by a plank. I was fatigued, and had no inclination to assist at it; but as it was evident that sleeping was out of the question, we thought it best on every account to purchase tickets and go there. There were some pretty women, and the thing went off as well as we expected. I left the affair about ten, but M. remained, and entered into the spirit of the thing. Meantime, I reclined patiently on my bed, listening to the stamping and laughing that were going on above me, until about three in the morning, when M. entered the cellar, and said the ladies had gone home "considerable lively."

In the morning I went, after breakfast, to visit some quarries which I had not seen, and had the good fortune to procure some exceedingly beautiful fossils of the same genera I had taken from the beds at Quincy, on our way to this place, most of them undescribed species of corallines. It was late in the evening before I got to the hotel, having purposely abstained one day from the too luxurious table. About seven p.m., M. and myself, accompanied by M. Nicollet, went to the promised musical party, at a French gentleman's, named D——. This was a very agreeable family. Madame was a well-bred woman, and, with two pleasant daughters, did the honours of a very neat supper. Upon retiring from table, we adjourned to the music-room, where we had some good quartetts, M. D—— playing an unexceptionable first fiddle. The rest of the performers were amateurs of the place, members of respectable French families. The organist of the cathedral, Signor Marellano, an Italian, afterwards presided at the piano, and we had some very good vocal music. It was quite delightful, in this remote part of the world, to hear some of the finest passages of Cimarosa's *Matrimonio Segreto* very tolerably executed. The organist was full of enthusiasm, and obliged us all to contribute towards the amusement of the evening, which passed off charmingly.

Amongst the guests was a Monsieur P——, a Parisian, who had resided several years at St. Louis, a very eccentric and amusing person, full of music,

but not a musician. The sarcastic and droll remarks
he made upon the manners of the Americans established at this place amused us all very much, and
were exceedingly relished by the French part of the
company. The truth is, that the Americans have
established themselves here in such numbers, that
they have thrown the French, who were the original
settlers, into the shade; and, being all Presbyterians,
or Baptists, or Dissenters of one sect or another,
had, by their austere and greedy mode of life,
seriously interfered with the lively and amusing tone
of society which had once been universal in the
population; and, by their denunciation of Christmas-
day, Easter, and the festivals which the French
delight to honour, had created a great disgust
amongst them. " Ces Messieurs," said M. P——,
" ont toujours raison, et c'est pourquoi ils ne font
pas scrupule à vous voler : je pense qu'ils font
leur compte de traiter le diable au bout du chapitre,
comme ils ont traité votre bon Roi d'Angleterre, de
s'insurger contre lui et prendre possession des ses
états." A traveller, who perceives how much they
are wounded at heart by the restraints which the
Americans impose upon them, cannot but sympathize
with them, especially when assisting at such a pleasant party as this was ; but the extraordinary energy
and enterprise of the Americans are not the less to
be admired on that account.

The weather continuing very fine, I rode out the
next day to dine and pass the day with my worthy
friend, General Atkinson, at Jefferson Barracks. I
found most of the officers there whom I had seen

when on my way to Arkansas, and passed a very pleasant day with them, returning to St. Louis late in
the evening. The succeeding day M. and myself
made two or three excursions to various points, and
in the evening went to another musical party at
M. P——'s, the eccentric Parisian; but although
our *petit souper* went off pretty well, we felt
the want of the female society which had made
the other party so pleasant, and came away very
early.

November 13.—This day M. and myself were
joined by a relative of his, who perhaps does not
yield in eccentricity to any person living. This was
Captain, now Sir William D—— S——, an exceedingly adventurous person, who had served in the
British army on the glorious day of Waterloo.
Perfectly *blasé* with European life, he had been
wandering about two years amongst the Indians of
the Rocky Mountains, and the north-west coast of
America, and only reached St. Louis this morning
from the Missouri River, which he had just descended.
I was delighted to make his acquaintance, his conversation being exceedingly attractive. Of Indian
life he spoke with the greatest enthusiasm, declared
that it was infinitely more satisfactory than civilized
life, and that it was his fixed intention to return to
it; a singular declaration to come from one allied
to some of the most illustrious families in Great
Britain, and to whom the most agreeable career in
Europe would seem to have been always open. We
passed the day together conversing about the nations
and the countries he had visited, of which and his

adventures he gave me a most interesting account.
The Riccarees at one time surprised him and his
party, and robbed them of their horses and every
thing they possessed, leaving them destitute, upon a
lonely prairie, hundreds of miles from resources of
any kind.   A person with less spirit and enthusiasm
than himself would have perished upon this occasion ;
but resolved not to give up the only chance that
was left to save himself, he attacked a fellow who
was making off loaded, amongst other things, with
the holsters containing his pistols. The Indian, who
had never seen holsters before, and had not remarked
the pistols in them, was not a little surprised to see
one of them drawn out, cocked, and presented to
his head. Without this persuasive argument he
would never have been able to obtain his horse again,
which he now did, and thus procured the means of
delivering himself from this one of the most lawless
and insolent of all the tribes.

November 14.—The succeeding day was excessively rainy and uncomfortable. St. Louis, as long
as fine weather lasts, is agreeable enough for a residence of a few days.   I certainly never was in any
other place where there were so many people remarkable for the adventurous lives they had led. Almost
all of them had been engaged as trappers in the
recesses of the Rocky Mountains, and some of them
were notorious for the desperate encounters they
had had with the Blackfeet and other formidable
Indians. The days passed very pleasantly when I
could get out to talk to these men, and listen to
their wild and rude narratives ; but, confined to the

house, with incessant heavy rains, and no place to go
to but the public room, frequented by the disgusting
people who are always smoking, chewing, and spitting, accustomed to make no difference betwixt the
inside and outside of a house, the moments passed
heavily, and our cellar was becoming so damp that
we were getting very tired of it.

November 15.—On the morrow we had no abatement of the rain, and the air in the cellar began to
smell so unwholesome, that we were forced to go
to what the servants called "up stars;" but up stars
was as bad as down stars, so vulgar and filthy had
everything become; and, going from one to the other,
at length both M. and myself began to feel unwell.
I began to fear now that one or both of us would
have a fit of sickness, and determined to go on board
some steamer, and proceed to the Ohio, if the weather did not change.   I accordingly went to the
quay and engaged a berth in the steamer Potosi,
bound for Louisville.   On my return we found an
invitation for M. and myself to a soirée, the next
evening, at Mrs. B——'s, a rich widow, whose husband had been killed in a duel some time before.
As this would help to get over the time, we were
glad of it, and accepted the invitation.

November 16.—The weather happily cleared up
to-day, so that we could get out and breathe the
fresh air.   Immediately after breakfast I sallied
out to the quarries, where every thing was nice and
clean, and working away vigorously, I got rid of my
headache, and acquired some fine fossils and a good
appetite for the excellent dinner I found on my

return. In the evening we dressed and presented ourselves at the fair widow's, who received us most graciously. The rooms were filled with company, and I had no idea that such a collection of well-dressed and agreeable people could be got together in St. Louis. Every thing was done in the best manner; the refreshments were various and good; we had vocal music, both Italian and English, and many of the ladies were agreeable in their persons and pleasing and cheerful in their manners. I was told that this was one of the handsomest parties that had been given in St. Louis, and was almost equal in brilliancy to one that Mrs. B. had given to General Lafayette when he paid his last celebrated visit to the United States.

This distinguished person, whose career had been so extraordinary, who had done so much to overthrow the monarchy of his own country, and who had all but brought his own neck to the guillotine in his vain efforts to save the life of the sovereign he had assisted to ruin, and to guide the storm he had too inconsiderately been one of the first to set in motion, had a conspicuous failing in his personal vanity, which sometimes exposed his *amour propre* to be greatly wounded. His ambition was to be considered in France as a French Washington, and to be looked upon in America as an American Frenchman. He professed to love the Americans as much as he did his own countrymen, if not more; he always called himself an American, and indeed he was consistent in his conduct to his adopted brethren, extending to them individually, when in

France, more hospitality and kindness than all mankind collectively did. During his triumphant tour in the United States his popularity was unbounded; the government at Washington, those of the different states—all of which he visited—the citizens without respect of party, all considered him the national guest, being at that time the only surviving general officer of the American army, when Washington commanded it soon after the commencement of hostilities. Wherever he went, his table was found at the public expense, and all his expenditure during his journeys through the continent was defrayed by the authorities of the states through which he passed. During many months it was a perfect holiday and public rejoicing wherever he appeared. Long before he reached St. Louis his name was familiarly known to every man, woman, and child in the United States.

But as there is an exception to every thing, so there was in this particular instance, for a very worthy old lady of St. Louis, who was proof against enthusiasm of every kind, had never even heard of Lafayette until the moment that public fame asserted that " General Lafayette was coming to St. Louis," and from that time indeed nothing else was talked about. Mrs. B., however, was to give this great man a great party, and the old lady, being a friend, was invited with everybody that was respectable. Overpowering was the reception that he met with at this party; every individual there was personally presented to him, and had the honour of shaking hands and listening to a few honied

words from his practised lips. When it came to
the old lady's turn, the General took her hand
affectionately, and expressed a tender hope that she
was in good health. "Lord, General," said she, "how
well you speak English; was you ever in America
before?" This tremendous state of innocency of
the past almost overcame the General; the chief
that had never flinched before a cannon faltered,
for the first time; his vanity was disturbed, and he
knew not what to answer. To relate to her his
first furtive departure from France, with all his
achievements, including the battle of Brandywine,
or to advise her to read the newspapers for the
last six months, where every paragraph spoke of
hardly any thing but Lafayette, and his movements,
was too great an undertaking. He thought it best,
therefore, to make her a respectful bow without
answering her, and, as my informant said, "looked
very *scary*" when the next person presented was
about to address him, apprehensive lest St. Louis
had not been sufficiently penetrated by his fame.
This looks like a story got up for the occasion,
but it was related to me by a lady who was standing next to him when this eminent person was
thus sadly disconcerted.

Nov. 16.—It was a late hour before we left the
party and reached our cellar. In the morning I
fell into a frightful dream, and struggling with it,
awoke : casting my eyes around, to my great astonishment I observed the room filled with tobacco-
smoke, and three slender-looking Indians sitting in
silence upon our trunks smoking their pipes as

earnestly as if they were attempting to suffocate us, which, no doubt, they might have accomplished in time, the space being very small and without any chimney to carry off the poisoned air. I immediately jumped out of bed, drove them out of the room, and opened the little window which communicated with the yard. Who these Indians were, and where they came from, was a mystery to us until Capt. S. made his appearance, and then we learnt that they were Nez Percés from the western side of the Rocky Mountains, who had left that country with him, but who had only reached St. Louis in the night. Hearing that we were Captain S.'s friends, they took it for granted that where we were he would be found, and, therefore, established themselves in our room whilst we were sleeping, just as if it had been a tent. They were gentle, intelligent beings, corresponding with the accounts I had received of them from Captain S., who had resided a long time in their country. After breakfast I got a fair vocabulary of their language from them. When they were first called Nez Percés I do not know, but the Indian name by which they are known is Sah haptinnay.

Having seen so much of St. Louis and its society as we were desirous of doing, we determined to leave it immediately; but as my friends proposed visiting New Orleans and other places which I had already seen, before they returned to the Atlantic cities of the United States, we separated here with the hope of meeting again at Washington during the winter. Bidding them adieu, I sent my luggage on board the Potosi bound to Louisville on the Ohio, and embarking early in the afternoon, got once more upon the ample bosom of the Mississippi.   From hence the route by which I proposed to return has been partly described in the tour I made in 1834, and indeed has been so well described by other tourists, that it would be foreign to my purpose of only laying before my readers an account of regions of country comparatively unknown, if I were further to extend the narrative of this year's excursion, which will close here.

CHAPTER XLII.

RETURN TO GALENA.—A SINGULAR LONDON COCKNEY METAMORPHOSED
INTO AN AMERICAN COLONEL AND DRIVER OF A STAGE-COACH. —
MANNER OF MORRIS BIRKBECK'S DEATH.—REACH MINERAL POINT.—
AN OBLIGING JUDGE.—LEAD AND COPPER "DIGGINGS."—THE SUDDEN
GROWTH OF TWELVE LARGE CITIES IN TWO YEARS.—THE CITY OF THE
SAINTS.

May 19.—On my first visit to the Wisconsin
territory in 1835, it will be seen, in the preceding
pages, that I approached it by the way of the
Great Lakes, and descending in my birch-bark
canoe the river which bears that name, got into the
Mississippi at Prairie du Chien.   The extraordinary
extent of the district in the western country from
which galena is extracted, and the great quantity
of it, which I afterwards learnt at Galena was
annually produced in the territory, made me very
desirous, as I have before stated, at page 36,
of inspecting it personally.   Accordingly, in the
spring of 1837, as soon as the proper season had
arrived, I put myself in motion again, and after
travelling more than 2,000 miles, reached the town
of Galena, in the state of Illinois, on the 19th of
May.   On my way there I had the pleasure of
meeting, at St. Louis, a scientific friend,* well
known to English geologists, and, embarking in
a steamer, we reached the town of Galena together.
Having engaged a barbarous sort of waggon of a

* Mr. R. C. T.

curious, speculating person, called Dr. Phillyo, we left the town, as soon as we could get ready, for *Mineral Point,* a recent settlement in the interior, near to some lead mines, amongst which were intermixed, as we were informed, some veins of copper. Nothing could be more uninteresting than the prairie country we passed over. Regions of this character, whilst possessed by the Indians, have much interest attached to them: the traveller's movements are not without a touch of romance; and at night, when his camp is properly fixed, there is cleanliness and comfort to be obtained. But the advancing tide of white population, amongst which we had now got, had destroyed every chance of these: the miserable low taverns were kept by greedy, vulgar adventurers, who had come into the country to torment it with what they call "diggings," a name they give to the rude, shallow shafts, a few feet deep, which they sink in search of metal. Nothing could exceed the ignorance and filthy habits of the working miners; the greater number of whom, being without skill, and becoming finally disappointed in their expectations, had fallen into the lowest state of poverty.

Mr. Phillyo had given us as the "driver" of our vehicle, a droll Cockney Englishman, about five feet high, and near sixty years old, born in London, who, by his own account, had never had either father or mother that he knew, and who had picked up his living in the streets there from his fifth year. By some chance, he had fallen under the protection of Mr. Morris Birkbeck, who had brought him to

the United States; but since his death he had been
knocked about in various capacities, and had at
length reached what may be called the bathos of all
human desires for an Englishman, the situation
of *driver* of this most wretched stage, as he called it,
which was dragged by two lame, miserable horses,
through a country without the vestige of any thing
like comfort.

At the top of his strange physiognomy was stuck
the filthy remnant of what had once been a fur cap;
about his neck was a disgusting handkerchief that
had never been washed; an old, ragged, red blanket
coat, thrice too large for him, covered his person,
and beneath its ample skirts appeared two odd
boots, that had been patched and repatched so
often, that, as he said, they had been made no-
where.   One of them, he remarked, was so plaguily
large, that he had cut a hole in the foot to let the
water out; and the other was such a blessed sight
too small, that he had cut a hole in that to let
his toes out.   Everybody we met seemed to know
him, and called him colonel, except one person,
who said: " Ginneral, I guess it's a toss-up whether
your cattle or your stage break down first."

From this fellow I got a detailed account of the
manner of poor Birkbeck's death.   He was crossing
a very swollen stream on horseback, when he got
entangled with a tree that was coming down with
the torrent, and finding it doubtful, perhaps, whether
he could extricate himself, he endeavoured to dismount and swim to the bank; but, unfortunately,
as he was striking off, the horse, that was struggling

very hard, kicked him in the temple, and becoming senseless, he sank and was drowned.

At a place called Belmont, about twenty-eight miles from Galena, we stopped for a short time to rest our nags, and after driving about twelve miles further through a more wooded country, we reached Mineral Point, or rather its suburbs, where were various small wooden houses, stuck up at a distance from each other. With difficulty, we procured a room to sleep in at the post-master's; and, it being evening, had scarce got our trunks out of the vehicle, when we were marched to his brother's, who was an apothecary, to sup. The supper consisted of fried ham, coffee, bread and butter, and treacle, served up in a cleanly way, and being hungry with our drive, we made a very hearty meal. As soon as our repast was over, I walked out to look at the place.

The village of Mineral Point is built upon the edge of a coulée (as a ravine or valley betwixt two ridges is called in this part of the western country), a short distance from the upland containing the suburb at which we had stopped. It was an exceedingly miserable place, built there, apparently, on account of a small rivulet, which is a branch of the Peccatonic River. It contained two filthy-looking taverns, into which I ventured to enter for a moment, both of which seemed to be very full, a court of justice being held at this time, which had collected a great many parties and witnesses. We had been referred to these taverns for lodgings, as the postmaster had told me it was not possible for him to give us quarters for more than one night; but I was not sorry to learn that none were to be had, being thoroughly disgusted with the dirty appearance of every thing; and then such a set of " ginnerals, colonels, judges, and doctors," as were assembled there, was any thing but inviting, and most of these dignitaries, as I was informed, were obliged to sleep on the floor. This was exactly what I had to do at the post-master's, whose house, at any rate, was clean.

May 20.—On awaking the next morning, I found it exceedingly cold, and asked permission to have a fire lighted, which was very obligingly granted. Some wood was accordingly brought in, and just as I had got it nicely burning and was preparing to make my toilette, a dirty, unshaven, but confident-looking fellow, walked into the room, with nothing but his nether garments on, and immediately turning his back to the fire, engrossed it all to himself. His free-and-easy way was not at all to my taste, and threatened to interfere very much with my comfort. Under other circumstances, I should not have hesitated to have turned him out; but, situated as I was, it was far from a safe proceeding, or, indeed, a justifiable one. It was certainly very cold, and I should have been glad to have had the fire to myself; but I had been treated hospitably, and the least I could do was to be hospitable to others; besides, my bare-footed friend had an air about him that imported something beyond the low swaggerer, something that smacked of authority—for authority is a thing that, from

habit or from the dignity inherent in it, has a peculiar, inexplicable way of revealing itself.   This
might be the governor, or some great man, *en
déshabille*, so I thought it best to meet him in his
own manner, by slipping a pair of pantaloons on,
and then addressing him in a friendly manner.   It
was most fortunate that I acted just as it became
me to do, for he soon let me know who he was.   He
was no less a personage than " the Court," for so
they generally call the presiding judge in the United
States, and was beyond all question the greatest
man in the place.   He was, in fact, *the* personage
of the locality for the moment, and it turned out
that the postmaster had given him up his only good
bedroom, and that he had good-naturedly given it
up to me for one night, and had taken the " Majesty of the Law" to sleep behind the counter, in a
little shop where the post-office was kept, with
blankets, crockery, cheese, and all sorts of things
around him, and had very naturally come to warm
himself in his own quarters.

The Court and myself now got along very well
together; he had been bred to the law in the western
country, did not want for shrewdness, was good-
natured, but was evidently a man of low habits and
manners.   He was very much amused with my apparatus for dressing, which was simple enough ; a
nail-brush was quite new to him, and he remarked
that " it was a considerable better invention than a
fork, which he said he had seen people use when
they *had too much dirt* in their nails."   He " didn't
see why I wanted so many tooth-brushes."   He " once

carried one, but it was troublesome, though the handle was convenient to stir brandy-sling with." After a while he left me, to dress himself after his fashion, and a little after 6 a. m. I was called to the apothecary's to breakfast, where the same viands with which we had been regaled the preceding evening were spread upon the table, without any change.

I had at various periods investigated portions of the extensive western district containing galena or sulphurate of lead, but never had had sufficient leisure to make an accurate and minute survey of the strata, and their metallic contents. Having now with me a scientific friend, and being in a part of the country offering many natural facilities, we agreed to make something like a regular survey, and ascertain the real geological structure and nidus of the metallic contents of the rocks. As a preliminary step, we walked over to what they called the *Copper Mines*, and found that very little work had been done, and that altogether superficial. Very extravagant accounts of these copper mines had been circulated by interested persons, and we saw at once that they would require a great deal of gullibility on the part of purchasers to be got rid of; my description, however, of these, as well as of the beds containing the sulphurate of lead, will be thrown into a separate chapter. After wandering about the whole day, we returned in the evening to our quarters, and sat down again to ham and treacle. Here it was announced to us that we had to " shift" our lodgings, as the Court had only bargained to sleep behind the counter with the crockery and cheese one night. We had, therefore,

to make the best of it, and lay down on the floor of
the eating-room.   It was evident that every thing
was make-shift at Mineral Point, but certainly we
found everybody very obliging.

May 21.—My berth was both cold and hard, and
I longed for the morning.   About 5 a. m. a woman
walked into the room and told us we must get up,
for she wanted to sweep the room and "lay the things,"
as the family breakfasted at six.   Having borrowed
a bucket from her, I drew some water at the well,
and having made my toilet, came back to the room
to warm myself at the fire ; but, alas, there was not
even a fire-place in it; so I took to walking up and
down the middle of the high road to keep myself
warm.   Not a leaf was to be seen on the few stunted
trees here and there, and the chilly, comfortless state
of the weather was in perfect keeping with the dismal aspect of the place.   At length came the sum-
mons to the never-failing repast of coffee, rice, treacle,
and bread and butter. Having got into conversation
with some of the people of the place, I found that
the inhabitants produced nothing of any kind whatever for their subsistence, not even a cabbage, for
there was not a garden in the place, and that they
were as dependent upon others as if they were on
board a ship.   Every thing they ate and drank was
brought from a distance by waggons at a great expense.
Flour, the price of which in the Atlantic states was
five and six dollars a barrel, was as high as fourteen
here : fresh meat of any kind was altogether unknown ; and indeed everybody lived from hand to
mouth, without once dreaming of personal comfort.

The sole topic which engrossed the general mind was the production of galena and copper, especially the first, upon which they relied to pay for every thing they consumed, no one possessing capital beyond that which a transient success might furnish him with.

It was, in fact, a complete nest of speculators, with workmen following in their train; traders again upon their traces, to sell goods and provisions; doctors, to give physic and keep boarding-houses; and lawyers, to get a living out of this motley and needy population. With but few exceptions, the diggings for metal were quite superficial; such a thing as a steam-engine, to drain a shaft or hoist out the " mineral," as it was called, was unknown here; so that, as soon as the superficial diggings were exhausted, the population was always prepared to flock to another quarter. But change of place is not often accompanied with wounded feelings in the United States. Men do not always seem to select situations in that country with a view to live tranquilly and happily, but to try to find ready money by digging for it, or to live upon others; the moment they find there is no likelihood of success, they go to another place.

After our treacle and coffee, we started again for the copper diggings, and passed the whole day examining the ravines where any rocks presented themselves, to make ourselves masters of the stratification; visiting some shafts that had been sunk, and commencing a general levelling of the whole locality. This was a day of some fatigue to us, as we extended our examinations several miles down the Peccatonic, where we found a blast-furnace in operation, for smelting the galena.

We reached our quarters at the apothecary's at sunset, and just as I was going to the usual dose of treacle and rice, I became aware that I had lost my bunch of keys, all of them patent locks: a very serious misfortune in a country where it could not be repaired. I was exceedingly annoyed, as there was no remedy but to break open all my locks, including my secretary ; but remembering that I had stooped some time at a heap of copper ore, hammering some pieces for the sake of procuring some fine specimens of green acicular crystals, I announced my determination to return there at once.

Much pains were taken to deter me from this attempt, but in vain : the loss would be productive of so much inconvenience, that I was determined to make an effort to prevent it ; so taking a lantern with me, and matches to light it, if it should be necessary, I started at a round pace, and quite alone, for the place I had in view, which was about three miles off, on a lone sort of moor, where no individual resided, and reached it just at night. In vain did I search the whole locality for an hour, and was just about to depart, with the intention of making a more thorough search the next day, when, by the aid of my light, I saw something rather red peeping from beneath some ore, and, delighted at the discovery, I seized hold of it, and dragged forth my keys. I mention this trivial incident for the purpose of stating that in my excursions I always tie a piece of red official tape to the ring of my keys, for that is seen better, if you drop them, than they are. This was not the only time it had been so serviceable to me. On my return, I said nothing at first about having found my keys, and the party at the apothecary's, believing I had not succeeded, attempted to console me by saying I had done a very foolish thing in going at that time of the night to look for them. I could only answer them, that as I was not in the habit of only washing, shaving, and dressing myself once a week, my keys were almost as necessary to me every day as my food. When they learnt, however, that I had been successful, they very good-naturedly expressed their satisfaction, and I came in for my share of the treacle as well as themselves, the apothecary declaring that I deserved it, and that he would not have taken such a walk as that alone, at that time of the night—no, he guessed " not for a dollar."

On our way from St. Louis to this place, I had observed that the conversation amongst the other passengers in the steamer turned almost exclusively upon the value of lots or building-places in some new cities, upon a magnificent scale, which had been projected since I had visited this part of the world in 1835. These cities were so numerous, that at first I was completely baffled to find an adequate cause for such an amazing increase of population as had forced into existence at least a dozen new cities, each capable of containing 500,000 inhabitants; for towns in America, at least in the new parts of it, are only congregations of people who intend to live upon the surrounding neighbourhoods. But that those cities had a real substantial existence, no person, at least no European, could reasonably doubt; for elaborate engravings of them, executed with taste by artists in the Atlantic cities, were profusely circulated. Cathedrals, cottages, churches, institutions of all kinds, squares, theatres, and streets without number, all bearing the most attractive patriotic names, were set forth with a detail and minute accuracy that bade defiance to scepticism ; and to these engraved plans were annexed eloquent descriptions of the salubrity of the climate, the purity of the waters, the curative qualities of the rare mineral springs, with many other unparalleled advantages incident to these much-favoured localities.

It was quite impossible for any uninitiated person, especially if honest himself, to suppose that all this was architectural poetry, and that in almost every case the engravings had been made without any reference to the nature of the ground upon which these modern Thebes were supposed to stand ; and above all, to imagine it possible that in no instance had any survey of the ground, where all these squares and streets were laid out, been at any time made.

On approaching, therefore, on the second day of my departure from St. Louis, that most respectable metropolis called *Marion City*, I was perfectly certain of seeing at least the rudiments of a great city, and the sons of Hiram busily engaged with the level and the square. This wonder of the western world—which I had been told it was destined to be

—was projected by a well-known preacher, of very extraordinary piety, in one of the Atlantic cities. The title of the land upon which it was to be erected was first acquired at the government price of a dollar and a quarter an acre, which is about six shillings. A noble plan was then lithographed, containing churches, colleges, squares, and streets, all bearing evangelical denominations. It was to be a *City of the Saints,* and only to be inhabited by *the Elect.* God, it was declared, was to be glorified there as he never had been glorified ; and what was particularly attractive was, that wealth was to be amassed as it had never been amassed before. There were to be no profane dwellers in it and no paper-money, and salvation and specie-paying banks were to constitute an earthly paradise of Marion City.

The reverend gentleman who was the prime mover of so much worldly blessedness used his opportunities well, and the faithful purchased their lots freely of him. A well-known senator of the United States, who knew all about his proceedings, assured me that nothing could surpass the zeal of the pious proprietor to get the Chosen together into this happy Marion City, and that one of his reverend coadjutors in one of the western towns informed his congregation, after a very exciting discourse delivered from the pulpit, that the Rev. ——— was in the vestry ready to sell pious brethren lots in Marion City ; and so excited were they by the extravagant expectations they had been taught to entertain of the spiritual and other advantages which an interest in the City of Saints would give them, that they rushed to the bait, and again made a temple consecrated to the Lord a den of thieves and fools.

When, after hearing so much of this Marion City, my eyes first opened upon it, I saw nothing but an extensive bottom of very low land, *with a few straggling wooden buildings* scattered here and there. A more desolate and unpromising-looking residence I never beheld. The captain of the steamer, who from his constant voyages, was familiarly acquainted with the place, told me that it was inundated at every rise of the Mississippi, and that it was a place that never could become a "resting-place for man." The few persons that had attempted to settle there were, he said, perfectly wretched, and were already looking out for an abode blessed with fewer perfections.

May 22.—All this was forcibly brought to my recollection by the arrival of a person at the apothecary's, bringing with him some elaborately-engraved plans of various cities in the territory of Wisconsin, some forty miles from Mineral Point, in the vicinity of *Tychŏberah*, or the Four Lakes. These cities, this person insisted, had at least been surveyed, the lots had all been regularly marked out, and the settlements most flourishingly commenced. One of them, according to him—and our host confirmed this part of his story—was to be the seat of government of the future State of Wisconsin, and was named Madison. Judging from his earnestness that he was concerned in the success of these magnificent enterprises, I made no suspicious remarks, and merely asked for some information, as I intended to

visit those lakes, of whose beauty I had heard a great
deal said. But I missed my mark this time, for our
friend did not possess a tithe of the information
about the country that I had collected myself. All
that I could gather from him was, that they were the
finest cities upon the " univarsal arth :" which was
the best of them to live in he could not tell, but he
" guessed that any man that would lay out his money
in lots in Madison, it would tumble overtail twenty
times in five years, and you can't do better than that,
stranger, go whare you will." I learnt afterwards
that this fellow had never been in this part of the
country before ; that he had purchased some of
these engraved plans not long before at Louisville,
and with that prodigious stock of assurance that so
much distinguishes the " go-ahead" men in these
western parts, had started upon the very original
plan of offering for sale at least 100,000 city building-lots for any thing whatever he could get for them
from the dupes he might meet with, pretending to
have an office of business at Milwaukee, and giving
an engagement to deliver a title there as soon as
some formality or other had been passed through
the legislature. He had even paid his fare in the
steamers more than once with his lots, and had
sported them at the gambling-table.

CHAPTER XLIII.

May 23.—I was promoted from the floor of the
eating-room to a small apartment at the top of the
house, having reached which, I discovered it was
the apothecary's shop of our host, and the smell of
asafœtida being inconveniently strong just where I
was obliged to lay my head, I passed a most extraordinary night. The weather in the morning continued extremely cold, not a bud on the trees swelling.
I was informed that warm weather was so uncertain
in this part of the country, that many persons did not
take their fire-stoves down at all. After breakfast
I met with the vender of cities again as I was walking to the copper-veins, and got into an easy conversation with him, without pretending to question
the respectability of his vocation. Certainly, nothing
can be more disgusting than the barefaced frauds
practised by these "smart creeturs" that are roving
about wherever men are to be found, for the express
purpose of cheating their fellow-beings.

May 24.—In the course of the day I met with a very
clever sort of person, called Messersmith, uniting in

himself the vocations of miner and farmer. He informed me that his settlement was not much out of the way to Tychŏberah, or the Four Lakes, and invited me to call and see him on my way there. The account he gave me of the sufferings of the Indians from the small-pox was very affecting. He had found a chief dead in one of the purification lodges of the women: having become blind and helpless, his two squaws, fearing that he and they would perish from the infection, as the whole tribe had almost done, had abandoned him and endeavoured to reach another part of the country; but they also were found dead in the woods some time after, of the same disorder. I extended my excursion some distance down the valley of the Peccatonic, and having got out of the reach of the settlement, started a great many fine tetrao. The stream was now a mere rivulet, but flowed in an ancient channel 800 yards broad, which bore all the marks of being once filled with a powerful river. The adjacent country was almost entirely prairie, of a rolling and anticlinal character, the strata dipping N. E. and S. W., and sometimes presenting natural sections in the coulées or valleys, much dislocated and shattered, the face of the country sufficiently resembling the character of the Alleghany mountains to refer such configuration of surfaces to the same cause.

May 25.—This was an exceedingly cold morning, but having laid in my supply of coffee and treacle, I betook myself into the interior again, and after rather a fagging day, returned in the evening to the treacle-pot. In my various adventures I never had been more curiously fed than at present; and what appears rather odd now is, that I began to take very kindly to it. The fact was, that, knowing there was nothing better to be had, I followed out my old plan of being contented with the best, which is the true way of getting accustomed to the worst.

I had heard much of a trial for murder that was to take place in the evening, and as amusement and characteristic manners are usually to be found upon such occasions, especially in the western country, I went to the court-house, which was a log building made of squared timber. It was but a sorry exhibition of a court of justice, dark, and filled with filthy-looking men, spitting about in every direction. The prisoner was an impudent, ill-looking fellow, of the name of McComber, and it appeared on the trial, that in a revengeful spirit, for some supposed injury, he had steadily followed up one Willard, a nephew of General Dodge, the governor of the territory, and seizing his opportunity, had shot him. The *court* was my old friend with his breeches on; but, sorry I am to say, he was ill-dressed, excessively dirty, unshaven, and had his jaws tied up in an old silk handkerchief, having, as he told the jury, "got the mumps." The prosecuting attorney, who summed up, exceeded all the pleaders I ever listened to for absurdity of language and bad grammar, and had evidently come from the very lowest class. The following was one of his grave passages, intended to be very impressive.

"Yes, gentlemen of the jury, he is proved to have been maliciously and aforethought contriving this here business. He was seen walking up and down, backwards and forwards, with solemnity, and to make the act more solemn, he did the solemnest thing a man can do when he is coming to a solemn thought, and determines on it, by the smoking of the pipe. Yes, he concluded by the smoking of the pipe; and if that beent, as you may say, putting the cap a top, why then, I don't know what is." The twang, the appearance, and gestures of the orator are wanting to do justice to this eloquent passage. At the conclusion of this speech the court adjourned the proceedings until the succeeding evening, and dismissed us, to go where we pleased, jury and all.

May 26.—This day my companion and myself, having procured some assistance, continued our levellings, and at the conclusion of our labours we returned to our quarters, where we learnt that the jury had sent a sealed verdict to the judge, having found the prisoner guilty, and that sentence was to be passed upon him at eight o'clock. The court, my old friend, had not arrived when I entered the court-house, and I was occupied looking at the convicted prisoner, whose eyes were glancing in an unquiet manner about the room, when the judge, his person in the greatest disorder, his neck-handkerchief awry, and his clothes partly unbuttoned, entered the court-room, *staggering drunk*, and after the most frightful exhibition of impotent inebriety, just managed to reach his judgment-seat without falling.

I have been present at many rare and curious

spectacles, but never before assisted at one so peculiarly and intensely shocking as this; most of the persons present evinced great dissatisfaction, and some of them proposed to lead him away. Leaning sideways, and not looking at anybody, he attempted to address the jury, but he was too far gone even to "talk straight." This horrid burlesque was gradually creating a strong feeling of indignation in the spectators, and I thought it probable at one time that they would seize him and duck him in the stream, which would certainly have been putting the "cap a top," as the solemn attorney said the preceding evening. As to the prisoner, who no doubt was turning the chances in his mind, he looked at his judge and seemed quite baffled at the probable nature of the coming sentence which the fiery dictates of whiskey might suggest. The prosecuting attorney, now feeling that his own dignity was at stake, addressed him, and entreated him to defer the sentence until morning. As it was out of his power to utter any reasons against the court's adjourning until that time, the attorney directed proclamation to be made, and we left the court, the reeling majesty of the law being led publicly to his lodgings by two of the constables.

May 27.—After breakfast I returned to the court-house to witness the conclusion of this disgraceful affair. The judge arrived and took his seat with that wretched and haggard appearance that individuals bear who are far advanced in mania potu; and, after a few absurd phrases, sentenced the murderer to pay a fine of three hundred dollars, and to be imprisoned until the fine was paid. The disgusting farce being over, the convict was conducted to the log hut which was appointed to be the jail, and as soon as they opened the door to let him in, I saw him make a couple of ground somersets, the last of which carried him into his lodgings. These consisted of a solitary log-house, with one room on the ground and a window with some iron bars. No sooner had they locked him in, than he began to crow with all his might. His numerous friends now went to talk to him at the window, and during the day brought him food and whiskey. In the course of the night he evaporated, and so ended the affair; for as to apprehending him a second time, few persons would be found to attempt that, it being universally known that when frontier bloods of his calibre once imbrue their hands in blood, they entertain no scruples about taking the lives of those who come with hostile intentions against them.

May 28.—Having finished our investigations in the course of the day, I began to pack up my fossils and minerals, preparatory to an excursion to Tychōberah. A more melancholy and dreary place than this Mineral Point I never expect to see again : we had not tasted a morsel of fresh meat, or fish, or vegetables, since we had been here. There was not a vestige of a garden in the place, and the population seemed quietly to have resigned itself to an everlasting and unvarying diet of coffee, rice, treacle and bread, and salt butter, morning, noon, and night, without any other variety than that of occasionally getting a different cup and saucer.

May 29.—Having engaged a waggon, we took
our places in it very early, and I turned my back,
not unreluctantly, upon our late quarters, leaving
my luggage to keep company with the assafœtida
until my return.   We were now bound to Tychōberah, and to those prairies and lakes whose beauty
had been so much extolled to me. *Madison City,*
too, was an attraction before us ; in truth, we had
been so wretchedly off at our apothecary's, that we
were convinced any change would be much for the
better, and were ardently longing to see new faces
in the shape of potatoes, fresh fish, and meat. As to
architectural expectations, I was cautious enough, in
consequence of my late experience, not to entertain
any very exalted ones, and therefore limited my
anticipations to the larder of the best tavern of the
metropolis of the territory, where it was clear there
must be something better than treacle and assafœtida.
About five miles from Mineral Point we called upon
the governor, General Dodge, at a quiet cabin he
had built for himself in a small secluded valley, tolerably well wooded, and spent half an hour with him.
This gentleman, at that time the chief magistrate of
the territory, was said to be a perfect western *character*. I had seen him on horseback in the streets
of Mineral Point, and was struck with the appearance of his accoutrements, having, although dressed
in plain clothes, immense horse pistols staring out
of his holsters. He had been brought up on the
frontiers, and since his manhood had been rather
notorious for his desperate feuds with various individuals, many of whom still surviving, he always

went armed, the invariable practice of bloods of his calibre being to fire immediately at any hostile approach.

On taking our leave of his excellency, we passed some " diggings," with a few miserable huts erected near them, dignified with the name of *Dodgeville.* From hence we pursued our way across a rolling prairie, covered with charming wild-flowers, and then came to some woodland, where the country became somewhat hilly. Here, at noon, we were met by my acquaintance, Mr. Messersmith, who was on the look-out for us, and who conducted us to his farm-house, situated at the bottom of a little wooded dell, near a copious spring of delicious clear water. We were received in the kindest manner by his family, and after partaking of a homely repast, served to us with unceasing kindness, we set out on a long ramble to visit *his* diggings, which appeared to be very productive. On our return to the farm we were surprised by a hurricane and a heavy storm, accompanied with torrents of rain, in which we had to walk about four miles drenched through and through. We were glad to get back to our host's cabin, and repair our misfortune as well as we could at a rousing wood fire. Mrs. Messersmith then gave us a cup of coffee, and we lay down whilst our clothes were taken care of by the good lady.

May 30.—At the dawn of day I rose, and, finding my clothes comfortably dried, dressed, and went to the beautiful spring, where, having made my ablutions, I took a stroll before breakfast ; and, having taken our cup of coffee and thanked our friends for their very hospitable reception, we again got into our waggon, and drove sixteen miles over the prairie to the Blue Mounds, two considerable elevations of rock, consisting of a silicious hornstone, resembling that which I had seen in 1834 in the lead district of Missouri. The galena procured in this neighbourhood is so very white and brittle, and contains such a superabundance of sulphur, that upon breaking many of the cubes, I generally found crystals of pure sulphur within. We here found an old bachelor, named Brigham, living in a log hut at this solitary place, following, as everybody does in this territory, the occupation of a miner. He gave us a couple of hard-boiled eggs and some stale bread, and charged us about ten times what they were worth for them.

Pursuing our journey, at one p.m. we passed the military road leading to Fort Winnebago and Navarino, and soon afterwards got into one of the most exquisitely beautiful regions I have ever seen in any part of the world. The prairie that had hitherto been distinguished by a regular rolling surface, here changed its character, and took the form of ridges somewhat elevated, which frequently resolved themselves into masses of gracefully-rounded hills, separated by gentle depressions, that occasionally became deepened valleys. In these, some of the heads of a stream called Sugar River, a tributary of Rock River, took their rise. In whatever direction our eyes were turned, the most pleasing irregularities of surface presented themselves. But that which crowned the perfection of the view, and imparted an indescribable charm to the whole scene, from the knoll where we stood to the most distant point where the alternate hills and vales blended with the horizon, was the inimitable grace with which the picturesque clumps of trees, that sometimes enlarged themselves into woods, embellished this rural landscape from the hand of Nature.

Here a thick grove hanging upon the slope of a hill, distinguished by its symmetry from its numerous companions, impended over the amenity of the valley beneath; whilst, further on, a more robust line of dense foliage betrayed the ample volume of some pellucid stream whence it was nourished. Turn where we would, every object within the ample range concurred to cherish and to establish more indelibly the pleasing impression caused by the whole; whilst the softness of these attractions contrasted here and there so strikingly with the noble rock escarpments peering out from the bluffs, that Nature might be said to speak to you in a voice that must be listened to, and to tell you that she had here surpassed the most polished efforts of English park scenery, the most difficult of all her achievements. America will justly boast of this unrivalled spectacle when it becomes known, for certainly it is formed of elements that no magic could enable all Europe to bring together upon so great a scale.

The aspect of this lovely country at once accounted for so great a population flocking to the lakes, on whose enchanting banks those cities were founded of which we had heard so much, and to which we were now advancing. Four noble lakes in the centre of a region of such unrivalled beauty must constitute perfection itself. Our expectations were exceedingly raised; every moment produced a new excitement; the occasional glimpse of the shy deer, with their elegant fawns, and the more frequent flushing of the prairie-hen from her nest, gave animation to the still beauty around us. Enraptured with all I saw, I could not but occasionally reflect on the oddity of *seven* large cities, each capable of containing a population of half a million of people, having congregated so close together. There was *Madison City*, which was the metropolis. Adjacent to this was the *City of the Four Lakes*. A short distance beyond this was the city of *North Madison*. Close upon this again was the city of *East Madison*. Then there was the city of *West Madison*, the city of *South Madison*, and, finally, the *City of the First Lake*. Of each of these I had a beautifully engraved plan, with all its squares, streets, institutions, and temples.

The path we were upon was an ancient Indian trail, holding its course steadily from the waters of the Mississippi to Tychōberah, or the Four Lakes; and, as if all things rare in their nature had here gathered together, to enhance the interest which was inspired by this romantic country, we came to some Indian monuments of a very remarkable character.

CHAPTER XLIV.

AN EXTRAORDINARY SERIES OF ANCIENT INDIAN MOUNDS. — GREAT
EXPECTATION OF GOOD FARE AT MADISON CITY.—THE SEVEN CITIES
ALL CONTAINED IN ONE SMALL LOG HUT, WITH A SINGLE ROOM.—
MRS. PECK SWEETENS OUR COFFEE.—TWO SMART QUAKERS.—A WIN-
NEBAGO BEAUTY AND HER CAVALIER.

THESE were figures of animals and men, formed
of the soil upon the surface of the ground, about
six feet high, in alto-relievo, all of them perfectly
distinct, and covered with a sod that appeared to be
coeval with that of the prairie itself.   Not one of
them appeared to have been opened ; and this circumstance, with the novelty of the spectacle, could
not fail to detain me until I had examined, measured,
and sketched these interesting objects.   They were
very numerous, and extended more than half a mile
on each side of our road, which, as before mentioned,
was an ancient Indian war-path, leading from the
waters of the Mississippi, in the direction of the
Four Lakes, to Lake Michigan.

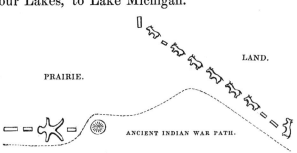

PRAIRIE.

LAND.

ANCIENT INDIAN WAR PATH.

At a point very near to the trail, was the figure of a man, amidst some oblong mounds, his arms extended north and south, his head lying to the west, and his legs to the east. East from this figure, about 200 feet, was a round tumulus, sufficiently high to overlook every thing around; and about 600 feet east from it was a line of seven buffalo mounds, each representing distinctly the head, horns, neck, fore and hind legs, body, and tail of that animal. Each of these animal mounds measured, from the nose to the tip of the tail, about 120 feet, of which the tail alone measured thirty-six feet. The figure of the man was about 150 feet long, from one extremity to the other, the limbs twenty feet apart at the east, and all the parts stood in bold relief, about six feet high from the face of the prairie. To the left of the trail was a circle, about sixty feet in diameter.

As we proceeded westward, we found other mounds of a similar character; a few, however, differed from them, and appeared rather to take the form of a beaver, as others, in distant parts of the Wisconsin territory, did that of the turtle. At one point near to the trail, was a large animal mound, embossed upon the prairie, betwixt a rampart of earth at least 200 yards long, and a vertical escarpment of incoherent sandstone, of the same quality with the friable sand-rock I had seen on the banks of the Wisconsin, which underlies the metalliferous limestone.

From the great abundance of mounds, of various kinds, which exist in this fertile territory, it is evident that it must have been in ancient times a

favourite abode of powerful tribes, remarkable for
their ingenuity.   We know that, having separated
into tribes, the buffalo, the turtle, the beaver, and
other animals, became the totems or badges of the
Indians ; and that, after their rude and simple manner, they used them as heraldic symbols.   Amongst
the various Indian nations, of which we have any
knowledge, in the continent of America, we find its
principal beasts and birds selected by them to desig-
nate their races, just as those objects in nature, the
lion, the eagle, the horse, have been adopted in
various parts of the old world ; and it deserves notice
that the presumption that the horse was not indigenous to America is strengthened by the fact that
no Indian tribe has ever taken that animal for its
totem or badge, and that no ancient name for it is
to be found in any of their languages.

  That these mounds, whatever form has been given
to them, are deposits of the dead, has been proved
upon numerous occasions.   Some of them, of all
kinds, have been opened, and have uniformly been
found to contain human bones.   Nor is each mound
the tomb of one individual, for bones are found
distributed throughout, and in such a manner as to
shew that layers of bodies have beeen placed side by
side, then covered over with earth, and another
layer deposited.   I can speak with certainty of this,
having been present at the opening of more than
one of them.   A collection of such mounds, then,
is to be regarded as an Indian cemetery, placed near
one of their great war-paths ; whilst those representing men may really have been so figured in

honour of some conspicuous warrior, whose tomb, thus situated, could be seen and honoured by all who passed up and down the war-path.

Having stopped to make the preceding sketch of these interesting objects, the first of the kind I had ever seen, we hastened on, as the day was drawing to a close, and we had yet some distance to go to Madison City. For some time I had kept a good look-out for some of the enterprising farmers, who must have come from great distances to this fertile country, and was rather surprised that we should hitherto have met with no one. We had not passed a single farm, and concluded that, being an Indian country, the settlers had clustered round the great city we were bound to, and had established them-selves near that lake where the best fish abounded. Fresh fish! prodigious varieties! cat-fish, pike, pickerel, salmon, trout, buffalo, perch! What anti-cipations for men who had for so many days been bolting pieces of tough fat bacon, cured 1,000 miles off. At length we came to a belt of open trees, and, passing through it, we reached the flat, marshy shores of the largest of the four lakes: we could see almost entirely around it, and much did we look; but, alas! no vestige of human dwelling was in sight.

This considerably changed the current of our thoughts, and materially impaired the beauty of the prospect. Not being disposed to express all we felt, we reluctantly took to the woods again, along the margin of the lake, in the hope to stumble upon some one or other. Night was gradually drawing her veil over every thing, and it became rather doubtful whether we should not have—in the language of back-woodsmen—to camp out. Keeping, therefore, all my visions of fried fish in the background for a while, I felt for my box of matches, and, finding it safe, turned my attention—as old Indian travellers always do—to the next best thing, a rousing fire to lie down by. Black clouds were forming in the horizon; we had been drenched thoroughly the day before, and it became pretty certain there would be another storm. Groping our way, and occasionally jolting over the fallen trees, we, at the end of an hour and a half, got to the shore of the third lake, having somehow or other missed the second lake, where *Madison City* was supposed to be. We now changed our course again, and keeping to the north-west, and meandering, and wondering, and shouting for my companion, who had got out of the waggon to follow a small trail he thought he had discovered, I at length gave up the attempt to proceed any further, and, selecting a dry tree as a proper place to bivouac near, had already stopped the waggon, when, hearing my companion's voice shouting for me in a tone that augured something new to be in the wind, I pushed on in that direction, and at length found him standing at the door of a hastily-patched-up log hut, consisting of one room about twelve feet square.

This was *Madison City!* and, humble as it was, it concentred within itself all the urban importance of the seven cities we had come so far to admire, and to which, according to our engraved plans, Nineveh of old, Thebes with its hundred gates, and

Persepolis, were but baby-houses. Not another dwelling was there *in the whole* country, and this wretched contrivance had only been put up within the last four weeks. Having secured our horses, we entered the grand and principal entrance to the city, against the top of which my head got a severe blow, it not being more than five feet high from the ground. The room was lumbered up with barrels, boxes, and all manner of things. Amongst other things was a bustling little woman, about as high as the door, with an astounding high cap on, yclept Mrs. Peck. No male Peck was on the ground, but from very prominent symptoms that went before her, another half-bushel seemed to be expected.

My first inquiry was, whether she had any fresh fish in the house. The answer was " No !" Inflexible and unwelcome word. No fresh fish ! no large, delicious catfish, of twenty pounds' weight, to be fried with pork, and placed before the voracious traveller in quantities sufficient to calm those apprehensions that so often arise in Indian lands, of there not being enough for him to eat until he falls fast asleep. " Why, then," exclaimed my alarmed companion, " what's to be done ?" " I calculate I've got some salt pork," rejoined our little hostess. " Then, Madam, you must fry it without the fish," I replied. So to the old business we went, of bolting square pieces of fat pork, an amusement I had so often indulged in, that I sometimes felt as if I ought to be ashamed to look a live pig in the face. Our landlady, however, was a very active and obliging person ; she said she would make us as comfortable as it was possible for her to do, and "she guessed" she had a little coffee, and would make us a cup of it. Whether it was acorns, or what it was, puzzled me not a little; it certainly deserved to be thought tincture of myrrh, and, as we drank and grimaced, dear Mrs. Peck, in her sweetest manner, expresssd her regret, that she had no other sugar for our coffee, they having, "somehow or another, not brought any with them."

Whilst we were at this repast, the thunder-storm broke over us, and a deluge of rain came down, streaming through the roof in various places. In the midst of the confusion two other vagabonds came in; one of them a ruffian-looking fellow, who said he was a miner, on his way across the Indian country from Milwaukee: the other, a stupid, boorish, dirty-looking animal, said he had not tasted any thing for two days, having lost his way on the prairie; and, having been overtaken the preceding night by a very heavy rain, whilst making his way up a coulée or vale, had been afraid to lie on the ground, and had passed the whole night sitting on a fallen tree. Fortunately, there was pork enough for us all, and when our landlady had put the frying-pan to bed, she did the same to us by the act of blowing the candle out. Where she stowed herself was her own secret. Choosing a place between two barrels, I lay down, and drew my cloak over me; of sleep there was very little to be had, for it rained in torrents almost the whole night, and, not having pitched my camp skilfully, it poured upon me from the unfinished roof as I lay stretched upon the floor, not daring to move in the dark, lest I should pull some of the articles of Mrs. Peck's museum upon me, or break some of her crockery.

May 31.—With the first ray of light I jumped up from my uncomfortable berth, and, having procured some dry clothes from my carpet-bag, strode over the two hang-gallows-looking fellows that were snoring near me, and gained the door. The illusion was now dissipated, and I had completely awoke from my dream of the Seven Cities, wondering how I could have ever thought it possible to have so deceived myself. *Smart* as I knew these western Americans were, I had not thought them so systematically and callously fraudulent as to cause engravings to be made of cities, with all their concomitant appendages, in countries where not a human being was to be found, and where not a single tree was cut down ; and this for the purpose of robbing their own countrymen. To rob strangers might, from the prejudice of education, be considered even meritorious ; but to rob their own countrymen so remorselessly argued an absence of principle so universal and total, that I do not know where it is to be paralleled in history.

The all-absorbing passion for money, which the absence of those moral distinctions that so much protect society from it in Europe has established in the American mind, has, with this class of men, obliterated every sense of that feeling that naturally inclines men to obey the divine injunction of " doing unto others as ye would they should do unto you." If a smart man cheats any one, no part of the dis-

grace of knavery falls upon him ; and if one smart
man cheats another smart man,* he receives the most

* An apt illustration of this was familiarly spoken of and
admired when I first visited New York, near forty years ago.
An active, extremely shrewd, and " considerable smart" Quaker
merchant expected the arrival from India of a valuable ship and
cargo belonging to him ; and she was so much out of time, that
he partially insured her at a high premium of twenty per cent.
The policy, of which a very large portion remained uncovered,
was in the hands of a brother Quaker, of great reputation for
sagacity and caution, but fond of large premiums.   One morning,
Friend Jacob B——, the insurer, was seen out very early, laughing
and chatting, as if in one of his happiest moods.   The other
"Friend," who still hesitated about taking the risk, was in the habit
of having Jacob's movements watched, for he calculated, very naturally, that his temper would be affected one way or the other by the
news that he would receive of his ship, and would be a safe guide,
in the absence of other information, for his determination about
covering the policy.   Learning that Jacob had been seen in such
a very lively mood, he began to think seriously about the premium ; and whilst he was meditating, a note was delivered to him
from Jacob, which ran thus :—
    " Friend ——
    " If thee has not signed the policy, I wish thee to send it to
me immediately by the bearer.   Thy friend,
                                        " JACOB B——"
    " Verily, Jacob," said the good man to himself, " thee did
not put on cheerfulness for nothing this morning ; thee hath private news of the arrival of this ship, and I may as well have the
premium as not."   Saying this, he filled the policy, and giving
it to the messenger, said, " Thee may tell Friend B—— that I
have taken the risk."   A quarter of an hour afterwards, another
friend dropped in to tell him, that news was in town that Jacob's
ship was a total loss.   His state of mind may be imagined, when
he found himself thus overreached.
    Setting aside the undoubted *smartness* of this transaction, a
more fraudulent proceeding, on both sides, it would be difficult

unbounded admiration; so that these smart fellows, having no motive whatever to be commonly honest, at last become callous, and forget even the nature of justice, living only to carry out their own base and selfish manœuvres. The vender of cities spoken of at page 79 took no particular pains to conceal from me the atrocious nature of the occupations he had followed, and was hardy enough, in an argument with me, to attempt to justify his practices. " Men," said he, " that keep a bright look-out are never taken in; it is only fools that take themselves in, and they are of no account."

It is fearful to reflect what will be the condition of society here when honesty retires altogether from the field of action, and leaves fraud, *smartly* perpetrated, to be the principal feature in all transactions; how much is to be apprehended from the future, when the generations of men, that will have no good examples before their eyes, may abandon even the intention to be respectable.

Having now fully made up my mind that I was in an Indian country as wild and unsettled as any I had yet visited, I hastened to the shore of the lake to espy what truly turned out to be the nakedness of the land, not a vestige of any human being or habitation being to be discerned. Rambling, however, along the lake-shore, picking up unios and

to produce. The insured, knowing his vessel was lost, assumed a cheerfulness he did not feel, and by his fortunate finesse, tempted his *brother* Quaker to underwrite the policy. And his unlucky victim, convinced the risk was over, signed the policy, when he must have felt he could not honestly claim the premium.

anadontas, I came upon a wigwam, inhabited by a
squaw of the Winnebago tribe, and learnt from her
that her mate was a French Canadian, and was
fishing from a canoe a little lower down. Thither
I hied, and having found him, engaged him, with
the assistance of his squaw, to procure us a mess of
sunfish. This being accomplished, I sent them to
Mrs. Peck, and following my messenger to Madison
City, requested her to prepare them for our breakfast. No time was lost in doing this, and we made
a very hearty meal without putting her to the trouble
of preparing us any coffee. Sallying out again, I
walked across a tongue of land which separated this
from the fourth lake, and soon reached its shore,
from whence I had a view of an extremely beautiful
sheet of water.

Advancing along, I found more signs of humanity:
two men were cutting some poles down; the one a
Canadian, the other a somewhat desperado-looking
young American, with cropped hair. Near to the
lake I observed other poles laid aslant upon a fallen
tree, forming a sort of shed, and looking beneath,
beheld a youthful Winnebago squaw lying down on
a filthy blanket, thoroughly drenched with the rain
of the preceding night. She was pursy and im-
mensely fat, but had some good features. Near to
her was a bower of a similar character, containing
an elderly squaw, with only one eye, as hideously
wrinkled and frowsy as she could well be. Whilst
I was standing near to these creatures, the men
came up, and I soon saw that the young American
was the cavaliero of the fat squaw, and that the

couch where she was lying was their bower of bliss. This fellow, having a canoe, agreed, for a dollar, to take me out upon the lake, and down a channel that connects the fourth with the third lake, and thence to Madison City. Accordingly, getting into a badly-constructed log canoe with his fat beauty, we paddled off.

After visiting various parts of the lake, and being more than once nearly upset from the awkward management of this youth, at whom the squaw laughed heartily, we entered the channel which connects the two lakes. It was about three miles and a half long and about forty feet in breadth, and we found the current so very strong at the entrance, that we shot down it with great rapidity, the shores on each side being, for the greatest part of the distance, a swamp very little raised above the level of the stream. At length we came to a piece of ground where a part of the band of Winnebagoes had their wigwams. Three horrible-looking frowsy she-savages were eviscerating fish, which they were curing by fire on some stakes. Their matted, coarse, black locks stood out at right angles, like the strands of a mop when it is twirled; scarce any thing was to be discerned in their lineaments that was human, and more loathsome and disgusting objects I never beheld. Every thing about the wigwams was in keeping with their re-volting and odious persons; ordure and dead fish in the last stage of corruption made a perfect pes-tilence around, amidst which they moved in the most contented and philosophic manner. Alecto,

Megara, and Tisiphone, the far-famed furies, must
have been beauties compared to these hags. I just
stayed long enough to purchase from them a fine
alligator gar (*Esox osseus*) for the sake of its skeleton, and then came away. Just as we were starting, one of these she-devils, wanting to visit the
one-eyed squaw we had left behind, strode into our
canoe, and a pretty inside passenger we had of her.
The canoe itself was a wretched, tottering affair,
imperfectly hollowed out of a small log, and wab-
bled about in such a doubtful manner that we had
been several times near upsetting in crossing the
lake. In this "dug-out"—for that is the expres-
sive name they go by—I had taken my seat on
the bottom near the prow, with my face towards
the stern, holding the sides with my hands; thus
situated, this she-monster, clapping herself immediately in front of me, and seizing a paddle, of
which she seemed a perfect mistress, most vigorously began to ply it. At first I was amused by
her motions; but, alas! my satisfaction was of short
duration, for warming with the exercise, every time
she raised her brawny fins to propel the canoe, she
at each stroke almost bobbed a particular part of
her person into contact with my nose, when such
lots of unknown odours came from her that I soon
became wretchedly sick at my stomach, and was
delighted when we arrived at dear little Mrs. Peck's
paradise.

These Howchungerahs, or Winnebagoes, well de-
serve the name of " Puants," which the first French
adventurers gave them. Establishing themselves

where fish is plentiful, they never change the site of their wigwams, at the entrances to which they throw down the entrails and offal of their fish. They have thus become notorious amongst the other Indians for the filthy existence they lead. I learnt from our hostess that the young Adonis, in whose canoe I had been, had deserted from the American garrison of Fort Winnebago, had been apprehended, flogged, his head shaved, and then drummed out of the fort to choose his own mode of life. He had wandered about until he fell in with this band of Indians, and, rejected by his own race, had found refuge and a mistress amongst the savages.

As soon as we had taken a good reconnaissance of the country around, and packed up the unios, and other fresh-water shells I had collected, we bade adieu to the little inhabitant of Madison City and turned our faces to the prairie again. It had been part of my plan to strike across the country to a branch of Rock River, being desirous of examining the remains of an ancient city which I had heard a great deal about, and to which the name of Aztalan had been given. This had been described as of large dimensions, having archways and casements made with brick and mortar, as if a city had in ancient times existed here, built of cal y canto, like those which Cortez found when he advanced into Mexico. But having spoken with various Indians well acquainted with the country, who declared they had never seen or heard of any thing of the kind, or indeed any thing but some mounds near the supposed locality, and considering the small success I had had in my researches after modern cities, I gave up my intention of looking up this ancient one. It would have taken us at least two days to reach the mounds, and being without a guide in a region where there was neither road nor inhabitants betwixt the lakes and them, we inclined more willingly to the supposition that it was quite as likely that the whole affair was a poetical speculation got up to establish a modern Thebes upon the ruins of the older one for the purpose of selling the lots; an ingenious device, of which we soon had a curious and instructive instance.

CHAPTER XLV.

WE had advanced about seven miles from the lakes into the prairie, when we met with the old bachelor, Mr. Brigham, whose cabin we had stopped at, at the Blue Mounds, accompanied by another person, holding various papers in his hand, and who appeared somewhat agitated as we came up with them. This man's name was Picketts, and his story was as follows. He had left New York on a trading expedition for Milwaukee, on Lake Michigan, and on arriving there, had sold and delivered to a person there, of the name of Glennie, butter, bacon, and other commodities, to the amount of nine hundred dollars. Mr. Glennie, it appeared, being desirous of introducing respectable settlers into the western wilderness, and being gifted with very persuasive powers, had induced Mr. Picketts, when in a remarkably verdant state of mind, to receive in payment for his goods nine lots admirably situated for erecting city buildings, in the city of West Madison, which, as the engraved map most forcibly exhibited, was advantageously situated upon the banks of the Third Lake. Mr.

Picketts had thought it one of the best bargains
that had ever been made, which was probably also
Mr. Glennie's opinion; who, in addition to his
deeds in fee-simple, delivered him a handsomely
engraved plan of the city of West Madison, with
its imposing squares and streets, and the most
charming of lakes lying in all its quiet beauty in
front of the city.

Now, these deeds were bounded by certain ranges
and lines that had been surveyed by the surveyors
of the general government, so that, of course, the
lots were there. Having obtained from the Land-
office some directions and instructions as to the
numbers of his lots, he brought Mr. Brigham with
him to identify that part of the township where
they were situated. Mr. Brigham, who understood
all this machinery very well, had just communicated to his companion, that the lots described in
his deeds were exactly where he was standing. Mr.
Picketts, therefore, had all that satisfaction that a
man can have who has found a mathematical point;
but as to its value to him, which depended altogether
upon its being in a city founded on the bank of
a large lake, it was as clear to his comprehension, as
any thing could be, that it was *nil;* for, however
true it might be that the lots were there, it was no
less so that the lake was seven miles off, and could
not be seen from them.

Upon looking over his papers, I saw into the fraud
at once. The plot of ground where we stood had
been laid out into squares and streets *on paper*, and

the building-lots in the streets had been regularly numbered and conveyed in the deeds, in which no mention whatever was made of the lake. By way of embellishment, the vender had added the lake to the engraved plan of the city, and had called the city West Madison. This was the best that he could do for his customers; he had brought the lake and the city very prettily together on paper, and it was most unreasonable to ask him to bring two points together in any other way that nature had so far divided. He had merely sold the lots by their numbers and bounds, and there they were: to be sure, there was not a drop of water, nor a tree, nor a being, within seven miles of them, and it was pretty certain that there never would be; so nothing was left for Mr. Picketts but to make the most of his wrinkle, and to part with them to some untravelled friend in New York, who had a romantic turn for lake scenery.

The issue, however, of all these projects, raised upon such unexampled frauds, cannot but suggest serious reflections; for the amount of fictitious evidences of credit that thus get into circulation is incredible. Besides these unsubstantial cities, railroads, as shadowy as themselves, have, by the manœuvring of speculators, become incorporated by the state legislatures, ostensibly to connect these imaginary towns. Hence, bonds, and mortgages, and promissory notes, railroad shares, and other apparent evidences of property, have got into circulation by the ingenuity of shrewd indivi-

duals, and the connivance of those who have the
management of banks with nominal capital; indeed,
I have been informed, that in many instances
evidences of credit, having no basis whatever, have,
in the intemperate haste of speculation, got so mixed
up with *bonâ fide* securities, that they have been
received equally in payment with them in the liquidation of real transactions. Thus do fraudulent
transactions receive direct encouragement, and are
continually on the increase, and the knowing individuals connected with them, as well as the culpable
banks that facilitate their operations, become en-
riched; but the moment cannot be far distant when
these false securities will have increased to such an
amount, that they will no longer be convertible, and
an explosion must take place that will force all the
ramifications into a liquidation; it will then be
found that half the banks in the country are rotten
to the core, and an immense number of persons
must be ruined. This moment may, to be sure, be
deferred by the ingenuity of individuals, especially if
they succeed—as many are now attempting—to get
American securities into circulation in England: the
high rate of interest they will profess to pay will
tempt many persons there, and if they only manage
to pay the interest a few times, the distinction
between the real and fictitious securities may be
lost sight of for a long time.*

* This passage was entered in my Journal in these terms, in
1837, since which period the world has witnessed the ruin of the
Bank of the United States, with the squandering of all its power-

Leaving the outwitted New Yorker to his reflections, we rode on to the buffalo mounds which had attracted our attention the preceding day, and having re-measured several of them, pursued our way to Brigham's, where we had to content ourselves with such wretched fare as this parsimonious old fellow had provided.

June 1.—Hard boards and an empty stomach had not assisted me to sleep during the night. I rose at early dawn, and took a walk on the prairie, where plover were feeding in the freshness of the morning, and where I started several tetrao. As soon as the horses were put to, we started again, and reaching Mr. Messersmith's about eight a. m., got a substantial breakfast. Being desirous of riding across the country to the Wisconsin River, about twelve miles distant, our kind host volunteered to accompany us, and we set off immediately after breakfast. The surface of the country was very irregular with hill and dale, and one of the valleys we crossed was singularly beautiful. The whole distance consisted of ridges, coulées, and vales, the escarpments often exhibiting an anticlinal state in the gaps occasionally separating the ridges; which,

ful capital, consisting of thirty millions of dollars, or six millions sterling. When President Jackson severed its connection with the general government, by vetoing the renewal of the charter, speculation was let loose in every direction, and, if this were the place to undertake it, it could be shewn, that the ruin of the bank, and the universal injury sustained by American credit, were greatly produced by the state of things here described.

however, our guide informed me, were often continuous for several miles.   It was very evident that the stratification had been much modified, either by an undulating movement from below, or from superficial pressure, from causes analogous to those which have acted upon the strata of the Alleghany chain.

On reaching the shot-tower, on the bank of Wisconsin, I found every thing much improved since my visit there in 1835.   Although called a tower, it was, in fact, a perpendicular cylinder cut from the top of the escarpment, through the incoherent sandstone, to the depth of 180 feet, and the adit below, from the surface of the escarpment to the water-tub, was 90 feet long. Their method in the manufacturing of shot was to put 10 lbs. of arsenic to every 1,000 lbs. of galena, to make the lead brittle and disposed to separate ; three-fourths of this arsenic evaporates whilst melting, and does not combine with the lead. The lead, when melted a second time, is poured through a perforated ladle, and falls from the top of the tower into the water below, in all sorts of sizes and shapes.   When taken out and dried, it is poured over a series of inclined planes, separated by small troughs.   Those globules, which are quite orbicular, run over all the planes, whilst the imperfect ones waddle along, and being sometimes double, and having no spring in their movement, drop into the troughs, and are melted over again.   The perfect shot are finally sifted in a machine containing various drawers with their bottoms perforated in holes of all sizes, from buckshot to mustard-seed. This machine is moved by the hand. The shot, when separated into sorts, is glazed and put into bags.

But a very short time ago, the whole country was a wilderness, containing only a few roaming Winnebagoes, and already the white men had established a well-conducted and prosperous manufactory. The colony of swallows, too, which I had observed in 1835, had increased greatly, continuing to make holes in the face of the soft sandstone with their beaks, and filling them with nests of clay, having small orifices ; in some instances the nests were built upon the face of the vertical escarpment. Many hundreds of them had established themselves in the rock ; some of the nests had eggs, and from others young birds were peeping out. It was truly a very pretty sight. Having got something to eat at the house, we lay down to sleep on the floor, and surrendered ourselves to myriads of pitiless mosquitoes.

June 2.—What with the mosquitoes, and the heavy thunder and rain that were performing almost the whole night, I rose at the dawn, sleepless and feverish.

The Wisconsin River, which interested me so much when I came down it in my canoe in 1835, was as beautiful as ever. Having got a cup of coffee, we left its banks about nine p.m., and returned to our guides, where, taking leave of our hospitable friends, we proceeded on our return to Mineral Point, which we reached about four in the afternoon. Here, I found, by the newspapers, that all the State banks, including that of the United States, had suspended the cash payment of their notes.

June 6.—We remained at this place, reviewing our investigations, and making a few more excursions, until this morning, when I paid my bill to the worthy apothecary, in whose house I had been staying. To have a decent place to remain at as your head-quarters in such a wretched village as this, was an advantage I felt daily, and which deserved to be well paid for. But our host's bill was twice as high as it would have been at a good hotel in one of the Atlantic cities, and many more days were charged than I had been at the house. This I remarked in a friendly manner to my host, who listened to me politely. Not wishing to dispute with him, I placed the amount of the bill on the table, and told him to make what deductions he thought proper. Upon which, coming to the deduction that I was a greenhorn, he conveyed the whole of it to his pocket, and leaving the room, I saw no more of him. I therefore left a house, where I had been treated in a kind and obliging manner, with a reluctant disgust, which, but for this instance of rapacity, I never should have entertained.

I now proceed to give a brief general account of the geology of this lead-bearing district.

In a part of the work referred to in the note below,* notice is taken of a bed of sandstone of an incoherent texture, which underlays the galenifer-

* *Vide* Excursion through the Slave States, vol. i. pp. 304—307.

ous strata of the State of Missouri, about thirty miles west of the Mississippi, in N. lat. 38°.

The lead district of Wisconsin, distant about 350 miles from that point, lies in a direction from it similar to the general strike of most of the metalliferous districts of North America, viz., a few points east of north ; a circumstance which, aided by the geological affinity of the rocks along the whole of the distance which separates these two districts, and by the strong fact of the galeniferous rocks in Wisconsin being also underlaid by an incoherent sandstone, encourages some probability that galena may hereafter be found at many points along that line of 350 miles, although until this moment it had only been found at its extremities.

The peculiar arrangement of some of the galeniferous and cupreous beds in Wisconsin, and the remarkable simplicity in the order of the rocks inclosing them, will render a somewhat detailed account of them acceptable to mineralogical and geological readers.

It has been already stated in vol. i. chap. 19, that in descending the Wisconsin River, its escarpments consisted of a friable, incoherent sandstone, resembling that in Missouri ; and that on approaching the Mississippi, the sandstone on the left bank supported a loose, fetid, calcarious rock, not dissimilar to that which inclosed the galena in Missouri ; and as it was only twenty miles from this point to the " diggings " in the interior, where the metal was obtained, I always kept a good look-out for this sandstone, believing it to be the key of the stratification of the country.

The " diggings " in the vicinity of Mineral Point, where our survey was conducted, were situated in a prairie country, sometimes rolled out into ridges 1,500 feet long, interrupted occasionally by great depressions of the surface, the slopes of the ridges being steep, especially where truncated by the transverse valleys. This state of the surface was favourable to making out the stratification, the valleys generally cutting down to the sandstone, through the metalliferous and fossiliferous limestones of the annexed vertical section, which represents the stratification of the country.

STRATIFICATION OF THE WISCONSIN GALENIFEROUS DISTRICT.

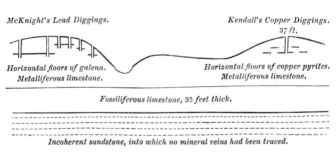

McKnight's Lead Diggings.

Horizontal floors of galena.
Metalliferous limestone.

Kendall's Copper Diggings.
37 ft.

Horizontal floors of copper pyrites.
Metalliferous limestone.

Fossiliferous limestone, 35 feet thick.

Incoherent sandstone, into which no mineral veins had been traced.

As the greatest quantity of the copper ore was stated to have been extracted from "Kendall's Diggings"—referred to in the vertical section— we first turned our attention to them, and found

that the deepest shaft sunk at this locality was
only thirty-seven feet. In going down, the
miners had followed an earthy, ferruginous *lead*
for eighteen feet, consisting of clay, silicious
matter, and oxide of iron, to which the Cornish-
men who had been employed had given the
provincial name of gossan : here they struck a
floor, dipping slightly to the south, consisting of
oxides of iron, light, earthy, cupreous carbonates,
and coarse, harsh lumps of sulphuret of iron, much
intermixed and coated with green carbonate of
copper, and occasionally blended with sulphurets of
the same metal. These lumps were characterized
by a vesicular structure, the fracture of which disclosed small cavities filled with diverging acicular
prisms of green carbonate of copper, of great beauty,
and not unfrequently coated with small but brilliant
crystals of blue carbonates. From this floor the
workmen had pursued the lead of gossan seven feet
further down, to a second floor of cupreous matter,
much superior to the first. Intermixed with this
ore, were found cubes of galena. The general appearance of the contents of both these floors was
that of a ferruginous scoria, much coated with
cupreous carbonates, of a low value, the assays of
the first not being rated higher than 8 per cent.,
and of the second, not higher than 20 parts in 100
of copper. Having emptied this second floor, they
had pursued the lead about four feet further, and
then abandoned the undertaking. These floors are
no doubt irregular expansions of true veins, such as

are common in all mining countries; and, indeed,
south of a vale through which the Pekatonica flows,
at a place called Ansley's South Copper-diggings,
we found a small vein of hard, substantial, grey copper ore, which yielded upon assay 50 parts in 100
of good copper.

The diggings and excavations which had been
made at all the places in this district did not appear
to warrant much expectation of present profit, taking
into the account the nature of the country, the great
scarcity of fuel, and the high price of labour and
provisions.

The deposits of galena, however, at *McKnight's
Lead-diggings* (see vertical section) had already
rewarded the miners. Various shafts had been sunk
upon the summit of the ridge, down which the workmen had successively come to different floors of
galena, all perfectly horizontal, from a few inches
to a foot in thickness of metal, accompanied with a
dry red earth, that seems to be the general concomitant of all galeniferous deposits, both in Missouri
and Wisconsin. The workmen stated that when
they had emptied the floors of the metal, they had
generally found a lead of galena running down at a
sharp angle, in the form of a vertical vein, to another
floor. This was repeated so often, that it had become
a preponderating opinion amongst the miners that,
whatever the form of the flat floors and their ramifications, all of them were connected with a descending
lode, gossan always leading down from them where
galena was not present.

At other localities, twenty miles east from this place, I found the floors also horizontal. Still, this is not the constant form of the deposits, for in the vicinity of Fever River, veins of galena came to the surface, through hard limestone rocks, in strong vertical lodes. I made the observation at the time, that where the metal was found in horizontal floors, the rock was of a soft, rubbly character, and easily excavated; as if the direction of the metal, when projected from below, had been governed by the state of induration of the rock through which it passed, diverging into floors where there was the least resistance.

The vertical section (at page 114) represents the circumstances under which deposits of galena may be expected to be found in any part of the galeniferous district, the chance of finding the metal depending upon the presence and thickness of the metalliferous bed nearest to the surface. At McKnight's Lead-diggings, the thickness of the bed, from the surface down to the fossiliferous limestone, was 118 feet : here, as elsewhere, were various floors of galena, but in no instance did I learn that any had ever been found, either in the fossiliferous limestone, or in the inferior sandstone. In whatever part of the lead-bearing district this metalliferous bed was shallow, not exceeding a few feet in thickness, no metal was to be found. This was the case in the district where the Snake-diggings—hereafter to be mentioned—were : there the bed was thick, and, at a distance of not more

than twenty-five feet from the surface, a quantity
of metal, amounting to about 800,000 lbs., had
been collected in a superficial area not exceeding four hundred yards in length; whilst in the
vicinity, at places where the bed had thinned out,
no galena had ever been found. Whilst the sandstone, therefore, is to be considered as the key
to the lead-bearing district, the presence and
depth of the metalliferous limestone is to be taken
as a sure indication of the probability of finding
galena.

It deserves a remark also, that whilst in the
Missouri galeniferous district, the galena is frequently found in solid horizontal bands of bright
metal, encased in a moist, waxy, red clay, in the
Wisconsin country it is as frequently found in floors,
in the form of masses of aggregated cubes, of a dull
aspect, and generally accompanied by a quantity of
red, argillaceous earth, perfectly dry. In both cases,
the red clay appears to have been projected along
with the metal.

Resuming our waggon, we finally left Mineral
Point, and proceeded on our visit to some more
" diggings," intending to descend to the Wisconsin at a place called " English Prairie," which had
attracted my attention in 1835. We found the
country cut up by ravines and coulées, and soon
broke down at a place called Pedlar's Creek,
where we had to remain a couple of hours to repair
damages.

We next traversed a naked prairie, on which

shallow excavations had been made in every direction, and reached Parish's, a settlement in a small
valley, with a few straggling trees. From hence
we went to the diggings on Blue River, and got
on a good hard prairie road: for the last six
miles the country was very picturesque as we descended to the low lands on the Wisconsin, and there
was a great deal of wood, until we reached the English
Prairie, an extensive sandy bottom. On nearing
the river, a Mr. Stevenson, the agent of a gentleman
named H——, who had a lead-furnace there, conducted us to a sort of hut, filled with countless
myriads of mosquitoes; at the door of which was a
negro attending a fire, and creating as much smoke
as he could, with the vain intention of preventing
their entrance into the hut. What they had to eat,
though not inviting, was hospitably offered; but,
having a distressing headache, I lay down as soon
as I was permitted to do so.

June 7.—I arose at half-past four, in a perfect fever
with the mosquitoes, and, on looking around, saw that
six other individuals, the negro amongst the rest, had
been pigging in the small tenement, which I afterwards
learned was the private room of Mr. H——, when
here. There was no looking-glass, no washing furniture, no towels, and, indeed, nothing to minister
to human comfort: on standing up, however, my
face was almost in contact with a shelf, containing a few odd volumes of Voltaire's writings.
Such was the retreat of one who submits to
all these inconveniences for the sake of the "al-

mighty dollars" that his lead-furnace produces him.

After partaking lightly of a most filthy and disgusting breakfast, we drove away from this wretched place, consisting of a badly arranged log-hut, and a very inefficient smelting-furnace, together dignified with the title of "City of Savannah."

The mosquitoes seeming disposed to devour us on this low prairie, we hastened to gain the upland, and at eleven a. m. got to the Blue River diggings. There is a deep ravine here with a perpendicular escarpment of sandstone, curiously disturbed, and of a brick-red colour at the top, which is very crumbling. Upon this lies about twenty-five feet of fossiliferous limestone, supporting about the same thickness of galeniferous rock. The greatest quantity of galena is found at eighteen feet from the surface, lying in flat floors, and mixed up with what they call "dry bones," and "black Jack." From this place we got upon a sort of blind road, twisting and turning in every direction over the prairie, sometimes going due east, sometimes due west, the only encouragement we had to proceed being that it must lead to some place or other.

At length, having wandered about twenty miles, and our horses and ourselves being heartily tired, we came to a settler's, called Morrison. Finding a good spring of water, and civility, we determined, with the permission of the mistress of the house, to remain here the night. She provided us with some bread made of Indian corn, and, for the rest, I drew upon my store of good black tea and loaf sugar.

June 8.—I awoke much refreshed by my night's rest, in what appeared a strange sort of sleeping-room. There was no door to it; my bed consisted of a few rags that the family could no longer wear —but clean—strewed on the floor, some pieces of harness for a pillow, and every thing else to correspond. I rose, however, cheerfully, and went to the spring, which was quite a luxury. The mistress of the house offered me every facility to accomplish my ablutions, and was unwearied in her obliging attentions. She was in a rapid decline, and, from her appearance, could not survive beyond the autumn. She expressed her apprehension of this to me, and attributed her condition to having had a numerous family too quickly. As soon as we had breakfasted, we started again, passing, soon after, a place called Lancaster, about twenty miles from the Mississippi and the Wisconsin. The soil around was excellent, and promised to make a fine agricultural country.

About noon, we reached "Snake Diggings," so called from a nest of rattlesnakes being found there in a cave. Galena had been found in great quantities in this neighbourhood. From one floor, not more than twenty-five feet from the surface, upon a length not exceeding 400 yards, they had already collected about 800,000 lbs. of galena, in masses of small aggregated cubes, of the first quality. I was permitted to select some curious and beautiful specimens of these masses. Here I learnt that some of the diggings had been carried to the depth of sixty feet, in consequence of the thickness of the galeniferous rocks.

About two p. m., we reached a settlement called Paris, where a Frenchman, called Detun de Baratz, had a store and some poor buildings. The houses here were excessively dirty, and the people seemed stupid and drunk, which is generally the case where rum and whiskey are sold in the stores. The natural situation of this settlement was very interesting, being an extensive cove near the forks of the Platte, surrounded by lofty bluffs. Having crossed the Platte in a ferry-boat, we ascended a very steep road to the summit of an escarpment about 250 feet above the valley, from whence I had a fine view of the cove below, with the Platte and its branches. Just below me the little Platte ran at the foot of the escarpment, with a lofty and narrow ridge to the north on its right bank; at the southern base of the ridge the north branch of the river flowed, with lofty bluffs to the north. To the west was the spacious cove, extending half a mile from N. to S., evidently scooped out by the stream in ancient times.

From the summit level we crossed the prairie to the Menominy Diggings, and about sunset reached Sinsinnaway Mound, the residence of Mr. G. W. Jones, a member of Congress from the territory of Wisconsin; here we were very hospitably received by himself and lady. Every thing in this

house was the very reverse of what we had lately
been accustomed to, and we sat down to a very
nice repast, enlivened by the agreeable manners of
the mistress of the house, and a most pleasant sister
of our host, who had been educated in Wales, and
had only just returned from a visit to England.

CHAPTER XLVI.

June 9.—I rose at the dawn of day and sallied
out to examine this mound, which, like the Blue
Mounds, rises far above the general level of the
prairies.   It consisted principally of the fossiliferous
limestone, and after collecting the characteristic
fossils, I returned to breakfast.   This repast being
over, we reluctantly took leave and drove to the
town of Galena, where we found the beastly tavern
full of all sorts of low people, and not a bed to be
had, unless I would consent to share one with an
animal of my own sex, in a room into which five
other beds had been crowded.   I therefore made
up my mind to wait until the canaille had retired
to roost, and then to lie down on the floor of the
bar-room with the " waiters."   Seeing me about to
shake a bearskin down on the floor, the landlady—
what acts of kindness are women capable of in all
countries !—would not permit it, and, listening only
to her own compassionate feelings, insisted upon
giving up her bed-room to me.   To be sure, it was
not half wide enough to swing a cat in, and the

small window which opened upon the yard was
exactly over the pigstye; but the luxury of being
alone overbalanced these disadvantages, and upon
her assuring me that she had another place to go
to, I consented to the arrangement.

June 10.—I got through the night tolerably
well, and was in the street again at daylight, the
pigs not being very agreeable neighbours, and after
breakfast, having paid my bill, with many thanks,
I got on board a dirty little steamer, called the
Envoy, bound to Dubuque and Prairie du Chien.
My trunk was placed over the boiler in the ante-
room, where, with its contents, it became, as I afterwards found, quite hot through. The steamer was
filled with low gambling vagabonds, and had not a
place in it clean enough to sit down upon; nevertheless, I was delighted to exchange the stench of
Galena for the pure air of the Mississippi. From
Dubuque we pursued our way to the Wisconsin,
enjoying the charming picturesque views furnished
by the bluffs on the banks of the river. The occupation of the passengers on board the steamer was
unremitted low gambling and cursing and swearing during the voyage; the captain permitted every
one to act as dirtily and as coarsely as he pleased,
and the various little boys on board, from seven to
ten years old, appeared to me to be as accomplished
blackguards as the men. Towards evening one of
our paddles got out of order, and we moored at a
wood-yard on the left bank to repair it. Here,
being obliged to remain all night, the musquitoes

literally took possession of our vessel, so that it was next to impossible to obtain any sleep.

July 11.—At the dawn of day we unmoored, and pursued our voyage, enjoying as much as I ever did in my various trips in this part of the river the curious and rare appearance of the banks, the strata often running great distances in straight ranges like the cornice of a room, and sometimes breaking out into huge bastion-like masses, giving to the whole the appearance of a ruined fortification. We stopped at Cassville several hours, and did not get away until nine p. m. It had improved very much since I first saw it in 1835, some substantial wooden buildings having been run up, and the foundation laid for a large hotel, to be constructed of stone. Some wealthy persons, I was informed, had taken an interest in it, so it may possibly succeed. I saw no preparations for gardens, the want of which is a great defect in all American settlements in this part of the country. Two gaily-dressed females, however, were walking about dressed in white gowns, with parasols in their hands, and were singularly contrasted with some Indian women near them, with their filthy blankets over their shoulders.

Things looked so unpromising on board, that I did not venture to lie down : this was not the first time that I had had the bad luck to find myself on board one of the numerous class of low, dirty steamers that ply on the Mississippi. Those of the first class are noble vessels, clean, comfortable, generally well commanded, and provided with every thing necessary, and nothing permitted on board that can be reasonably objected to. The Envoy was one of a class of disreputable steamers, not seaworthy, usually commanded by low, drunken fellows, who run about from place to place, picking up freight and chance passengers amongst the coarse dissipated gamblers that abound on the western rivers and frontiers, and who, committing excesses at every place where they land, are happy in opportunities to escape from punishment. Many of these fellows live on board, and are the colleagues of the captain in various kinds of villany. They are eternally playing at a low game of cards, called poker, sleeping two or three hours in the daytime. The chance passengers we took on board seemed to want very little pressing to sit down to the gambling-table, and I presume were vagabonds no better than the rest.

During the confusion on board I had kept as near the stern as I could, seated on a large, loose bench, which, in the expectation that we should explode, and that I might have to float myself ashore, promised to be of some use; fortunately, perhaps, we ran aground after midnight, and remained stuck fast until near five in the morning. In this Pandemonium, how many of our passengers and crew were drunk, and how it came to pass that we were not blown up or set fire to, was not explained to me.

June 12.—The morning was beautiful when we got under way; the degraded beings on board had, at length, discontinued their orgies, and were asleep, and I saw no more of them; for at eight a. m. we reached Prairie du Chien, looking as beautiful and picturesque as ever, with its magnificent bluffs, and its ample and verdant plain bounded by the noble river with its graceful islands.

Remembering the smoking I had got here in 1835, from my worthy host, Mons. R., I went quietly and secured myself a clean lodging in a private house, before I made any calls; and having transported my luggage out of the filthy steamer, and installed myself in my quarters, I called upon my old friend, whom I found with a cigar in his mouth, as usual; a drunken band of Winebagoes were rolling about in a high state of intoxication, and others were prostrated on the ground in front of his house literally sewed up in perfect oblivion. One of their party, who had been concerned in the murder of a white man not long before, had been arrested that morning; and this being an exciting event, they had made the most of it, after their own way. Towards evening I called upon the commandant, Colonel Taylor, and had a long and pleasing conversation with that worthy and intelligent officer.

June 13.—With a room to myself, a good bed, and clean sheets, I could not fail to pass a good night; and having breakfasted, I went to the Bluffs with my hammer and memorandum-book. At two p. m., having made a frugal dinner, I went to the French village to consult M. Rolette about making arrangements for an excursion across the Mississippi, to the heads of the Iowa and De Moine rivers. This matter was discussed over claret, champaign, and countless quantities of cigars, all smoked by himself. My jovial friend had engaged to remove every difficulty, and procure me every facility; and, accordingly, he began with the first and most necessary want, an efficient guide. The man whom he sent for, however, and whom he represented as equal to any thing, was a little copper-coloured Canadian, as pert as it was useful to be, at least, but whose qualifications were not much better than my own. My plan was to cross the country from hence to the Missouri River, and to visit on my road the head waters of the Makatoh, or Terrebleu River, and the locality of the Red Pipe-stone Rock. The difficulties I should have to contend with were the necessity of carrying our subsistence on our backs, this being the season when all game was breeding, and the want of an interpreter. The little Canadian could neither talk Nacotah nor Sauk and Fox; he was a stranger to the country, and seemed weak and unequal to the task. I saw at once that he was not the man for me, and felt greatly the want of Milor. During my examination of the qualifications of this man, Rolette had smoked a prodigious number of cigars, and upon finishing my inquiries, and saying to him, " Eh bien, qu'en pensez-vous ? " he replied, " Si vous aimiez le tabac, mon cher, vous pourriez aller au bout du monde : pour moi quand je fais des voyages, je fais toujours une bonne provision de tabac et je mange ce que je trouve. En cas de besoin je sais manger le diable et boire son bouillon. " This is a valuable secret of the Canadian voyageur.

June 14.—I rose at five a. m., and it being a beautiful and refreshing morning, went to the Bluffs to enjoy the interesting spectacle of the night fog rising from

the waters of the Wisconsin and Mississippi.   One of
the most pleasing natural sights of this country, intersected by so many streams, is enjoyed when you stand
upon an eminence and see the night-mist gracefully
rising as the sun ascends in the heavens; as if the earth,
in its matutinal revolution, flung those long horizontal
and airy columns from the bosom of the numerous
lines of waters where they had reposed.   During
the day, I made many inquiries respecting the prac-
ticability of my excursion to the Missouri at this
season. Colonel Taylor did not approve of the means
I should have of accomplishing it ; and discussing it
again with M. Rolette, with whom I dined to-day, I
found he was of the same opinion. I therefore at once
determined to give the excursion up for the present,
and to employ the remainder of the summer in descending the Mississippi, exploring the iron and lead
region of Missouri a little more, and then finish the
season amongst the Cherokee Indians, and in the
gold regions of Dahlonega, in Georgia.

June 15.—I arose before five, and going, as usual,
to the Bluffs, saw the smoke and steam of the Palmyra
steamer at a considerable distance to the north, descending the Mississippi from Fort Snelling; and
nearly at the same time that I observed this interesting
object, the smoke of the Burlington, another large
steamer expected from St. Louis, appeared advancing
to the prairie.   This, which would have been a
beautiful sight anywhere, was a most interesting
one in this remote Indian country.   I now hastened
to my lodgings, breakfasted, and sent my luggage on
board the steamer bound to St. Louis, and following

it, secured a clean and commodious state-room to myself. On board the Burlington I found Mrs. Hamilton, the widow of the celebrated Alexander Hamilton, and mother to the gentleman in whose hut I had lately slept at English Prairie. This lively old lady, now about eighty years old, told me that, knowing she might not have a long time to see things of this world in, she had determined to avail herself of the great facilities for travelling, and pay a visit to her son; and having an inclination to see all she could, was determined to ascend the Mississippi to the St. Peter's. I could not but admire her spirit and vivacity.

At half-past ten I bade adieu to the pleasant and, with me, favourite shores of Prairie du Chien: the Mississippi being full of water from the melted snows and ice of the upper north country, we were rapidly borne along. The islands were so overflown, I could scarcely recognise them, and on passing the mouth of the Wisconsin, I could not but deplore the melancholy fate of one of the noblest of those magnificent cities, intended (on paper) to be the ornaments of this interesting country. In old times, before the enjoyable romance of this Indian country was destroyed by the introduction of the white man's improvements, I had often wandered on the beach where the Wisconsin joins the Mississippi, collecting fresh-water shells, and little dreaming of the mighty metropolis that was to be raised within so short a period on the identical spot. But to those who resided at a distance, it was now announced, that the "city of Prairie du Chien," with all its architectural wonders, was

" located" at the confluence of these mighty
streams.   This city the " Father of Floods" had
now taken under his especial care, converting it
into one vast cold bath; all the streets, bearing
the illustrious names of Washington, Jefferson,
Madison, &c., being at least twelve feet under
water, and nothing indicative of what sober people
call " real estate" being visible, except the tops of a
few willows, which wriggled about as our noble
steamer shot rapidly over them.

With much interest did I look upon this beautiful country as I left it behind, never, most probably, to be revisited by me.   The selfish, vulgar,
white man had got possession of it, and had destroyed the *prestige* which once made it so attractive.
It will take many generations to civilize and refine
the descendants of the present settlers, and make
them as agreeable as the educated people are in the
old American settlements.   Only eighteen months
ago, when I passed through this country, something
of romance was still left for the sanguine traveller,
and all the incidents of his life were more or less
connected with Indian adventure.   Then, on arriving
at the Indian posts, the universal topic was sure
to be the Indians, their manners and customs, and
the stirring incidents continually arising amidst
their doomed race.   Then, you were asked if
you had seen the celebrated *Howchungerah* chief,
" Whirling Thunder."   Now, you are asked if you
have seen " Governor Dodge."   Ere long, the
whites will tread upon the graves of the whole
red race.   At six p. m. we reached Dubuque, but got

aground, the waters of the Mississippi having covered all the landmarks, and made the pilot mistake the channel, nor did we get afloat again until eleven p.m.

June 16.—Awoke very early this morning, lying at the wharf at Galena, the steamer touching here to take a cargo of lead on board. Nobody being up in the town, I walked to a quarry and got some fossils, from the beds that appear to be the equivalent of the Wenlock limestones. After breakfast I called upon my old acquaintance, Mr. Gear. He has been a practical miner here eighteen years, and informed me that the veins or crevices at his " Diggings," as they are called here, are vertical, and run nearly north and south. Sometimes the sulphuret failed, and the vein closed ; at other times it was filled with gossan, but he had always followed it downwards, and, hitherto, with success, though always without intersecting any floors like those which prevail near Mineral Point. Sometimes he had found lumps of galena at the surface, weighing 1,000 lbs., which he supposed had been thrown out of the crevice, but which, more probably, were left behind when the surface had been degraded, and the earthy matter carried away. I suggested to him to run adits from the lowest valleys, or coulées, and intersect them by shafts through the lower sandstone, which he seemed inclined to do. In the neighbourhood of Mineral Point, no shaft had ever been sunk through this sand-stone, and the metal had invariably been found in horizontal floors in the metalliferous limestone, super-incumbent upon the fossiliferous bed. Supposing, therefore, the metal to have been injected from below in both cases, it is to be inferred, from the circumstance of the galena being found here in vertical crevices, that the causes which produced these vertical fissures did not extend to the beds near Mineral Point.

June 17.—We left Galena before daylight, and soon got into the Mississippi, and having passed another city, called *Savannah*, consisting of *two log houses*, came, soon after seven o'clock, to a pretty prairie, with two more log huts upon it, dignified with the name of *New York*. At another place, on a slope with a few trees, was a solitary log hut, called, in honour of the president of the United States, *Van Buren*, and, a short distance from it, was a settlement, consisting of two huts, called *Albany*. Plans of these flourishing places were in circulation, but I was told that the lots of places with New York names did not sell well. We passed a settlement, however, called Bloomington, which had been formed under curious circumstances, and which may possibly succeed. By the theory of the law, all lands belonging to the federal government must be advertised to be sold at public auction, by order of the President, at the minimum price of one dollar and a quarter an acre, which is about six English shillings. Those who intend to settle in a particular part of the country usually pay a preliminary visit to it to suit themselves, and, having done so, erect a log hut, and make a small clearing, where they establish their families, until the appointed period of the public sale. But the speculator, who watches the movements of the

bonâ fide settler, appears, as the time draws near,
and announces to the farmer that he means to bid
against him at the sale.   To prevent the price running very high, the poor man is frequently induced
to give the settler a heavy gratuity in some form or
other.   Where, however, this last is a man of spirit,
he often contends with the speculator, but in vain ;
for in these distant parts of the United States,
where the agents who conduct these land sales are
so far removed from the eye of the government,
they often collude with speculators, and, by various
frauds and devices, make the settler pay five dollars
or more an acre, for what ought not to have cost him
more than one dollar and a quarter.   These malprac-
tices, which had been too common of late, had irri-
tated and disgusted the *bonâ fide* settlers, and, at this
particular place, had driven them to a mode of de-
fending their interests, quite as illegal as the proceedings of the others were dishonest.   The settlers, then,
at this Bloomington, having agreed amongst themselves to occupy an allotment or farm not to exceed
320 acres each, and to mutually guarantee the possession to each other, offered the minimum price at the
public sale, and if they were overbid on the part of the
speculators, took possession of the land nevertheless ;
and, when the person to whom the farm was knocked
down at the sale, or his assignee, came to claim it,
a jury was summoned, by the person in possession,
from amongst the fraternity of settlers, which was
sure to bring in a verdict that the land belonged to
the person in possession.   If the claimant was disposed to be troublesome, they brought him before

Judge Lynch ; and the alternative being then put to him, to surrender his pretensions, or undergo due process of law, upon his bare back, with a cat-o'-nine-tails, a compromise usually took place. No doubt, this scheme will occasion much litigation, when regular courts of justice are established ; but as it will be a long time before they have the power to enforce their decisions, the first attempts to do so will probably give rise to much violence. In the mean time, the speculators have been very much baffled.

CHAPTER XLVII.

REACH THE OLD FRENCH SETTLEMENT OF ST. GENEVIÈVE.—AN EXCUR-
SION TO THE PILOT KNOB.—RECEIVED BY AN AMIABLE FAMILY THERE.
—DESCRIPTION OF THIS REMARKABLE MASS OF IRON.—THE CITY OF
MISSOURI.

June 24.—After a pleasant passage I reached the
town of St. Louis again on the 19th, and remaining
there a few days, embarked on the 24th, on board
the William Glasgow, a fine steamer bound up
the Ohio. Intending, however, to make another
excursion into the interior of the state of Missouri,
I landed at the old French settlement, called St.
Geneviève, on the right bank of the Mississippi, where
the steamer stopped for a few minutes at the wharf,
and walking about a mile to the village, was very
hospitably received for the night by an acquaintance
residing here.

June 25.—I arose very early, and walked out to
look at this interesting place, which is an ancient
French settlement. The streets are narrow, and the
houses almost all built after the humble but grotesque
fashion of the people of Normandy, whose descendants
form a great majority of the inhabitants. Each
cottage had its fertile and productive garden, full of
vegetables and fruit-trees. When Louisiana was
transferred to the United States, the Americans took

possession of this place ; but very few had been induced to settle at it, the religion, manners and customs of the French being so different from their own,
and there being no opportunities of pushing trade
at it.   The few, however, who did reside here, lived
upon very friendly terms with their French neighbours, and the settlement was said to be a very happy
one.   Adjacent to the village was a very extensive
alluvial bottom of rich soil, upon which the inhabitants
plant their Indian corn and pulse, and as the river, by
rising a foot in the course of the past night,
threatened to inundate their crops, some anxiety
was expressed on that account.   In consequence of
every one possessing great abundance of cereal and
leguminous products, and raising their own poultry,
there was no market held in the place for any thing
whatever.   When any of the inhabitants caught any
fish in the river with a seine, which is easily done,
every one who was desirous of having fish could have
it without purchasing.   Neither were vegetables,
turkeys, chickens, or any kind of poultry, sold in this
place, the surplus quantities being sent by the passing
steamers to be sold at New Orleans.   But this is
only done when the waters of the Ohio are so low
that no supply can be furnished from that quarter.
At such times, the people of St. Geneviève can sell
their turkeys at New Orleans for five dollars each,
and their fowls for twelve dollars a dozen.

 There was a good school in the place, kept by an
intelligent Frenchman, where French, English, music,
dancing, and many useful things were taught; so
that the young French and Americans, educated there,

not only could acquire each other's languages, but be respectably educated. Judge Bogy, a very well-informed inhabitant, of the French stock, informed me that the two races lived in the most amicable manner together; and indeed he gave me a most pleasing account of the place and its society. The adult inhabitants, with an exception or two, had not yet learnt to speak each other's language, though a certain degree of fusion was commencing, if one may judge from the following notice, which I saw over a door.

BENEZOIT TIENT

GROCERY.

In the course of the day, I hired a clever-looking little pony, and having managed to procure a rather inconvenient saddle, I left my luggage and started for the lead-mines, and crossing some bad and miry branches of a stream, called the Vase, got upon a barren sandstone country, where I rode fifteen miles without finding a human being. There being various tracks leading to the " diggings," it was not difficult to lose myself, which I contrived to do ; being, however, quite indifferent about it, as the whole country was new to me, and knowing from long experience that every road leads to some place or other, I rode confidently on. Instead of Fredericton, however, to which I was bound, I came to Farmington ; so, riding up to the house at which I had alighted in 1834, when going to the Mexican frontier, I found Mr. Boice, the landlord, who recognised me, and gave me a tolerable supper and a clean room to sleep in.

June 26.—I arose early, and making a hasty breakfast, pursued my way to Mine Lamotte, distant
fifteen miles, and having passed a couple of hours
examining the excavations, which are described in
another work,* I remounted my slow, lazy pony,
who often obliged me to dismount and lead him by
the bridle, and rode on towards Fredericton. A remarkably thick, smoky atmosphere had prevailed
for some days, which was said to be unusual at
this season.　On reaching Fredericton, a little after
five p. m., I met in the street an old acquaintance, in a senator of the United States, who conducted me to, I think, one of the most wretched
taverns I almost ever entered ; but, for the sake of
his society, I agreed to remain there for the night.
In the evening, he took me to sup at a Mons.
Pratte's, the son of an old French trader.　Here
Madame Pratte, a young Frenchwoman of lively
and engaging manners, gave us a very comfortable
repast, and we talked French and were very gay.
I was sorry when the hour came to retire, for I had
a perfect horror at the idea of sleeping at the beastly
tavern ; but there was no remedy, and only one
room, with six or seven detestable, filthy beds, upon
one of which I lay down, surrounded with all sorts of
disgusting people. To be sure, I had merely stretched
myself on the coverlid, and drawn a cloak over me ;
but I scarcely got asleep once, for if I happened
to doze, I felt the bugs crawling on my face, or
fancied I did.　My companions, it appeared, had
taken their clothes off : one fellow, who, with
another, occupied the bed next to me, was constantly

* Excursion through the Slave States, vol. i. p. 322.

doubling himself up on his hams, to scratch away as energetically as if he was paid for it. If the little animals who were trying to penetrate into his hide had understood English, they could not but have admired with me the various compliments he paid them, which for original deep blasphemies were unequalled. How I got through the night in this ruffian-like hole, kept by a tall, lazy hulk of a Yankee fellow, called Idson, I know not; but the dawn at length came, and I rushed down stairs before it was light enough to see the horrors of the place where I had passed the night.

Finding a well, with a pail near it, out of doors, I kept possession of them for half an hour before anybody was stirring, and having dried my towels and partaken of a breakfast prepared by the land-lady, that was almost as disgusting as herself, I joy-fully mounted my pony again, and, taking advantage of an old Frenchman, named Le Saint, who was going in my direction, turned my back upon these brutal people, who were quite as filthy in their habits as any Indians I had ever been amongst.

My companion, who was an old inhabitant of this mineral country, had, like many others in the neigh-bourhood, his head full of dreams of silver-mines, which he believed he should find some day or another; and this induced him to pick up every glit-tering stone, hoping it might turn out to be gold or silver. He had heard something of my pursuits, and had formed a little plan of his own, to draw me to a hut he had in the woods, and get my opinion of his treasures. When, therefore, we reached an

obscure fork in the road, which was altogether in
the forest, and where we had to separate, he entreated
me to accompany him to his cabin. "Ce n'était
qu'à deux pas, et de là je vous remettrai moi-même
sur votre chemin. J'ai trouvé de l'argent, j'en ai la
conviction, et je crois aussi avoir trouvé de l'or, mais
je ne suis pas si sûr, vous pourrez me resoudre cela,
et vous pouvez penser, Monsieur, combien je serai
redevable à votre politesse."

With even a slight inclination to be obliging,
there was no resisting this; so, in my capacity of
savant, I rode through a bridle-path in the woods, at
least two miles, to his domicile, where he had a
patch of cleared land. His treasures, unfortunately,
turned out to be pieces of iron pyrites; and, on
leaving him, I was sorry to think that my visit had
not contributed to his happiness, for the last thing
he said, when I had remounted my horse, was:
" Vous pensez donc que mes pierres ne sont bonnes
à rien ?" "Absolument," I replied, and rode away.
When I had got about ten or twelve miles from
Fredericton, I came to the St. Francis River, which
was full of water, and the current very strong. Seeing a cabin at no great distance, I rode up to it, to
inquire if the ford was safe, when another Frenchman
came out, and before he would give me any defini-
tive answer, insisted on my going into his house, to
see "des échantillons magnifiques d'argent qu'il
avait trouvés." I told him to bring them out and I
would look at them ; but, like the others, they turned
out to be worthless; and whether this man, who
told me his name was La Guerre, was angry at

my decision or not, he certainly directed me to a part of the river where my pony and myself crossed with difficulty and in doing which I got completely wet. Pursuing my road, I crossed several branches of what is called *Stout's Creek*, and, as evening drew on, came to a lofty and precipitous ridge, about 650 feet high. Having scrambled over this, I came to a valley of fertile soil, and extremely well wooded.

Night was rapidly approaching; I was very wet, and, looking anxiously and vainly for a settlement, began to fear I should have to pass the night on the ground. The pony followed the blind path we were upon with more spirit, however, than he had shewn during the day, and I was comforted with this, having had numerous proofs of the undoubted intelligence of horses upon similar occasions. At any rate, I determined to go as long as he would, and on we jogged until we came to a more open part of the country, when I saw, at no great distance before me, a lofty conical mountain, which, from its shape, I supposed to be the " Pilot Knob." Being apprized that there was a settlement near to it, and seeing the track of wheels, I followed and came to a fence, and having got through it, came at length in sight of a large log cabin. Riding up to it, I learnt it was the dwelling-house of a Mr. Pease, an enterprising person, who, with some of his friends, had projected the establishment of some iron-works here. Mr. P. and his family, consisting of his wife and her sister, two amiable and very clever females, from New England, received me in the kindest manner. The cabin was neatly furnished, had two rooms on the ground-floor and two above. They lost no time in giving me a very refreshing cup of tea, with very good fried meat and bread, and then shewed me to a nice small room, containing a comfortable, clean bed. Having laid my clothes at the door to be dried, I laid myself down in the most perfect confidence that none of the Idsonian species were to be my companions.

I arose at six, thoroughly refreshed, after a charming night's rest, and full of admiration at the tidiness with which these worthy ladies had arranged every thing in their cottage. This I determined to make my head-quarters for a day or two, if I should be permitted to make them a compensation for their hospitality. After breakfast Mr. Pease and myself made preparations to ascend the very remarkable phenomenon I had come to see, and which deserves a detailed description.

This Pilot Knob is a well-wooded cone, about 650 feet in height from the base, and may be estimated to contain, from the base to the summit, a circumferential area of 500 acres of land. But what makes it so rare and curious a phenomenon is, that it entirely consists of a micaceous iron ore, which yields from 50 to 65 per cent. of pure iron. It is, in fact, a mountain of iron, and how far the metal extends beneath the base, must be of course unknown. The skirts of the base are covered for a considerable distance with ponderous masses and pebbles of this ore, and the ascent to the top is everywhere strewed with broken fragments of the same, some of them exceedingly sharp. About half-way up, on the S. W. side, is a depression or ravine, both sides of which are piled up with enormous masses of iron-stone, as though a fissure or crater had once existed here; bands of silicious stone are found alternating with the oxide of iron, but in such instances the ore always appears to be very heavy.

On the east side is a steep escarpment of about 150 feet in height, at the foot of which is a terrace, succeeded by another escarpment. Towards the top, the ferruginous rock appears to turn in broad flat plates to the S. W., whilst the natural cleavage has separated it into thin seams, which resemble strata on their edges. At the summit, where I found whortle-berries and wild vines growing in great profusion, the cone divides into two pinnacles, each about thirty-five feet high, and much weather-worn. The view from the top was, of course, very extensive, the whole country being at your feet. I now perceived that this Pilot Knob stood at the north edge of a basin, surrounded by mammillated hills, less lofty than itself, describing a circle to a considerable distance, whilst beyond it was a universal forest. It formed a most pleasing picture, and I hastened to make a sketch of it (*vide* frontispiece). Many trees upon the mountain had been struck with lightning, but none of the specimens of ore which I examined were magnetic in the slightest degree. On the east side the ore lay in courses not more than one or two inches thick, and the grain was so fine, that Mr. Pease had used it successfully as a hone for razors and knives. Here the beds dip to the west, in such a manner as to lead to the inference that the whole mountain has been heaved in that direction, and that the huge fragments lying on that side had been shaken from the top when the pinnacles were separated. I found some tolerable crystals of specular iron ore on the south side, though far inferior in beauty to those of Elba; and at the base, on the east side, was a cool chalybeate spring. I did not visit the mammillary cones I have spoken of, but Mr. Pease informed me that they consisted of a silicious rock, sometimes very much impregnated with ferruginous matter. From the general appearance of things, all the cones appeared to me to have been produced at the same time, by an eruption from below.

Having passed the greater part of the day examining this extraordinary mass of iron ore, which, without taking into calculation the subterraneous portion no doubt subjacent to it, would suffice several thousand years for the consumption of the United States, we returned to the house with a collection of specimens, and having taken some refreshment, rode to a waterfall on Stout's Creek, where Mr. P. contemplated erecting some works. This was situated at the confluence of several mountain streams, the water coming brawling along over the rocks with great rapidity. The silicious rocks here passed into a sort of porphyritic granite, containing prodigious quantities of irregular crystals of red felspar, the quartzose matter being an opaque flint-looking substance, intermixed with occasional seams of micaceous iron.

Many geologists would class these with metamorphic rocks.

From Mr. Pease's conversation I perceived that he was an enterprising man, and very sanguine as to the result of his operations in smelting the unlimited quantity of iron ore in his possession. Of this it is true he holds an entire mountain, which if iron ore were a scarce mineral would be invaluable; but it is, as it appears to me, too plentiful in the Atlantic states to be valuable at present, especially in Pennsylvania and New York, where canals and railroads abound to take it to market, so that competition with them from this quarter cannot be attempted without an immense expenditure of capital in roads and works, and it is very problematical whether the iron would not cost more than it would sell for. In the evening Mr. Pease took me to see a Mr. Van Doren, another settler, with whom he appeared to be connected, who, with his wife, son, and three daughters, had moved from the Atlantic states into this remote part of the world, to live upon the iron mountain. In this day's rambling I became wet through twice, but my comfortable bed made amends for every thing.

June 29.—I rose early and prepared for an excursion of twenty miles to that extensive deposit of micaceous oxide of iron which I had visited in 1834, and which, without being quite a mountain, is also called the Iron Mountain, whilst this true mountain is called Pilot Knob. On leaving Mr. Pease's house I offered him a bank note for my entertainment, which he politely but promptly declined, adding that he thought it a duty to entertain respectable strangers, but that he took no money for doing so. I was somewhat embarrassed at this, as I had rather unceremoniously ordered grain for my pony, and perhaps too much conducted myself as travellers usually do when they are at houses of entertainment kept by respectable farmers; but as he offered to accompany me as guide in the ride I was about to take, I thought some method of obliging him might present itself before we parted; so, accepting his offer with pleasure, we rode away together through a beautiful and fertile country. On our way we visited a picturesque outlier of huge masses of granite, loaded with crystals of red felspar, which my guide said was called—and I thought oddly, the " Grindstone Quarry." We came suddenly upon it in a flat woody bottom, which had evidently been denuded, and it presented a curious appearance. In one part the rocks towered up to a great height, assuming all sorts of grotesque forms, and presenting a picture which became still more interesting by the appearance of a beautiful deer, which came and gazed upon us from one of the masses. All these rocks were exceedingly bright and smooth at the surface, as if water had passed rapidly over them for a long period.

We remained a couple of hours at the Iron Mountain, which is in fact composed of two distinct hills of micaceous oxide; both of them perhaps contain together an area of 500 acres of land. In many instances the ore was composed of a mass

of imperfect crystals, with a bright fracture of a
steel-grey colour ; and there was an unequivocal
character of fusion in many of them. Immense
masses of ore were laid at the top of the two hills,
the spaces between them being filled up by fragments that had been broken from them, with angu-
lar edges a little rounded by the weather. Some
portions of the ore were mixed up with quartzose
matter of a flinty character, and in some instances
crystals of iron were imbedded in the quartz. The
other hills which I examined adjacent to these two,
consisted of a dark-coloured coarse quartz and red
felspar without mica.

Mr. Pease at this place disclosed to me a project
in which he was concerned with the Van Doren
family, viz. the building of an immense city at this
place, to be called the " City of Missouri," and
conducted me to a brick-yard where a person
named Chapman was making bricks. He shewed
me also a beautifully engraved plan of the city,
evidently destined to be larger than the largest
size. The universities, the colleges, the cathedrals, the churches, and the streets were innumerable. In the mean time there was not the
foundation of a single house yet laid, nor could I
conjecture for what purpose a house, much less a
city, should be built here ; but it was difficult to
object to what might take place hereafter, or to
the intention of the projectors, because there really
was a live man on the ground making bricks, which
was a step far beyond any preparation I had witnessed at any other pseudo metropolis. I avoided

conversing about it as much as I could, because if a fraud was not intended, the affair appeared to me the most extravagant piece of folly that ever came under my notice. There was not a drop of water near the place, nor any satisfactory reasons to be given why even a village should be built there. Iron ore at such a place had no more marketable value than the granite that abounds everywhere, and must remain valueless for centuries. Men might as well try to put all the coal-fields in the world into operation at once, as all the iron ore. These remarks, however, I kept to myself, as I had before had proofs that a traveller is hardly ever safe from the resentment of speculators if he crosses their purposes by his observations.

CHAPTER XLVIII.

ITINERANT PREACHERS.—NEGRO ACCOUNT OF THE FIRST WHITE MAN.—
NEGRO DRIVERS.—A MAN-KILLER FROM CHOICE.—BEAUTIFUL FOSSILS.
—MISSISSIPPI COVERED WITH DRIFT WOOD.—EMBARK AGAIN IN AN
INFERIOR STEAMER, AND TRICKED BY THE CAPTAIN.

AFTER a pleasant ride, I came at night to Mr. Van Doren's, where I had promised to alight, and found, besides the family, two travelling Methodist ministers there. One of them had been amongst the Indians on the Missouri, and had seen enough of life in other situations to make him a practical and rational person. The other was a coarse sort of country preacher, with manners appropriate enough for a back settlement apostle. His conversation was ever of the shop. Not an observation could escape from any of us but he instantly brought us back to the necessity of " glorifying God." He was a violent abolitionist, and spoke very freely, considering that we were in a slave state; but I believe he was quite safe, for the whole family entertained his opinions. It is the practice of these itinerant preachers, during their journeys, to stay only with those families who agree with them in religion and politics, for many of them are active agents in canvassing the votes of back settlers, and circulating party newspapers. Brother McDougall, for so they called this man, expressed, amongst other things, an

opinion that the blacks would have been just as
white as ourselves, but for the crime of their ances-
tor Cain, and that the penal mark set upon him was
his black complexion, for, as he forcibly observed,
"there aint no mark under arth equal to the black
face of a nigger." Upon which I told him the following story, that I had heard of a black preacher,
when holding forth to his congregation. He said:
"It was berry kurous how peopel wid de same
parent should be sum of dem black, and sum of dem
as white as a turnip. Now, de Scriptur, my bredren,
says dis is de way dat it kum about. When Cain kill
his brudder Abel, Goddermity meet him one day
and said, 'Cain, what is become of your brudder?'
So said Cain, 'Massa, it an't none of my business to
look arter him.' And den he meet him anodder
time, and he say jist de same ting. Well, den, I
tell you, he git considerably angry, and said, 'I know
what you been about, as well as yourself, and I set
a mark upon you dat won't kum off so easy.' Den
Cain get frightened, and have de cold chills, and
when de fever and agy left him, his face was jist as
pale as a snowstorm, and he was de first white
man, my bredren, what ever lived." They all
laughed most heartily at this, and brother McDougall shook his sides over and over again.

After this we had prayers and a hymn, and, to
wind up, brother McDougall gave us a tremendous
long prayer, in which he specially mentioned every
individual of the family, complimented each of us,
spoke of our intelligent conversation, and sent us
all to bed exceedingly well pleased, I suppose, both

with the orator and ourselves. The two reverend gentlemen and myself were shewn to the attic, where two beds with clean sheets were spread on the floor. I tucked mine into as narrow a compass as I could, flung off my clothes, got into it, and bade them good night, in a tone to make them comprehend that I meant to sleep by myself; but I had no occasion to apprehend any interference, for they got very cozily into bed together, and I heard no more until about three in the morning, when we were all roused by a contest betwixt Mr. Van Doren's dog and some wolves, that had come into the yard; and it must have been a sharp one, for we found in the morning that the poor fellow had been severely bitten.

June 30.—I rose at five a. m., and taking my towel in my hand, found my way to the well, and having shaved and brought up my notes of the preceding day, I went to the breakfast-table. Having finished our repast, we had prayers, after which the family bible was circulated, each of us reading two verses and passing it to his neighbour. I was much pleased with the manner in which this was done. There is nothing which unites human beings so thoroughly into a brotherhood as a knowledge of the bible, and I believe we all rose from our exercise most kindly disposed to each other.

Having heard of an extensive tract of statuary marble, some ten miles off, in a direction where I had not been, I expressed an intention of visiting it, and Mr. Pease kindly offering to accompany me, we mounted our nags, and had ridden some miles through the woods and valleys chatting along, when suddenly we saw a huge black she-bear with her two cubs, on a hill-side a short distance before us. We immediately alighted, and having tied our horses to trees, led our dog up the hill, and pursued her; every now and then she would turn and rear upon her hind legs to look at us, and then rush through the woods with her young ones. When we reached the top of the hill, we lost sight of her, and the dog being, I suppose, intimidated, refused to go any further, knowing that when they have young ones, it is very dangerous to contend with them. Having remounted, we rode on to the marble, which turned out to be a ridge of altered silurian limestone in horizontal strata, some of it being partially coloured red, and the rest highly crystalline, of a dullish white colour, resembling statuary marble. There appeared to be about 1,000 acres of it exposed at the surface. On my return, I stopped again at Mr. Van Doren's, and after a cheerful supper, we went to prayers, the master of the house officiating, and the ladies singing very pleasingly.

July 1.—Breakfast being over, I took leave of this kind family and departed, admiring the simplicity and tranquillity of their lives, and sorry to see that they were involved in speculations that, according to my judgment, could produce no useful results. On my way, I called to repeat my thanks to the worthy members of the Pease family, and then directed my course N. E. by the east flank of the granitic hills, here composed of a dark red felspar, and a small quantity of quartz. I had a pleasant

woodland ride of five hours, enlivened by the occasional sight of deer, to Farmington, which I reached
about four p.m. Here I hoped to have Mr. Boice's
nice clean room to myself, but was afraid I should
be disappointed, as a dirty spitting insolent fellow,
with the most offensive manners, was playing the
great man at the tavern, and I began to dread that
it would be proposed to me to sleep in the same
room with him. On being called to supper, however,
I found a woman at table, who was called his wife,
and her presence relieved me for two reasons. First,
I was delighted, because it was probable he would
sleep with her in the room generally provided at
these places for married people ; and secondly,
because I should not have to sleep in the same room
with her, for a more unfeminine she-jack I never
met with : their conversation was entirely about
runaway negroes, the state of Mississippi, and yellow
fever. I soon came to the conclusion that he was
what I afterwards found him to be, an agent for
purchasing refractory negroes to drive to the sugar-
mills at New Orleans.

After supper, I called to see a son of Mr. Van
Doren, who was a Presbyterian minister at this place ;
but he was gone on a journey, and I only saw his
wife. I think I never looked upon a more beautiful
young woman than herself, and upon her repeated
invitation, I walked in and sat down. She must
have thought that I was one of the brethren, for she
several times urged me to stay all night, adding that
there was nobody at home but herself, and she could
accommodate me very well. When a man contends

against a she-bear, and prevails against her, he is generally thought to have performed a great feat ; but what sort of a feat is that compared to resisting the temptation of sleeping in a suburban cottage, with no other person in it but a lovely young woman, who in the innocency of her heart would draw a man into so perilous an adventure.   And as if the temptation were not dangerous enough, nothing could be neater and cleaner than the inside of the cottage, which promised infinitely more comfort than was to be had at the tavern. But, believing that her guilelessness and hospitality deserved the best return I could make her, and remembering the great kindnesses I had received from her friends, I told her that I was not a minister of the gospel, but an English traveller, who had been entertained by her father-in-law; and as her husband was from home, I would, if she would permit me, decline her kind offer, and return to sleep at Mr. Boice's.   She seemed to understand me, for she pressed me no more, and I took my leave.   I passed a very indifferent night at the tavern, a strong smell of tobacco prevailing during the whole of it, which I have no doubt proceeded from the negro-driver and his woman, who slept in a room about eight feet long and six feet wide, and who comforted themselves with smoking, and cursing, and swearing at the hot weather.

July 2.—I arose at the dawn of day, and after breakfasting with the negro-driver and his companion, mounted, and took to the woods again, meeting with nothing but deer and wild turkeys until I reached the Vase River.   It was a prodigiously hot day : during my first stage of twenty-two miles, I stopped a few moments under the shade of a tree, and, suspending my thermometer, found that it stood at 91° of Fahrenheit. It was three p. m. before I reached St. Geneviève, and upon returning to my old quarters, I found that both the master and mistress of the house had gone on a visit to Kaskaskias, an old French settlement in Illinois, but had left word that I was to consider myself at home. I had engaged to spend the 4th of July with them, the great American festival ; therefore I took possession of my old room, and contriving, with the aid of a negress, to get a quantity of water into it, I made a sort of sponge shower-bath, from which I had often received great relief in such hot weather. This is effected by loading a large sponge with cold water, and placing it on the top of the head, and pressing it gently. A quarter of an hour's exercise of this kind refreshed me greatly, for I had become so inflamed with riding in the sun, that my head was rather disordered. Having further refreshed myself with a comfortable cup of tea, I strolled out into the village.

How different the tranquil existence of this primitive French village from the busy excitement of a populous city ! At nine p.m. there was not a soul to be met in the streets; here and there the chords of a guitar, accompanied by a French voice, agreeably interrupted the general silence, whilst the only tread that was audible was that of cows slowly moving up and down the streets. Returning to the house, I sat upon the steps until a late hour, hoping that a breeze would arise, or that I should become sleepy. There was no door to the house, but in its place was a large piece of striped calico, which served as a curtain, and which reminded me of those exhibitions I had seen in my youth, where an Irish giant, or a lady cutting watch-papers with her toes, was sure to be placed, to the high gratification of my juvenile appetite for wonders. Here, at least in the house where I was, there was no door to be locked, a fact that spoke volumes for the habits of the lower classes of French and mixed negroes, who, indeed, living in the midst of abundance, are not under the necessity or temptation of stealing.

July 3.—Here I remained until the arrival of the master and mistress of the house. On the 4th, they had company to dinner, to celebrate the day; when some striking anecdotes, characteristic of the country, were related of a notorious person, once well known here, by the name of John Smith T. What the T stood for I could not learn, but this was the name he went by. In the course of his career, he had killed fourteen men either in duels, or by unceremoniously blowing their brains out. He was said to take great pleasure in manslaughter, and to be in the habit of killing men with as little remorse as others would deer, and had, not a very long time ago, put a ball through the head of a young man, whilst sitting at a table, for merely differing in opinion with him. These repeated cold-blooded murders caused him to be so much dreaded, that although he had been more than once put upon his trial, no jury had ever been bold enough to find him guilty. He used to say, openly, that if any man injured him, he had a right to take his life, and as everybody knew that he was equal to carrying his words into effect, he was respected accordingly. The man with whom he had had the longest feud, was General Dodge, the governor at Wisconsin, whom I had visited near Mineral Point. Inhabiting the same part of the country, they always travelled with horse-pistols in their holsters, in expectation of meeting, and it was for this cause that Dodge had his pistols with him when I first met him in the street at Mineral Point. He was a half-brother of the senator in whose house I was staying, and who, although a most obliging and amiable person, was, as I was afterwards informed, a decided *dilettante* in that line, having figured in a great many adventures. One of our party was an ex-member of Congress, by the name of S., a well-informed man. The day being hot, he had come to the party dressed in a light jacket and loose waistcoat, which being open, everybody could see what indeed he took no pains to hide, a pair of pistols and a bowie-knife stuck in a belt that went round his waist. I was told afterwards, that he also invariably went armed in that way, having some ancient feuds yet unsettled. In the evening, I went to a ball given at a French house in a room about fifteen feet square; there was a room full of these French creoles dancing most vehemently to a wretched violin, with Fahrenheit at least at 100°.

July 5.—The morning was tremendously hot.   I
walked to the landing-place to see if there was any
steamer bound down the Mississippi, and leaving a
person stationed there to bring me information, I
returned to breakfast, under one of the most fiery
suns I ever experienced.   Our repast being over, I
observed my worthy entertainers engaged in close
and low conversation, after which my host apologized
to me for having an engagement that would detain
him an hour or so, and I took leave of him with
many thanks for his kindness, expecting my messenger within that time.   Soon after I heard pistols
firing, and in twenty minutes the master of the house
returned, and told me he had been out on the
ground, in the capacity both of second and surgeon
in a duel ; the principals were two young Frenchmen of the place—one of them, named Rozier, a
youth of nineteen years of age ; happily, the parties
having fired without hurting each other, became
reconciled, and thus acquired their glory very cheaply.
Upon my asking how he could reconcile his taking
such a part with two boys, with what was due to his
character as a senator of the United States, he said
that he went out with no other intention than to
give them a lesson how to manage such affairs by
preventing mischief, and that he did not think the
parties would have been reconciled without his
interference.   This was certainly very humane in
him, and shewed that he had more consideration for
them than for himself ; for if one of the parties had
been killed, one would deem it difficult for a man
turned fifty years of age, and a senator of the United

States, to justify himself with the sober portion of his countrymen, for taking so principal a part in a duel between two inexperienced boys. No boat having arrived, I went again to a singular bed of limestone in the neighbourhood, containing some beautiful large fossils of the genus *Bellerophon*, in jasperized silicious nodules of a red colour. In many parts the limestone, for a great extent, was brought into the same jasperized state.

July 9.—During the last three days no steamer touched at the landing, and I was compelled to remain at this place, to my very great regret, for the heat was overpowering, and for the last forty-eight hours we had constant exhibitions of heavy thunder, vivid lightnings, and surprisingly heavy rains, so that it was very difficult to stir out of the house; nevertheless I always went to the landing after breakfast to watch for a steamer. The current of the Mississippi was furious; its waters were loaded with sediment, and were constantly rising. Enormous quantities of floating drift, covering at times the whole breadth of the Mississippi, were passing down at the rate of five or six miles an hour. This was a state of things which explained clearly to a spectator how the alluvial bank of a river, formerly deposited when the stream was perhaps three or four times the present volume, was again worn away by the river now moving in a confined channel below the surface of its ancient bottom. Masses of the bank were washed away before my eyes, and I was informed that about six acres of land had thus been abraded and carried away within the last five years. I have before observed, that north of the mouth of the Missouri, and especially north of the Wisconsin, the Mississippi is crowded with islands formed of its ancient bottom, when it occupied the whole breadth of the channel between the bluffs; but that south of the Wisconsin, and more especially south of the Missouri, few or no islands are to be observed, the torrent having carried them away. Here, in the countries south of the Missouri, the Mississippi is gradually doing that to the alluvial bottoms, which it has already done to the islands that were contemporary with them; restoring to the diminished flood its ancient dominion by again occupying at a shallower depth the whole area lying between the bluffs, and bearing to its mouth, and there spreading into new alluvial bottoms, the ruins of the older ones.

This process can be observed, in times of great floods, upon all the tributaries of these great rivers. With the falling masses of the alluvial banks, the forest trees also come down, plunging into the torrent, and borne along into the main stream : thus, many are carried out into the ocean, others sink, and are covered with silt, as in the case of the great raft on Red River. Such, probably, has been the origin of the great deposits of lignite at Bovey-Heathfield in Devonshire, and in the banks of the Upper Missouri. It is in this new world that a geologist has those opportunities of studying the origin of phenomena, which do not explain themselves in the more limited fields of Europe, especially in England. In America, there are forests and rivers two and three thousand miles long, where the beginning and ending of such phenomena can be witnessed; whilst the area of England, which presents a fine specimen of European formations and geological systems, communicates very few hints as to the causes which have either brought them there, or modified them.

After watching for a steamer from seven in the morning, and contemplating the tumultuous state of the river, which was rising at the rate of an inch an hour, a steamer, about three p. m., bore in sight, and I gladly got on board of her without asking where she was bound to, or what she was ; this was a hasty step, and one that I should not have taken, if I had not been wearied out with my protracted stay at Geneviève. The boat turned out to be one of the very bad old ones, and dirty enough. On we went, however, borne by the furious flood at the rate of twelve miles an hour. She was bound, as the captain informed me, to Louisville, so that I could land at Paducah, and from thence proceed up the Tennessee River. With this I was very well satisfied, and when evening came on, I lay down in a berth which was assigned to me, and soon fell asleep.

July 10.—I awoke about a quarter past four a.m., feeling no motion, and hearing a voice as if it came from the shore, went upon deck, when I found we were at the wharf of a place called Bird's Point, in the state of Illinois, near the mouth of the Ohio. Having shaved and washed before the other passengers turned out, I landed, and found a couple of frame houses, on a very low piece of alluvial ground, thickly timbered, and filled in a most extraordinary manner with mosquitoes. The papaw trees (*Asimina*) on this bottom were taller than I had ever seen them before, many of them being nearly thirty feet high, and all the trees were covered with elegant creepers. It resembled a fertile and thickly-wooded bottom in South America, and I tried to penetrate into it a short distance, but was soon obliged to give it up on account of the mosquitoes, that invaded, in the most resolute manner, my ears, my mouth, and my nostrils. Calling, on my return, at one of the frame houses, I was informed that this was a very sickly place towards autumn, and that the present hot, moist weather would probably produce cases of fever. This was not pleasant ; but I now made another discovery equally disagreeable, which was, that our steamer was not going to Louisville, but had come here for a cargo of plank, with which the captain intended to return to St. Louis. I immediately went on board to see him, and going below, found the steamer almost as full of mosquitoes as the shore. I now saw into what a trap I had fallen by my too great haste, and that to look before you leap is quite necessary, however tired you may be of the place from whence you are going to leap.

The fact was, that our captain had advertised to go to Louisville at a very low fare, and had by that means succeeded in getting passengers, who, tempted by the prospect of saving money, neglected the opportunity of going on board one of the regular Louisville boats. It was not for me to reproach him : I was a voluntary passenger, and it was my interest to be upon good terms with him. I therefore, in a good-humoured tone, asked him if his going to Louisville was really a joke ; upon which he frankly told me, that the advertisement he had put out at St. Louis was only a decoy, adding : " Why, doctor, you must see, that if I had advertised for such a place as this, I shouldn't have got not a beginning of a passenger in a month." Why he had chosen to call me doctor, I was unable to tell ; but it was of no consequence, as a traveller meets with all sorts of titles in this part of the world. He comforted me, however, by saying that a steamer was to leave St. Louis for the Ohio soon after him, and that she was sure to " turn up" this morning. As to the passengers, they were outrageous when they found out the " fix " they were in, and if he had not had a good share of humour, he would have found it difficult to pacify them, which he at length did, by promising to abate something still more of their fare, which was the tenderest point with them, for he was obliged to keep us all as long as we were on board him, and they had got so far on their journey for very little money, and time being of as little consequence to them as personal comfort, they saw an advantage in being kept at his expense.

CHAPTER XLIX.

LAND AT A SETTLEMENT AT THE MOUTH OF THE TENNESSEE RIVER.—
TRANSITORY STATE OF THE POPULATION.—A GENTLEMAN BLACKSMITH.
—SUSPECT THE MASTER OF THE STEAMER OF AN INTENTION TO LEAVE
ME IN THE WOODS.—CAPTAIN AND MISS KITTLE.—SENSIBLE WAY OF
DRYING THE HANDS AND FACE.

ABOUT noon we saw a steamer bearing down
towards us, which he told us was the Lady Marshall,
and that she would come alongside. " That you may
be quite sure of," said he, " for she knows I have
got passengers for Louisville." " Then," said I, " you
always set this trap for people, and they know it,
I suppose, in yon steamer ?" " Why, doctor," replied
he, " I know it ain't right; but you can't get on no
how on this river without lying a little." Such are
the morals of the Mississippi, and the unscrupulous
manner in which they are avowed. I now tran-
shipped myself on board the Lady Marshall, one of
the regular Ohio steamers, and in five minutes we
entered the Ohio, which, mighty a stream as it is,
appears small upon leaving the ample Mississippi;
the current, too, although the river was full, was
gentler, and the water much less muddy. At half-
past seven p.m., I landed at Paducah, a pretty settlement, built on a fine dry bank, about fifty feet high,
at the mouth of the Tennessee River, another of
the noble streams of this continent. Here I was so
fortunate as to secure a comfortable bed-chamber

to myself, at the house of a Widow Piles; and, having books and paper with me, I proposed waiting contentedly until a steamer should present itself, to ascend the Tennessee.

July 11.—The good widow gave me a clean breakfast, and though a very hot morning, she sallied out to reconnoitre and procure information as to the probability of a steamer soon appearing. It was an animated little place, and afforded another proof of the untiring enterprise of the Americans. Here, upon a piece of flat alluvial ground, where such a thing as a rock or stone was not to be seen, they had, in four years, run up a neat and comfortable-looking town, sufficient for their present population of 1,500 persons, with a large brick court-house for the lawyers, and an imposing-looking brick hotel, called the Marshall House, for travellers; in addition to these, there was an excellently-constructed steam saw-mill. The ground upon which the town was built commanded a fine view of the Ohio, upon which numerous steamers were constantly plying.

The population of such places, being brought together by speculation, is necessarily transitory, and constantly changing. At the time I was here, the proprietorship of the ground upon which the town was built was disputed in a lawsuit, yet every one went on making his improvements with as much apparent confidence as if he had a substantial title in his possession. When causes of this kind are decided, they then set about making a compromise, and generally effect their purpose to some extent or other, the party who has not received perfect satisfaction flying to some new place or scheme. If all the doctors, lawyers, tavern-keepers, itinerant priests, tradesmen, speculators, and bankrupts, that are roaming about this great western country, "seeking whom they may devour," were to congregate into one place, it would be the most populous and extraordinary city out of China.

In walking the streets, I saw the words "coffeehouse" painted at almost every tenth house, which I was told were all low, gambling dram-shops, frequented only by the most profligate and desperate, who always went about armed. Quarrels with such men are not light matters, for, as the saying is, "they always go for killing." In the evening, when I was writing quietly in my room, I could not but consider myself fortunate in having escaped the Marshall House, which was also frequented by these fellows. At the widow's I was safe and quiet, and from her I was sure to learn every thing that was passing in the village, my worthy hostess seeming to know everybody, to be up to every thing, and to be incapable of containing her knowledge long.

July 12.—In the United States, the best friends the trunk-makers have are the "drivers" of stages and the hands on board the steamers. On landing here I had requested the captain to let one of his men put my trunk ashore, it being too heavy for myself, who had a carpet-bag and a portfolio to take care of. Accordingly, one of the men took it upon his back, and, when he reached the wharf, dashed it impatiently on the ground, adding, "If that aint heavy I don't know what is." I had been too much amongst the Sovereign People, and knew too well that a trunk crammed with minerals and fossils must be heavy, to dispute the point with him; but it came to the ground with such violence, that a large rivet in one of the iron bands at the bottom was started. On inquiring this morning if I could get it repaired at Paducah, I was answered "that a *gentleman* who boarded in the house could do it." I was rather curious to see such an animal before I emptied the trunk of its contents, and, instead of sending for him, I went down stairs to see him, and found a coarse, impudent-looking blacksmith, seated, without his coat, at the breakfast-table. This fellow, being under no restraint from religion, law, education, or decency, and who, in his way, was as proud as Lucifer, pretended to make a favour of it; so I told him, very quietly, that if he had been, as they had told me, a gentleman, I should have considered it a favour; but as he was only a blacksmith, and would expect me to pay him for his work, the favour would come from me for giving him the job in preference to another, and that I did not care whether he did it or not. The gentleman made no reply; but it did him good, for, half an hour afterwards, he came up stairs, and did the work cheerfully and well. I am persuaded that the better classes in the United States suffer by not checking the Sovereign People in their insolence, having observed, that if you are frank with them, and treat them with reasonable indifference, they usually come to, if there is any thing to be got by it. This evening Fahrenheit stood at 93° in the shade;

I walked out, but soon found it advisable to return, and sit perfectly still, with nothing but my shirt and trowsers on.

July 13.—This was another fiery day, every thing flinching from beneath the beams of the sun. I could do nothing but sit still the whole day, reading and writing, and using pocket-handkerchiefs. Towards evening information was brought me that the Warren steamer was arrived, and would proceed up the Tennessee to-morrow. Being heartily tired of the dull life I was leading, I was delighted at the prospect of pursuing my journey.

July 14.—The air was so hot and close in my room, that it was almost impossible to sleep until late in the night. At break of day I awoke to another blazing sun, and, going to the steamer, was informed she would certainly start during the morning. This time the master of the vessel kept his word, and at noon I joyfully received a message to embark, and went on board the Warren, a small, worn-out steamer, with a phthisicky engine, making a hoarse noise at every stroke of the piston, as if its lungs were worn out. There was no private state-room for me; but, by giving a douceur to the steward, he secured me a pair of clean-washed sheets, and a decent-looking mattress, to lie down upon. Having secured this principal point, I resigned myself up to the exquisite pleasure of beholding a country I had never seen before, to me one of the greatest of all enjoyments.

The mouth of the Tennessee River contains a beautiful island of about 350 acres, and as we passed along, I observed that both banks of the river were fringed with willows, gracefully hanging over the water in front of the dense woods. What a pity that so attractive a country should be so infested with mosquitoes and fever and ague! The captain informed me that he was bound to Florence, in the state of Alabama, distant from Paducah about 300 miles; that his steamer made about five and a half knots an hour, and that the first piece of rock that cropped out on the bank of the river was about twelve miles from Paducah. Everywhere the tall cane (*Miegia*) was growing plentifully around. Having made twenty-two miles, we stopped at a wood-yard, where there was a small open shanty, and as I knew it would take the steamer an hour to ship a supply of wood, I told the captain I would stroll meanwhile into the woods, who answered, " Very well." But I had not penetrated into the forest 100 yards, when I heard the bell of the steamer ring, and knew, from much experience, that it was the signal for passengers to go on board. I now set off as fast as I could run, and on reaching the wharf, found they had unmoored the boat, and were all but in the stream. Fortunately, I was in time to jump on board, but only just saved myself. There was no appearance of an intention to wait for me, nor was any interest expressed about me; on the contrary, the captain was sulky, and looked as though I had deprived him of some advantage he thought within his reach. If I had been a quarter of a mile off when the bell rang, the steamer by a turn of the river would have been out of sight, and

I should have been left in a perfect wilderness, without provisions, and without the means of getting backwards or forwards. It was now evident to me that the captain, who had been quite civil on my embarking, had conceived the plan of abandoning me on shore, and plundering my luggage. He knew that I was in the wood, and that I believed he would remain at the yard an hour; and certain it is, that if I had walked instead of run after I heard the bell ring, I could not possibly have reached the wharf before she was steaming on her way, and whatever noise I made, he would have pretended not to have heard me.

This was a lesson to me, and I lost all confidence in him. Not thinking it prudent to come to an open quarrel with him, I merely asked him why he had not taken wood in at the wharf, as he had proposed to do. His excuse was, that the man who had the charge of it asked more than it was worth. I did not believe a word of this, for he was almost the only steamer on the river, and being the only customer, it was not likely that the poor woodcutter would raise the accustomed price upon this occasion.

About thirty-four miles from Paducah we came up with some strong rocky bluffs in the banks, and as he had promised me to stop now and then at such places as I should point out, I expressed a wish to examine these rocks for a few minutes, but he was in a bad humour and refused. About six in the evening we stopped at a ferry on a high-road leading to Cadiz, in Kentucky, where there was a poor sort of settlement. I was told at this place that the Cumberland River was only distant eight miles to the east. The people here, especially the women, were scarce above the level of savages, either in manner or appearance, although, having slaves under them, they appeared to have a prodigious idea of their own importance. But this is an invariable consequence attending a state of slavery; for the white animal, however degraded, dirty, and illiterate, will always think himself a superior being where the black one is his slave. In this obscure place, inhabited only by a few of the lowest of our species, consisting of two ruffian-looking free whites and their equally repulsive-looking she's, political placards were stuck up addressed to the Sovereign People. The soil was very fertile here, and the clearing in the forest, which was extensive, was an old one, and might have produced them every comfort; but they had neither butter, eggs, milk, nor vegetables of any kind. Salt-pork, bad corn, bread mixed up with dirt, tobacco and whiskey, formed the whole list of their necessaries and luxuries.

The entire distance from Paducah to this place had presented an unvarying scene of dense woods down to the water's edge, the monotony of which was somewhat relieved and softened by a belt of willows that hung over the stream, with the exception of an occasional clearing at intervals of about twenty miles, made by woodcutters, who have piles of this fuel split up ready for the steamers, of which the price is one dollar and a quarter a cord.

As it is not my custom to eat more than once

a day, I had not gone below when dinner was announced, reserving myself for the evening's repast, when my appetite is usually less fastidious. The steamer was an unpromising looking affair; the captain's conduct had prejudiced me much against him, and I had certainly not formed any pleasing anticipations of supper. *Ne crede colori*, however, is a just maxim; for on going to the evening's repast, what was my surprise to find a clean tablecloth, coffee, sugar, dried beef, preserved apples, excellent bread and butter, with plenty of beautiful transparent ice. Besides these good things, there were two neatly-dressed and comely-looking women, perfectly well-behaved, whom, not having descended to dinner, I had not before seen. They were the wives of the captain and his clerk, and to them I justly attributed all this neatness.

I now transferred all the kind feelings I had once been disposed to entertain for the captain to his wife, and was very civil to her, knowing that if I made a friend of her, I should stand a much better chance of occasional indulgences in leaving the steamer to examine the rocks than if she had not been on board, for he was a very different animal in the presence of his wife than when upon deck; in short, every thing shewed that she played the first fiddle, and then when he sang to it, it was *sotto voce*. I have for an article of faith, that when a woman is neat and clean, she is good; cleanliness and godliness being said to be near akin. As to the clerk and his wife, they were young, had not been long married, and the lady

did not appear yet to have turned her attention to
the delicate science of government. She had fine
eyes, and appeared to have found out that she could
look at others besides her husband with them.
Music, too, she was not insensible to; for when we
were all upon deck in the cool of the evening, and
I had taken out my accordion and played a few
notes upon it, as we were gliding along, she said, in
a tone of most decided approbation, "Well, if that
ain't the leetelest piazzur-forty (piano-forte) I ever
seed: don't it beat all, now don't it, Miss Kittle?"
—this being the name our commander and his wife
rejoiced in.

As to my tidy friend, the captain's lady, for
it was most evident from her mate's subdued
manner that she was married to him, — she was
everybody else's miss, for by that title it is usual
amongst certain classes to call married women in
the United States; a very refined fastidious-
ness making them, as I have been told, object
to the word "mistress," not knowing, in their innocency, that the word "miss" has its faults too.
But in a country where the *legs* of the piano-fortes
are said to be sometimes covered with muslin
trowsers, from excess of delicacy, we may expect
very ingenious refinements in other things, especially where there is a total ignorance of the usages
of really well-meaning society. Be these things as
they may, I established such a capital understanding with the ladies this evening, by telling them
stories about the Indians, about storms on the

ocean, which they had never beheld, and especially about General Jackson, for whom, in common with all the people in this part of the world, they had an unbounded veneration, that when I went to bed I felt I was quite independent of the captain, and that he would never venture to leave a passenger in the woods a second time, who had seen both Ginneral Jackson and Mr. Van Buren, and who was decidedly of Miss Kittle's opinion, that the last " was a considerable leeteler man than the first."

July 15.—We were obliged to come to during the night, on account of a fog as dense as a cloud. On rising from my mattress at the dawn, where, from extreme heat, I had got but little sleep, I observed that the other passengers, who were lying around, were sleeping upon sheets as dirty as tarpaulins. Half a dollar had saved me that horror. Quietly rising, I went softly to the washing-place, where I not only got the first turn at the clean towel, but had the whole locality to myself, with plenty of elbow-room for my ablutions. Thence adjourning to the deck, my friend, the steward— who had a most remarkable pair of spindle-shanks—got me a tub of water for my feet, and the luxury of another towel. Having made myself up for the day, I saw my fellow-passengers turn up in succession : two of them got my wet towels, and after in vain attempting to find " a dry " upon them, went to the door of the boiler, to make them serviceable. But these were unsophisticated people, incapable of making themselves unhappy because a towel is not what we call a clean one ; it suffices for them to be able to accomplish their principal object, which is to dry their hands and face.

One of the passengers told me that he had been lately on board a steamer on Red River, where they allowed them no towels. " And how did you manage?" said I. " Why," replied he, " I washed my face with my hands, and when I had dried them in my pantaloons, I wiped my face with them." And I thought it very sensibly done, for travellers of his class have seldom but one handkerchief, and that they wear round their necks.

We were now 100 miles from Paducah, the banks of the Tennessee still preserving the same beautiful character, only being a little higher, and sloping gracefully down. Here and there, the universal wilderness was partially broken in upon by the intruding squatter, who, depending upon the sale of wood fuel to the steamers, and upon the sale of venison and deer-skins, hardly plants maize enough for the support of his family, preferring to take bread in pay for his commodities from the passing steamers. For some time the banks had consisted entirely of tertiary beds, apparently made from tranquil waters, when a great part of the states of Mississippi and Alabama were deposited. The catalpa was growing wild, and signs of southern vegetation were increasing. Occasionally I saw strong beds of gravel at the water's edge.

At half-past seven, we reached a settlement called Point Mason, with a plantation on the east side, some old buildings and a house for curing tobacco being on the west side. This plant is grown in considerable quantities about here, and when cured, is put into hogsheads and shipped for New Orleans.

A curious instance occurred this morning, of the extreme insolence of those uneducated, puffed-up sons of equality sometimes found in steamers, and of their equally extreme meanness when any thing is to be made by coming down from their high ropes. The steward of this steamer was a disgustingly conceited, long-legged, ill-made, cadaverous-looking youth, boiling over with self-importance, for no reason but that he was not a negro, and had got a vote. Whilst we were at table it was his business to wait upon every body; he had to make the beds, to sweep the floors, and to do the most menial offices; but when he was upon deck, to shew that he was a being altogether superior to the negroes who navigated the steamer, he ventured upon the most intolerable familiarity with the passengers, uttered the most horrible oaths, indulged in the most extravagant republican boasting, and seemed to consider himself not only equal to, but to be above, every one. Perhaps he was made worse by the court many of the passengers paid to him; these, knowing that he had it in his power to oblige or disoblige them, and unwilling to secure his services by paying for them in gratuities, endeavoured to propitiate him by mean submissions, courting his notice, and encouraging his insolence. Boasting that he was equal to "any man on arth," I was saved his familiarity and insolence by bribing his assurance.

Close to the corner of the floor where I slept, was a small table, with an ill-contrived mirror hanging over it, from the corner of which was suspended, by a string, an extremely filthy, broken hair-brush, probably contemporary with the steamer. In the morning, when I was dressing before the glass, this puppy, to give himself importance in the eyes of the other passengers, came and stood between me and the glass, seized the brush, and having taken a most approving view of his dirty shirt and conceited face, began to labour away at his hair. Whilst he was in the midst of his operations, I ordered him, in a decided tone, to leave the glass to myself, and to go on deck and fill a tub with water for me to wash my feet. I saw that his pride was wounded, and he hesitated. " Very well," I said; " I thought such a fellow as you would do any thing for money, and if you don't do as I order you, I shall give you nothing when we reach Florence to-morrow." This decided him; and he sneaked off with the big words rising in his throat. I told the captain's wife of this incident in the evening, who laughed, and said, " It will do him more good than his victuals."

Near ten a. m. we passed Reynoldsburgh, consisting of one farm-house. One of the roads from Nashville to Memphis crossed the Tennessee here by a ferry, and here we found a steamer called " Walk in the Water." Further on was another road at Kirkman's Ferry. At such places the steamers land groceries, &c. for the villages and settlements in the interior. At five p. m. we were about 150 miles from Paducah, and the channel had narrowed from 800 yards to about 450, the banks sloping down gracefully, and the trees in their freshest foliage. Altogether, the scene was very beautiful. The soil was a micaceous sand mixed with vegetable loam, and underlaid with strong beds of clay, and occasional beds of tertiary limestone. At six p. m. we reached *Perrysville*, a miserable-looking settlement on the left bank, consisting of two or three poor brick houses. There is an escarpment of thin, laminated limestone beds here, and the washing of the water has removed the seams of softer matter that separated them, so that the edges of the lamina appear with grooves between them from the top of the escarpment to the water's edge, whilst, below the surface of the river, the rock preserves continuously a smooth face, affording a curious illustrative proof of the river having worn its channel from the top of the calcarious strata to its present level. In other places I observed the beds were in the same state.

CHAPTER L.

WATERLOO.—WHY A LONE HOUSE WAS CALLED PALMYRA. — ARRIVE
AT TUSCUMBIA.—GO BY THE RAILROAD TO DECATUR.—AN OVERSEER
OF SLAVES.—PURE ENGLISH NOT UNDERSTOOD.

July 16.—On awaking, I learnt that we had been
steadily going on all night, which was very satisfactory, as the affair was beginning to be monotonous.
At five a. m. we came to a small place on the left
bank, about ten miles below Savannah, in Harding
county. Three women and five children were
standing on the bank, looking pale and sickly, as if
oppressed by fever and ague : one of the females
was smoking a pipe, with a wretched-looking baby
in her arms ; near them were two men and a boy,
all dismal-looking objects. An Arcadia of yellow
fever, and Corydons and Daphnes living upon calo-
mel and whiskey ! Unfortunate children, issued
into such wretchedness as awaits them in an
existence devoid of the smallest hope of comfort
or respectability ! Heavy beds of blue clay and
ferruginous sands, with stout lignites, began now to
prevail, and probably extend to the Mississippi.

Near eight a.m. we passed the village of Savannah,
at some distance from the right bank. I saw also
a large brick house, pleasantly situated on an eminence, with some fields of maize planted around.

The Tennessee, which for the first 150 miles had preserved a nearly north and south course, governed by the bluffs of silurian limestone, had been some time meandering amongst the tertiary beds. For a few miles it divides the states of Mississippi and Alabama. The further we went south, the language and state of the people became, as it seemed to me, more degraded. The people at the wood-yards had a peculiar set of slang phrases, larded with the direst execrations, occurring about as frequently as commas and other punctuations do in printed books. It was perfectly frightful to hear them speak.

Soon after four p. m. we passed a place called *Waterloo*, consisting of a few ruinous-looking framed buildings on the right bank. Betwixt this place, with its illustrious name, and the Mississippi, there is a similar monument erected to *Bolivar*. *Moscow*, a little south of this last, has not been complimented quite so much, having only one tenement. This is quite the American taste, for in creating the new towns and counties, which speculators endeavour to force into notice, there is scarcely a conspicuous name in the annals of humanity which they have not pressed into the service, and which is not displayed upon the maps. I once asked a magniloquent young fellow why they called a lone house which we saw, *Palmyra*, when he answered, " Stranger, I don't know no more than you, but I expect it likely that Jackson gave the British a most complete whipping there." This singular mixture of ignorance, impudence, and bombast, drawn in genuine draughts from the school of " Ancient Pistol," is unknown in any other part of the world, and certainly it is exceedingly amusing to hear some of these fellows " let their steam off." Equally certain is it that these wholesale whippers of men are very easily whipped themselves, for upon more than one occasion I have found that they relied upon big words, and gave it up when they would not do.

The river south of Waterloo acquires its first breadth of about 800 yards, the banks become more elevated, and greatly improve in beauty. About five p.m. we came up with some pretty islands in the stream, and the crest of a fine ridge appeared running nearly parallel to the left bank. Nothing could exceed the density of the foliage of the for-ever-extending woods, equal to any of the Indian countries I have ever visited: but the Indians that would have rendered this forest so attractive, have all been driven away by Moscow, Bolivar, Waterloo, and Co.

July 17.—At eleven last night, after I had retired, we reached a wharf, which is the terminus of a small railroad that has been constructed from here for a distance of forty miles, to a town called Decatur, built at the eastern termination of the Muscle Shoals. These shoals are formed by an immense collection of fragments of rock, the ruins of the former strata, which have been deposited in the bed of the river along a line of from thirty to forty miles, so as effectually to interrupt the navigation for that distance.

Upon going on deck at break of day, I found the steamer lying at the foot of a strong limestone bluff,

about seventy feet high, upon which the buildings
of the terminus are erected. Two miles from this
place was a small town called Tuscumbia, through
which the railroad passed. I availed myself eagerly
of this opportunity of liberating myself from the
monotony of the voyage, for time always passes very
irksomely where there is so little to compensate for
want of comfort and rational society. The ladies
had taken so decidedly to bolting immense quantities
of fried onions at every meal, that we had not been
very sociable of late, and the audacious blasphemy
that escaped from every individual on board was intolerable. I accordingly hastened to transfer myself
and luggage, at eight a.m., into a one-horse car, and
was driven to Tuscumbia. Here I found a new and
spacious brick hotel, called the Franklin House, of
which the landlord, Mr. Ransom, promised, in a
printed card, to make " travellers agreeable," meaning or despairing to make his house so.

Notwithstanding that Fahrenheit stood at 90° in
the shade, I sallied out to look at the place, which
is prettily situated. The place was laid out in broad
streets, at right angles to each other, and many
substantial brick warehouses were erected here and
there. I found also that they used bituminous
coal here, brought from a place called Moulton,
about forty miles from hence. The commerce of
the place was sustained by cotton, which is the
staple of the country, and finds its way down the
Tennessee, to New Orleans, to be shipped for
Europe. Later in the day I went to a limestone
quarry, the silurian rocks of which are composed

of a congeries of encrinites, flustra, cardia, and innumerable small fossils, almost entirely converted into calcarious spar. There is a magnificent spring near this quarry, twenty feet in breadth, which flows from beneath a limestone ledge. Having forgotten to bring an umbrella with me, and remaining too long at work in the sun with my hammer, and my back quite blistered with the heat, I suddenly felt an unpleasant sensation in the head, accompanied with sickness at the stomach ; and, apprehensive of the consequences, I hastened back to the tavern to the bed-chamber which had been assigned me, but it felt like an oven. Here I lay down, bathing my head and body from time to time, until my unpleasant sensations abated. Feeling much better in the evening, I descended, and asked for something to eat, and never have I been more agreeably surprised, than when they placed before me a nice little clean dinner, with delicious fresh milk, and excellent apple-pie to eat with it. At night, we had heavy thunder with rain, and the burning earth became cooler.

July 18.—I arose at five a.m., with the air in my bedroom so deadly hot, that, seizing my gown, I used the greatest haste to go down stairs to the well, where I desired a droll old negro slave, whom I preferred to wait on me because he never swore, to bring me two chairs and a bucket-ful of water, and a tumbler. I believe the old fellow thought at first that I was going to drink mint-julep, and to enjoy myself after the fashion of the gentry of the country, but when he discovered that I was only going to wash myself, he laughed as if he would split his sides; "Massa," said he, "I call dat make yourself berry greeable;" but when he saw me shave myself without a mirror, he exclaimed, "I don't believe, massa, dere a lawyer in all Albama can do dat." The landlord at this house was a very obliging person, and ordered a nice breakfast for me of coffee, cream, bread and butter. Few persons in this very hot climate have the courage to be clean and nice in their doings; exertion seems to be painful, and it is evident that the general slovenliness is very much to be attributed to the weather. On leaving the house, I thanked the landlord for his attentions to me, and I could see that he was much gratified with what I said. When I gave the old negro his gratification, he said he "was berry sorry massa was going, dat it did him so much good to hab a gentleman in de house, dat shave widdout a looking-glass."

At six a. m. the locomotive drew us out of Tuscumbia; it was a beautiful morning, and we had a charming breeze. The cotton plantations as we passed them looked just like potato-fields before they go into blossom, and a great number of slaves, particularly children, were in the rows weeding them. Horrible as slavery is, yet industry is always an agreeable spectacle, and since cotton must be had in this manner, it is most fortunate that these poor creatures can work in these fiery suns. The picture the fields presented would have been upon the whole a pleasing one, but for the sight of a swarthy ruffian-looking overseer, whom we passed, sitting on a fence, holding a short-handled whip with a knotted lash in his hand. Perhaps it was only to intimidate those who were idle, and, like the staff of the beadle, denoted that punishment was at hand for those who deserved it ; but the sight of this villanous-looking agent of tyranny excited my indignation ; I could no longer admire any thing, and saw nothing but slavery in its worst form grinding to the earth helpless beings who had no appeal from the cruel greediness of their oppressors.

In this frame of mind I had no relish for the society of the car I was in, consisting of white, yellow, and black, indiscriminately packed together in a long sort of omnibus, including some young men of the country, who cursed and swore every time they opened their mouths. I had often observed, that when I asked for information of those with whom I occasionally got into company, they stared without answering me : finding myself often obliged to repeat what I said, I sometimes thought they were rather deaf, and at other times, attributed their silence to their not being accustomed to my mode of articulating words : but here I became clearly convinced that they did not comprehend me for a different reason, and that it was because I did not introduce what I had to say with an execration suited to the taste of those I was addressing, a sort of seasoning, as it were, of the conversation to their liking. When I remarked that " it was very hot, and that I hoped there would be some cool water at the next stopping-place," it produced no more effect than if I had spoken Polish or Italian. From

what I heard of the communications betwixt my
travelling companions, I perceived that if I had
made my remark in the following approved form,
" I wish I may be roasted in to h—l if I don't call
this reel b—d hot," I should have been instantly
understood, and that a strain of eloquence would have
been poured out of a sympathetic character.   Certainly, the English language is in a strange way, in
the southern slave-holding portions of the United
States, which, in one way or another, may soon
claim to be a new Pandemonium altogether unfitted
for the few men of education, and sobriety of life,
whose lot is cast there.

We made the distance, which does not exceed
forty-five miles, in four hours, reaching Decatur at
ten a. m.   On getting out at the station, I walked
into the town to see if there was any steamer bound
up the Tennessee, and heard that one was expected
from Knoxville very soon.   Decatur is a rural little
place, on the left bank of the Tennessee, every
building in which appeared to be a store ; the only
one which looked like a private house turning out
to be a bank.   The principal tavern had rather a
promising exterior, but on entering the bar-room I
found the swaggering, cursing, and swearing gentlemen of the railroad car " carrying on there,"
and as this did not betoken much comfort for a
residence that might last several days, I sought out
another with a less promising exterior.

This was a very humble tottering-looking wooden
concern, at which I was received by a good-tempered old negro, named Adam, who led me up a

rather dangerous staircase into some rooms in a very dilapidated state, and containing no furniture. Not a single bedstead was to be seen in any one of them; but perceiving that there was an airy corridor or balcony, into which the rooms opened, I asked Adam if he would try to make me comfortable if I determined to stay here; upon which he engaged to sweep and wash out any room I might select, to lay a clean straw bed on the floor, and put clean sheets and pillow-cases to it; would keep plenty of water in the corridor for my use, and would put nobody on that side of the house as long as I stayed. Having thus secured myself, as far as I could, from vulgar intrusion and tobacco-smoking, I took possession, procured a table and a couple of chairs, and determined to be comfortable. I was now within one hundred miles of *New Echota*, in the Cherokee country; and, but for the impossibility of getting my luggage through an Indian country without roads, should have attempted to go there by land. This not being practicable, I was altogether dependent upon the arrival of the Knoxville steamer; any accident happening to which would leave me in an embarrassing situation. Whilst I was looking over the map, and pondering over my situation, the dinner-bell rang at noon, and although I had not eaten since six in the morning, I entertained no intention of assisting at the dinner-table, certain visions of dirty table-cloths and dishes of bacon presenting themselves; but being desirous of seeing how they were off for the articles I placed my chief reliance upon, viz., milk, and bread and butter, I

descended into a dark, unpromising-looking room
on the basement-floor, where I found locomotive
engineers, stokers, boatmen, and all sorts of gentry
of their caliber, discussing their dinners with their
coats off.   Great, however, was my surprise, to perceive, that not only the table-cloth was clean, but that
opposite to an empty chair was a nice-looking dish
of roast chickens, lower down, a very tempting-
looking ham, some exceedingly nice-looking vegetables, and sundry glass pitchers filled with milk.   I
immediately felt very hungry, and down I sat, and
made a most hearty and excellent dinner.   So much
for second thoughts, and for condemning people and
things before you know them !

Just as dinner was over, that monster, an American stage-coach and four horses, drove up, to take
passengers to Huntsville : it was the first machine of
the kind I had seen since I left Wheeling in the
month of May.   It looked as it does everywhere,
and as its brother, the French diligence does, like a
very clumsy contrivance ; but in the pestilent, miry
state of the roads, at some seasons, in the newly
settled parts of this continent, a machine less capable
of resistance would, perhaps, not serve the purpose.
It went once a week _viâ_ Huntsville and Jasper to
Knoxville, in Tennessee, and, if the steamer failed
me, was the only resource I should have.   I was
now in the last settlement adjacent to the Cherokee
country, where there was a railroad, a bank, merchants, a postmaster, and landlords, yet I had in
vain endeavoured to acquire some information as to
the best mode of getting into the Cherokee country.

I perceived that they took no interest in matters
that they could make no money by.   I had a strong
desire to get into the stage at once, and if it had
stopped an hour, I think I should have done so ; but
it soon drove off, and I was left to my only resource,
the river.   Towards evening, when it was less hot,
I strolled out, and found some limestone beds in the
vicinity, which were a continuation of those at Tuscumbia.

July 19.—Adam was as good as his word; he
gave me a wholesome bed and clean linen.   I slept
soundly until the sun had risen, and proceeding
immediately to the corridor, where the sweet air of
the early morning prevailed, I saw to my great
delight the expected steamer slowly descending the
Tennessee.   Hastily dressing myself, I descended,
and having made a very fair breakfast, went to the
wharf where the steamer had already arrived.   The
captain assured me that he should depart again
to-morrow, that his freight would be taken in to-
day, and that he had only to run down on the
railway to Tuscumbia and come immediately back.
All this he assured me of with great earnestness,
and not one word that he said did I believe.   I
was perfectly sure that he was going to Tuscumbia
to seek for freight, and entertained no hopes of
seeing him again until he had found some.   But
the steamer was here, that material point was
gained, so I secured a berth, and determined to
be patient.

CHAPTER LI.

A GUBERNATORIAL CANDIDATE.— AN ELECTIONEERING SPEECH.—GANDER-
PULLING.—EMBARK FOR THE CHEROKEE COUNTRY.—SITUATION OF THE
CHEROKEE NATION.—BITUMINOUS COAL.

IN the course of the morning a Mr. Bagsby, a
politician, on an electioneering tour with two
friends and a domestic slave, all on horseback,
came to the tavern I had put up at. He was a
candidate for the gubernatorial chair of the state
of Alabama, and, in conformity with the custom of
the southern states, was on a tour for the purpose
of declaring his political sentiments, and canvassing
the people. This declaration was to be made in the
open air, and we seemed to be all in the humour
to be either edified or amused by it. Dinner being
disposed of, the landlord assembled the inhabitants
by ringing the tavern bell. There was a flight of
steps that led outside from the street to the first
floor of the house, with a pent roof at the top to
keep off the scorching rays of the sun. Thither
the candidate went for the benefit of the shade,
and there the landlord had the kindness to place
me a chair.

His appearance was prepossessing; he had a dark
southern complexion, black hair, piercing black
eyes, was modestly dressed, and I saw at the first

glance that he was a southern *gentleman*. From the great pains he took to assure his auditors that he really was of opinion that General Jackson was a great man, I came at a very early stage of the speech to the conclusion that he had once thought differently, and that the most difficult part of his task was to remove that impression from the minds of his hearers. It was clear that he had ratted to the dominant party, and was now an excellent democrat. He pledged himself, in the event of success, that he would govern the state with a sole regard to its interests, and that he would act in the most friendly and liberal manner towards every individual in it, as the people of Decatur, whose votes he should feel himself greatly honoured with, would find reason to acknowledge.

Throughout his speech, which was an able one, he appeared in the character of a temperate politician well versed in the affairs of his state, and actuated by a Catholic kindness towards every body. Of those opposed to him he spoke with moderation, praising them for their good qualities, and following his commendations with justifiable reasons why they were not exactly the men the state wanted at this juncture. If it had been his premeditated intention to rat a second time, he could not have been more cautious to avoid giving offence. But the influence which men acquire when they observe a charitable and amiable conduct to those who are opposed to them, was much manifested upon this occasion, for, upon bowing to his audience at the end of his speech, he was heartily cheered by every body, although I was afterwards assured that many of his political opponents were present.

July 20.—An excessively hot morning: Fahrenheit at 92°. Going down to the steamer I was informed that she would certainly start at noon, as soon as the captain and his clerk arrived from Tuscumbia—an assurance that was soon belied by the arrival of the train without either of them, or even a message from them. I would gladly have got away from this place, for, notwithstanding old Adam's clean bed, I was very uncomfortable. It was so hot by day that it was painful to go out before sunset, so that I was obliged to keep the house. If I attempted to remain in the public room, I met nothing there but dirty, profane, smoking, spitting fellows, and the walls of my bedroom were so disgustingly covered with the tobacco-juice that its former occupants had squirted upon them, that I was obliged to drag my table to the corridor to escape the sight of them. Our landlord was a goodnatured Scotchman, named M'Kenzie, but dirt appeared to be so congenial to him, that I think he would have been unhappy without it. The proprieties of the table, which I had observed the first day of my arrival, had not been repeated; indeed the clean table-cloth of the dinner made its appearance the next morning at breakfast, in as filthy a state as if it had been in a pig-stye.

July 21.—Hearing that the clerk of the steamer had arrived, I went on board, when he told me very coolly that the steamer would not leave Decatur, at any rate, until the next day. The whole lives of these fellows are passed in lying and fraud; they no longer pretend to veracity; advertising their steamers for places they are not going to, and swearing every morning that they are going, without the least intention of keeping their words. A more contemptible state of society cannot be imagined than one in which the people you are obliged to deal with attempt to deceive you upon every occasion, and, perceiving your dependence upon them, swagger and swear, and attempt to bully you if you say a word. These bad habits and vices, of men of this class in the southern states, grow out of the combined causes of climate and slavery. The climate makes them too indolent to help themselves, and slaves being at hand to do all menial and laborious offices, they acquire, from their earliest years, extravagant ideas of their own importance, and being brought up in the belief that blacks are created to work for them, and constantly hearing about Liberty and Equality amongst white men, they bluster when they cannot reason. That class, therefore, which, in the northern states, sustains the different branches of industry, is too often resolved here into a vapouring, disgusting, and unprofitable set of beings, devoid of education, religion, or manners, and have the audacity to call those who correspond to their own class in the north, *white Niggers.*

In the evening a dance was got up at the tavern by some young persons of the place, and I went into the room to observe them. It was the first time that I ever was present at an assemblage of young persons of both sexes in the United States,

where the females did not greatly excel the males
in manners and personal advantages. The music
was execrable, and the awkwardness and extreme
want of grace of *tutti quanti* were not to be easily
paralleled.

July 22.—I was glad to find, on going down to
the steamer, that the captain had arrived, who assured me that he really should go to-day as soon
as he had embarked four hogsheads of sugar. " I
tell you this, stranger," he said, " because I know
you are asked to go to the gander-pulling this
morning, but you may depend the steamer will go."
It was true that I had been invited to this polite
amusement by some persons at the tavern, but
having seen it once I had no inclination to be present a second time, especially at the risk of losing
my voyage.

" Gander-pulling " is a sort of tournament on
horseback, and is, I believe, of European origin. A
path is laid out on the exterior of a circle of about
150 feet diameter, and two saplings are sunk into
the ground about 12 feet apart, on each side of the
path. These being connected towards the top
with a slack cord, a live gander with his legs tied,
and his neck and head made as slippery as possible
with *goose* grease, is suspended by the feet to
that part of the cord immediately over the path.
The knights of the gander having each deposited a
small sum with the manager of the game to form
a sweepstakes and to defray the expenses, follow
each other, mounted on horseback, at intervals
round the ring, two or three times before the signal

is made to pull. When that is done, the cavaliers advance, each fixing his eye steadily upon the gander's shining neck, which he must seize and drag from the body of the wretched bird before the purse is won. This is not easily done, for as the rider advances he has to pass two men, five or six yards before he reaches the potence, one of them on each side of the path, and both armed with stout whips, who flog his horse unmercifully the instant he comes up with them, to prevent any unfair delay at the cord. Many are thus unable to seize the neck at all, having enough to do to keep the saddle, and others who succeed in seizing it often find it impracticable to retain hold of such a slippery substance upon a horse at full speed. Meantime the gander is sure to get some severe " scrags," and for awhile screams most lustily, which forms a prominent part of the entertainment. The tournament is generally continued long after the poor bird's neck is broken before it is dragged from its body ; but some of the young fellows have horses well trained to the sport, and grasp the neck with such strength and adroitness, that they bear off the head, windpipe, and all, screaming convulsively after they are separated from the body. This is consi- dered the greatest feat that can be performed at gander-pulling.

At two p.m. we unmoored and got into the stream, pursuing our way through a flat country for about ten miles, when a fine ridge of land, running ap- parently at right angles to the river, came in view. A person on board told me that it was sandstone, and that there was a mineral spring of sulphuretted water, and another of chalybeate at its foot, not more than two or three miles from the river, which were resorted to by the gentry of Alabama. We reached Triana about five p. m. where the extensive clearings contrast themselves well with the deep wooded banks of the river : beyond this, and about twenty miles from Decatur, the country becomes very pleasing, lofty and graceful knolls rising up amongst the clearings. About sunset, we landed some rather livid-looking passengers at a place called Damascus Ferry, who were going to the mineral springs. The sandstone here lay regularly upon a silurian limestone. At night we had thunder and lightning in the distance, with a promise of rain, now much wanted, to increase the depth of the river, and without which, I was given to understand, we should be puzzled to get over a place called " The Suck."

July 23.—I arose at sunrise, and going on deck, found we were at Gunter's Landing, a collection of slightly-built, unpainted wooden stores, upon a high sandy bank, about thirty-five feet above the level of the river. Much rain had fallen in the night. We were now at the most southern bend of the Tennessee River, with the Cherokee country on our right. Various sandstone ridges were in sight. Fifteen miles further up, we stopped to take in wood, at the old Cherokee Coosawda village ; and seeing a rude log house in a small clearing hemmed in by the woods, I walked up to it. Some peach-trees were around, with green fruit on them, growing in a fertile, sandy, micaceous loam. On entering the hut, I found a stout Cherokee Indian, stretched out at his full length on the ground, near a hideous-looking woman, seated upon her haunches, and an Indian girl, her daughter, depediculating her mamma's head.

She asked me civilly, and in good English, to sit down; but, being apprehensive of carrying some of the live stock away, I advanced no further than the door. They said there were a great many Indians within two miles of the place, but that the whites had got possession of the country, and they all expected to be driven out of it. At this time the brave and intelligent nation of Cherokees was in a very distressing position. For the sake of tranquillity, they had not only in various treaties with the United States surrendered, as the Creeks had before done,* important portions of their territory to the state of Georgia, but had, *upon the urgent recommendation of the whites*, abandoned the savage life, had successfully entered upon agriculture, and universally adopted the Christian religion. A remarkable man,† who had appeared amongst them,

* *Vide* "Slave States, &c.," vol. ii., p. 305.

† This man, *Sequoyat*, called by the Americans *Guess*, was a native Cherokee. Having been informed that the characters which he had seen in the books at the missionary schools, represented the sounds made in pronouncing words, and pondering upon this, he finally invented a character for every sound in the Cherokee language, to the number of eighty-five. His countrymen soon acquired the knowledge of these characters, and all those whom I saw could read the books printed in them. As the distinct sounds do not modify each other, as the syllables in the Euro-

had invented alphabetical characters to express every separate sound in their language, and books of prayers, psalms and hymns, with the gospels, had been printed in these characters, in the familiar knowledge of which the whole Cherokee nation had been instructed. These poor people did more than possess the Christian religion; in the honest simplicity of their hearts, they endeavoured to live in conformity to its precepts, and were most exemplary in the performance of their religious duties.

In the treaties which the Government of the United States had made with them—the whole of which, on the part of the Cherokees, were treaties of cession—that Government always guaranteed to the Indians, in the most solemn form, that portion of their territory which was not ceded; so that they had the security for the performance of these treaties from the same people at whose instance they had embraced the Christian religion ; a moral security, which national faith on the one side, and their own friendless condition on the other, invested with high responsibility.

It is, I dare say, but doing justice to the Government of the United States to believe, that at first they were disposed to observe the stipulations they had entered into with the Indians, and that they would not have turned aside from so sacred a duty, but for the pressure of the population of those states whose territory was contiguous to that of the

pean languages do, every one who can pronounce the characters correctly can read the words.

Cherokees, to whom every successful encroachment served but as an incentive to further invasions upon the rights of the Indians, and whose political influence was brought to bear upon the general Government for the accomplishment of their cupidity.

This state of things got at length to such a height, that it became evident the whites would never remain satisfied until they had wrested every acre of land from the hands of the rightful owners. The discovery, too, of several alluvial deposits of native gold in the Cherokee lands had removed the last moral restraint from the people of Georgia, who entered, without leave or license, upon the best possessions of the Indians.

At the time of my visit, the Cherokees were almost incensed to desperation; they were yet about 18,000 in number; were brave, and had leaders of great ability. An outbreak was therefore expected. The general Government, which was well informed of the oppression the Indians were suffering, were reduced to the apparent alternative, either of turning the national arms against the people of Georgia in defence of the Cherokees, or of leaving the Georgians to perpetrate every sort of wrong against the poor Indians they had solemnly agreed to protect. But another plan, and, perhaps, the one that was now most consistent with humanity, was adopted. A powerful draught of the militia of the state of Tennessee was called out, and these, aided with a few United States regular troops, proceeded to occupy the Cherokee country, for the purpose of preventing an insurrection of the Indians, and a

collision betwixt them and the Georgians.   The
Cherokee leaders were also invited to cede the whole
of their territory to the Georgians, for a consideration to be paid to them by the United States,
which engaged to provide them with other lands
west of the Mississippi.

The proposition to abandon their native country
was abhorrent to the Cherokees, with the exception
of a very small minority of them, that had been
gained over by some subordinate chiefs, whom the
agents of the United States Government had induced
to enter into a contract to cede the whole territory
to the Georgians, with a stipulation that the entire
nation was to evacuate the country within a short
period.   In this contract, the legitimate chiefs, who
alone were authorized to transact public business for
the Cherokees, and who, in fact, constituted the
Government of the nation, had had no part.   They
immediately protested strongly against it, and at
least five-sixths of the nation adhered to them, under
the advisement of a half-breed, named John Ross, a
man who had received a good education amongst the
whites, had fine talents, great experience, an inflexible character, and who possessed unbounded
influence over his countrymen.   It was now more
obvious than ever that the Cherokees never would
leave the country voluntarily, and that their affairs
were nearly brought to a crisis.

Under all these circumstances, which had a great
notoriety, I felt a warm interest for this much-
wronged people, fully persuaded, however, that
although justice was not to be expected, the United

States Government would observe a merciful and humane conduct towards them. By landing at some point higher up the Tennessee River, I determined to avail myself of the opportunity of crossing the whole of the Cherokee territory, of examining its geology, and observing the real condition of a famous aboriginal race, with which Ferdinand de Soto communicated when, in 1539, he traversed that part of the American continent which extends from Tampa Bay, in East Florida, to the shores of Texas, in the Gulf of Mexico.

We continued to advance up the river to the north-east, a very extensive and well-wooded chain, called Racoon Ridge, holding a parallel course with us near to the left bank. The Sandstone Ridges appear to have been left behind by a great denudation which has laid bare the fossiliferous silurian limestone below. At half-past three p. m., we stopped at Bellefonte, forty miles from Gunter's Landing, to take in wood: here the Ridge, near 700 feet in height, came close to the river. At six p.m., we passed Crow Creek on the right bank, with a pretty island in front, and an hour afterwards we stopped at Caperton's Bluff, where a compact and sparry fossiliferous limestone cropped out on the right bank.

July 24.—Upon going on deck at five a. m., I found we were within the limits of the state of Tennessee, a short distance above Sequatchee River, and sixteen miles below the Suck. The scenery was very pleasing; the Tennessee had cut its way through the Cumberland mountains, leaving elevations of from 700 to 800 feet above our heads on each side. We had the same incoherent sandstone incumbent upon limestone, the mountain being densely wooded to the top, and abounding, as I was informed, with bears, deer, and wild turkeys. Veins of bituminous coal are said to be found in these rocks. Geological proofs were constantly presenting themselves of great areas of the sandstone having been swept away, previous to the deposit of a red earth upon which the cotton is raised, and the period of the deposit of which is probably contemporaneous with the red soils observed in other countries, as in Devonshire.

At half-past seven the scenery became exceedingly picturesque, and reminded me of the Upper Mississippi, strong escarpments of disintegrating sandstone appearing on each side of the river, which abounded in sudden bends, and having a strong current setting down. The stream now contracted to about 200 yards, and we reached a rapid called the Pan, where the current was so strong that we were detained two hours making preparations to warp the steamer beyond it. Whilst this was going on I amused myself collecting unios, with some fresh-water univalves I had not seen before. There were some bulima of a remarkable size. The animal of some of these shells of the turritella family was very curious, the inferior part consisting of a broad contractile fleshy disk, exceedingly flexible, resembling the cleavers made of leather which boys use to raise stones with. At the top of this the other part appears, its head with two lateral feelers about half an inch long, and a snout. The whole body was of a bright yellow colour, streaked and spotted dark brown, and the anterior portion was beautifully lined with neat brown stripes, crossing like the stripes of a zebra.

About noon, we passed another rapid, called the Pot, which is very difficult to traverse when the water is high. The hills here rose to about 1,000 feet in height on each side. We were, in fact, steaming through a deep ravine. There was a vein of bituminous coal, three feet thick, in the sandstone mountain on the right bank. A man on the shore informed me, that a youth in the service of the United States died near this place the other day from the bite of a rattle-snake. He was driving a stake into the ground, when the reptile struck him in the neck, and he never spoke afterwards. I got into a canoe to examine the Suck, a powerful rapid, with a fall of about ten feet. The Chute, at its head, divides itself into two branches, which, meeting lower down, force the water a foot above the common level.

CHAPTER LII.

PROCEED UP THE RIVER IN A " DUG OUT."—CONTRIVANCE OF THE TOR-
TOISE FOR HATCHING ITS EGGS.—THE LOOK-OUT MOUNTAIN.—REACH
ROSS'S LANDING.—TROOPS AT CAMP WOOL.—THE MORAVIAN MISSION.—
PROCEED INTO THE CHEROKEE COUNTRY.

July 25.—The steamer could get no further at
present, and it was necessary to provide, in some
way or other, for my further progress. Leaving her
moored to the bank, I walked into the country
in search of a man called Thompson, who I was
told had a canoe, in which, if I succeeded in
engaging him, I could continue my course up the
river. After wandering about for some time, I
found him, and after beating him down about one
half of the amount he required, I engaged him,
his canoe, and another man he was acquainted
with, to take me about fifteen miles up the river to
a new settlement called Ross's Landing. I had
been told that the militia of the state of Tennessee
had a post in this neighbourhood, where it would
not be difficult to procure information of the state
of the country, and perhaps the means of penetrating into it: at any rate, I must do something with
myself and my luggage, which was too heavy to
carry on my shoulders. Accordingly, returning
to the steamer, I ate a hasty meal, got a little
provision, in the event of being obliged to bivouac

for the night, and making a portage round the Suck, found my men with their canoe at the place we had agreed upon.

Our steamer, which was but a small one, was a huge leviathan compared with the simple convey- ance in which I now deposited myself and my effects. It was a log of wood roughly hewn out, called, in the language of the country, a "dug out." It had no seat except on the bottom, and having assumed the only position it admitted of in it, I found that if I stirred in the least degree, the centre of gravity would be so changed, as to set it rolling in a perplexing manner, and that, in my anxiety to re-adjust the balance, I was just as likely to upset it as not. I soon perceived that my only plan was to sit perfectly still. About two miles further up the river we came to another rapid, called the *Tumbling Shoals*, both broad and strong. Here I was greatly puzzled to consider how the men in- tended to force our canoe through the current, and this was by hugging the bank as close as possible where the water was least powerful, and so getting round a bluff that rather projected into the stream, and protected us from the current. In attempting this, the eddy took us, and threatened to whirl us into the wildest part of the furious rapid, where we should certainly have been upset, with scarce a hope of saving ourselves. I was already considering where the "dug out" would probably rise again, and what chance there was of my clinging to her, when, at the crisis of our fate, one of the men seized a point of the rock, and clung to it with desperation, whilst his companion seized a strong shrub that was growing in the rock. This enabled the first to get a more secure hold of the bluff, and using a paddle as a rudder to keep her head right, I called out to them to pull with all their might. In this way we forced the canoe round the bluff, and got into quiet water. I think I never was in more imminent danger.

The river now expanded to about 800 yards wide, and paddling pleasantly along we came to a high sloping bank of loose sand, which I landed to examine. It had an angle of more than 50°, had a south-west aspect, and was composed of loose sharp sand, derived from disintegrated rock. This was one of those tortoise-banks occasionally found on the margin of the rivers where that amphibious animal abounds. In the upper parts of the Tennessee and its tributaries they attain a large size, as I had occasion to remark when examining, upon a previous occasion, the country watered by the Holston. The contrivance of this species (*Trionyx ferox*) for providing for the hatching of its eggs forcibly shews the power of animal instinct; and the details respecting it which I am about to give, may be considered as illustrating some of the phenomena connected with the fossil footmarks found at Corn Cockle Muir, and at Craigs, near Dumfries, where the inclination of the strata is also about 45° S.W.*

Where a slope like the one I was now exa-

* *Vide* Dr. Duncan's Paper, in Trans. R.S. of Edinburgh 1828.

mining, exists near waters inhabited by this species, the animal, at the proper season, crawls up it, and when arrived at the top begins to make its nest. This is done by screwing its body repeatedly round in the sand, until it has scooped a pit sufficiently large: here it lays from twenty to forty round eggs, generally without a shelly calcareous covering, but covered with a tenaceous membrane. Sand is then scratched over the eggs to the depth of six or eight inches, which the tortoise pats down firmly by rising on its hind feet, and flattening the nest with its anterior extremities. When the sun has hatched the eggs, the young animals force their way out of the sand, and following their own instinct, and the inclination of the slope, roll down into the river.

Further up, I observed numerous wood-ducks (*Anas sponsa*) fly out of the trees: this beautiful bird often hatches in their tops, and conducts its young to the water in its bill. The country now became very interesting, and I began to regret that I should soon have to leave the canoe; a favourite mode of conveyance with all travellers who, like myself, have devoted much time to the exploration of the rivers of America. About ten miles from the Suck, we came to the Look-out Mountain, a noble pile of stratified limestone with a huge hump of sandstone at the top. I should have been glad to land here, but the men had become rather impatient at my frequent stoppages, and upon my inquiring whether it was possible to find a path of any sort up the mountain near to the river, told me there was nothing of the kind, that they wanted to get back, and that I could find somebody at Ross' landing to serve me as a guide. From the resolute manner in which they now began to paddle, I perceived their humour, and that our good understanding might not be ruffled, told them that I was obliged to them for the attention they had paid me, and was contented to proceed as fast as they thought proper.

After some time, they ran the canoe ashore at a beach where there was no appearance of a settlement, and told me that it was Ross' Landing. I was somewhat dismayed at first at the prospect of being abandoned on a lone beach, since these men having fulfilled their agreement had a right to be paid immediately, and time was important to them to get back that night. Upon parleying with them, however, I learnt that there was a small settlement not far from us, and that they would carry my luggage there for a reasonable gratification. Upon which I sent them immediately on, and taking a last look at the river followed the road they took. At length I came to a small village hastily built, without any regard to order or streets, every one selecting his own site, and relying upon the legislature of Tennessee to pass a law for the permanent arrangement of their occupations. The appearance of the individuals I saw was very unpromising, and addressing myself to one of them, he directed me to a small tavern kept by a person of the name of Kennedy.

Supposing, from the state in which the country was, that I should meet with all sorts of disorderly persons, and wishing in my heart that the Indians had continued in possession of their country—for wherever I had been, the Indians had been friendly to me—-I almost dreaded the idea of going to this tavern; but on reaching it, I was quite delighted to find that it consisted of three new log huts, built upon a high piece of ground that commanded a beautiful view of the surrounding country. The landlord was very civil, every thing was tolerably clean, and having made a neat and acceptable supper with good milk, bread and butter, and coffee, I considered myself a most fortunate person, and laid down to rest in a very contented state of mind, with the benefit of the wandering breezes of the night upon my face, that entered through the open logs of the hut I slept in.

July 26.—On awaking, I got a fine view of the country through the walls of my bed-room, which fronted that fine chain which on this side the river is called Racoon Mountain. The Look-out Mountain also was towering up with the numerous peaks of its extended line, that appeared wooded to the top. The rest of the landscape consisted of picturesque knolls of limestone, all densely covered with trees. Having made a hearty breakfast, I strolled out to look at the rocks. The limestone consisted of heavy compact beds of a blueish colour, much intermixed with chert and non-fossiliferous. Near the river it was horizontal, but here I found the anticlinal structure occasionally well marked, the beds not observing the steady horizontal position of the beds at Tuscumbia and Decatur. I was not surprised at this, always expecting that the nearer I approached to the Alleghany Mountains, the more I should find the beds influenced by that great movement which has modified the surface it operated upon into their ridges and valleys, and produced those flexures in the non-bituminous carboniferous beds.

How I was to remove my luggage from this place, and get fairly into the interior became now a matter for serious consideration. There was no such thing as a wheeled vehicle in the place, nor any probability of their being one ; and I found it equally impossible to engage horses. In this serious dilemma, I determined to go to Camp Wool, in the neighbourhood, to state my case to a Colonel Ramsay, who acted as commissary and store-keeper to the Tennessee mounted volunteers stationed there. I lost no time, therefore, in proceeding to his quarters, where the troops appeared to be comfortably hutted. He received me civilly, and offered to accompany me to the quarters of the commanding officer, Colonel Powell, where we immediately proceeded. With this officer, I found a Major Vaughan and a Captain Vernon, three persons, as far as I could judge, well suited to the responsible duty they were engaged upon.

They received me in a very friendly manner, and the commanding officer, on being acquainted with my situation and embarrassment, expressed his regret at not being able to give me any conveyance. He said that he expected an order every moment to take his command to a place called Red Clay, where Ross, the Cherokee chief, had convened his nation to meet on the 31st of this month. This piece of information, although it was the cause of a great disappointment, excited a strong desire in me to go to Red Clay also. To have an opportunity of seeing the whole Cherokee people convened together, to deliberate upon the resolution it was proper for them to take at this juncture was to me very tempting; and I determined, if possible, to shape my course for the accomplishment of it.

At the camp, I was told that the best chance afforded me of procuring a vehicle would be at the Moravian Mission of Brainerd, six miles distant, and determining to go there, I engaged a horse of a suttler for the ride as the heat was too overpowering to go on foot. But the animal turned out exceedingly vicious, and plunged and reared in such a furious manner, that part of the rotten bridle they gave me having given way, I was thrown, and came with the back of my head upon the bare limestone, receiving a very stunning blow that made me sick at my stomach for at least an hour. As this happened in sight of the encampment, several of the soldiers ran up to assist me, and the accident being reported to Colonel Powell, he sent Captain Vernon, who offered me every kind attention, remaining with me until I felt somewhat recovered, and insisting upon my mounting his horse to accomplish the excursion. The sun beat powerfully upon me, and I was quite ill during the ride, grateful, however, to Providence for not having fractured my skull. On reaching the Mission, which had the appearance of a farm-house, I dismounted, and an Indian woman called Mr. Buttrick, the resident Moravian missionary, a pious elderly person apparently out of health, with whom I had a very interesting conversation about his Mission and the situation of the Cherokees. On the subject of my visit, he referred me to a Mr. Blunt who managed the farm belonging to the establishment. This person, whilst he professed to be sorry for my embarrassment, did not seem disposed to give himself much trouble to relieve my wants. I soon found out that every one at the Mission was zealously disposed in favour of the Indians, and anxious to prevent their being sent out of the country, a measure that would of course be followed by its suppression. Not knowing me, they considered it to be very possible that I sympathized with their oppressors; and, therefore, rather politely, but coolly enough, declined assisting me. It was evident that the people at the

Mission had transferred all their natural sympathies for their own race to the persecuted Indians. I was not much surprised at it, and perceiving how matters stood did not renew my request.

In the meantime, I turned my visit to the best advantage I could by entering into conversation with Mr. Buttrick about the Cherokee language. Having been acquainted many years ago, at Bethlehem and Nazareth, in Pennsylvania, with some of the leading Moravians there, I spoke of them and of the great services that Loskiel, Zeisberger, and the excellent Heckewelder had rendered to the Aborigines. This inspired him with more confidence in me, and before we parted he laid down a great deal of his reserve. He told me that he had been twenty years amongst the Cherokees, and had paid much attention to their language. From his observations, I perceived that its structure closely resembled that of the Nacotahs and Howchungerahs, their compound ideas being expressed by polysyllabic words composed of fragments of simple words reduced into grammatical forms consistent with a peculiar euphony familiar to the Indian ear. He was kind enough to promise me some remarkable instances of this arrangement at a future day. Mr. Buttrick was a decided friend of the Indians, and considered the whites to have violated the most sacred of rights in dispossessing the Cherokee nation of their native country. It had not been found difficult he said to frame an apology for the conduct of those whites who had, in the earliest times, come amongst these defenceless men and taken their lands, for they had done it under pretext of converting them to Christianity ; but, in the case of the Cherokees, not only treaties had been trampled upon, but every wrong had

been heaped upon an unoffending Christian nation.   He
said he knew the Cherokees well, and thought they would
die on the spot rather than leave their country ; but, if it
came to that, the whites were the strongest and must
prevail.   " Nevertheless," added he, " God has his eye
upon all that is passing, and at his own time the Cherokees
will be avenged."

I was very much impressed by his manner, for he
evidently was sincere, believing himself in a deep decline,
as a bad cough, which frequently troubled him, too truly
indicated.   I remarked to him that none of the Indian
tribes had been able to stand against the tide of white
population, and that perhaps the hand of Providence was
in it ; for, although the people of Georgia had treated the
Indians wrongfully, yet a few generations hence, their
descendants might fill the land and be a good and religious
people ;   that the Indians would probably be a much
happier community in a distant territory, where they had
no white neighbours, and that I was of opinion that those
who had influence with them would render them an
essential service by advising them to submit where resistance was hopeless ; that to encourage them to resist
would be to assist in their extermination, and that I
sincerely believed the wisest plan would be to endeavour
to persuade them to throw themselves upon the generosity
of the United States Government, who had the highest
motives to deal in the most merciful and humane way
with them.   To this he merely observed, that the Council
of the Cherokee nation would determine what was to be
done.

I saw several young Indians of both sexes about the
Mission, and would willingly have remained longer, but I

was not encouraged to do so, and perceiving that my presence was an embarrassment, I took leave of the interesting Missionary, assuring him that the Indians had not a more sincere friend than myself. Mr. Blunt, the farmer, followed me to the gate, looking as if he was conscious that he had not acted a very friendly part towards me, and began an apology which I cut short by saying: " Either you have a conveyance, Mr. Blunt, or you have not. If you have not, that fact would render an apology unnecessary ; but if you have one, as I have been informed is the case, then you have lost an opportunity of obliging a traveller who has always been a friend to the Moravian Missions." Leaving Mr. Blunt to digest this I returned to the encampment; and having delivered the Captain his excellent horse with many acknowledgments, walked slowly back to my quarters, my head aching violently with the severe blow I had received in the morning.

July 27.—I had a restless night with some fever and great soreness in the back of my head; towards morning, however, I got some sleep, and was awoke by a refreshing breeze passing over my face. Having dressed and breakfasted I felt much better. The landlord had heard of the ruins of an old gig with wooden springs that belonged to a man of the name of Rawlins; it was under a shed, and had served exclusively for some time past for his cocks and hens to roost upon. Hoping that it might be possible to cobble it up in some way or other, I went to see it and its owner, a long-legged drawling fellow, who was a complete pendant to his vehicle. He said if I would go to the expence of having it repaired, he didn't care if he hired it to me but that he had no horse, though he had some old harness. As this was the only card I had left to play, and fearing that if the detachment left the camp, I should be left here without a resource or friends of any kind, I hastened to Colonel Powell's, who upon learning the discovery I had made of the gig, asked me what use I could make of it without a horse. " Why to tell you the truth," said I, " I know some of your suttlers keep yokes of oxen to move their things about, and as these men are always ready to make money, I have thought you would lend me your influence to hire a yoke to take the gig with my luggage to some main road where I can get a conveyance, and as to myself, I would rather walk than ride, for I want to examine the country as I go along." " Upon my word," he replied, " a man that is as ready to help himself as you are ought to be helped by others, and I will direct one of my blacksmiths to mend the gig for you."

Accordingly the Colonel mounted his horse, and with the smith and myself on foot proceeded to Mr. Rawlins'. Here upon inspection, it was reported that the gig could be mended, and Rawlins having paraded his harness before us, the Colonel said there was an old horse at the encampment which had been unwell, but was now better, and that he would lend him to me for three or four days. Thus was I, by the kindness of this worthy officer, put into an independent position again, and making a bargain instantly with Rawlins to accompany me and to bring the horse back, I took leave with many thanks of the good Colonel, who returned to his camp with the smith. Meantime, Rawlins and myself went to work to clean the gig, and mend the harness. Whilst we were thus occupied, the smith returned with the horse, a miserable looking creature that seemed to have every infirmity. But being an exceedingly clever and obliging man, in an hour, what with ropes and the

fragments of horse millinery belonging to Rawlins, and
the ingenuity of the smith, we had got the horse into the
shafts and drove to my quarters.

Here I took leave of my obliging landlord, and, sending
Rawlins to proceed and lead the horse, soon followed him.
It was a burning sun, and I was not yet free from headache,
but the excitement produced by getting up this equipage,
and by having the world once more before me had made
me rather indifferent to it. We reached the Moravian
Mission in three hours, which was two miles an hour, and
here I fed the horse whilst good Mr. Buttrick looked up
some Cherokee vocabularies for me. At 4 P.M. we started
again, but an unthought of difficulty soon brought us up,
for we had to pass the Chiguamawgah Creek: this was
rather too deep for Rawlins and myself, who were on foot,
so we were obliged to get into the gig, which had no seat
in it, and which was already filled with the luggage.
Alas! when we had got fairly into the middle of the creek,
our Rosinante could not muster strength enough to drag
us across. In vain we encouraged him, he would not
stir, and for near a quarter an hour it seemed certain that
we should have to lighten his load, by jumping out. At
the end of that time we tried the poor animal once more,
and setting up a great shout, and clattering the ropes upon
his back we got the steam up a little, and on we went
amidst the rocks and stones at the bottom, bouncing and
rolling from one to another, every instant expecting an
upset. Happily, we reached the opposite bank in safety.

The exertion I had made, and the breezes which became
very refreshing at the decline of day had abated my headache, and I enjoyed my evening's walk very much. The
country around bore a truly Indian character, short trees

sparsely growing amidst tall luxuriant wild grass, and occasional remains of Indian habitations. I saw no game of any kind. At night we came to a wretched hotel, kept by a person named Inman, and here we were fain to put up, our horse having more than once given symptoms of coming to an anchor. Having tea, and biscuit and sugar with me, I made myself as comfortable as I could, and then laid down contentedly on the floor, the room smelling like an ill kept hospital. In the night we had a furious storm, with thunder and torrents of rain that set me thinking of the creeks we had yet to pass.

CHAPTER LIII.

July 28.—I got out of this dismal, filthy place at 5 A.M., and having walked about ten miles, came to a chalybeate spring, where I found some of the principal halfbreed Cherokee chiefs with their families in log huts, these people having their watering places as well as the whites. In one of the huts was a tolerable bath, the water being led by wooden spouts from the foot of the hill whence it issues. Being a rural shady place, I remained here a short time for the purpose of conversing with the Cherokees. All of them, including the women, spoke English, these last being well dressed and good looking. Perceiving that they were not disposed to communicate very freely with me, I proceeded on, and my horse being in a tolerable willing humour, we at length reached an American settlement called Cleveland, newly made on the road leading from Calhoun, on the Hiwassee, in Tennessee, to Gainsville in Georgia. Being now on a stage coach road, and no longer in danger of being embargoed, I inquired for the best tavern, and was directed to a clean house kept by a person named Berry. Here I dismissed Mr. Rawlins and his machinery, and having washed and shaved, sat down to a very comfortable but late breakfast. Twelve months ago there was not a building of any sort here; but such is the activity of these people that already they had got a street, and a square, and a tavern, and stores upon the plan of the older settlements.

This spirit of enterprize, which somewhat astonishes the Europeans who witness it has nothing so very extraordinary in it, when we consider that every individual concerned is a speculator. The tavern-keeper, the trader, the doctor, the lawyer, the artisan, all build to allure others to settle near them, every one of them being at all times ready to sell his possession, and move to any other part of the country where he thinks he can turn a penny to greater advantage.

In the afternoon, a vehicle which they called the stage drove in from Calhoun, distant twelve miles: it was a singularly small affair drawn by two long-legged, raw backed horses, but I was glad to see it, small as it was, for it contained no passenger, and just held myself and my luggage. I was now once more upon a regular communication, and could look about me at my ease. We passed several small ridges consisting of a cherty non-fossiliferous limestone, and were evidently ascending an elevated primary country, on the skirts of the Unaykay or White Mountains, that separate Georgia from Tennessee. At the end of eighteen miles, we stopped for the night at another dreadful dirt-hole kept by a man named Osborne.

July 29.—The fatigue of the day made me sleep well, although on the floor, and at 4 A.M. we started again. As soon as we passed the boundary dividing the two States, into Georgia, we came upon shale and slate dipping to the S.E.; over this we rode fifteen miles, and then came upon limestone again. Lofty mountains were upon our left, appearing to form part of a chain bearing N.E. and S.W.

We met many parties of Cherokees of the lowest class going on foot to the great meeting. Some of them were very drunk and were accompanied by young women carrying their infants. Log huts now increased in number with clearings around them, surrounded by broken-down fences, and bearing evidence of slovenly farming. The white inhabitants were a tall, sallow, gawky-looking set, with manners of the coarsest kind; their children were all pale and unhealthy-looking, suffering, as the mothers told me, from bowel complaints, occasioned evidently by unwholesome food and filth. We passed several farms belonging to the principal Cherokees, containing fine patches of the sweet potato (*Convolvulus Batata*), maize and pulse of various kinds. Some of the Indian women spoke English, but generally they were shy, and in a few instances refused to answer me. I was not surprised at this at the present juncture.

About 8 A.M., we passed a substantial-looking brick house belonging to a man named McNair, who had an Indian wife and a progeny of half-breeds. Some miles further on we found him seated by the road-side with a waggon near him, and his family around him preparing their meal. He was an old man, and being struck with his strong resemblance to General Jackson, I stopped and spoke to him. He told me that he had a dropsy, and was now on a journey of one hundred miles to consult a famous doctor.

Before noon we reached a settlement prettily situated, called Spring Place, with the fine line of Cohuttie Mountains in view, and stopped at a tavern, kept by a person named McGaughky, who very obligingly, upon my request, gave me an airy room to myself up stairs. This I took possession of, and having made my toilette, descended to a comfortable breakfast. Here I learnt that Red Clay, the place appointed for the Indian meeting, was only twenty-five miles distant, and that I must proceed there from hence; but that I should be in time for it in four or five days, the chiefs not having yet arrived. Understanding that another stage would depart in the morning for Gainsville, in Georgia, a village distant about eighty miles, where I had directed my letters to be forwarded, I determined to go there and return to the meeting in the same vehicle.

I should have been glad to have made an excursion in the neighbourhood of this pretty place; but Fahrenheit stood at 90^0, and it was so excessively hot that I was compelled to keep the house; so getting my papers in order, I brought up my diary and wrote some letters.

In the evening I ventured out to look at an ample and most pellucid spring in the vicinity, from whence the settlement takes its name. The water flowed copiously from seams in the limestone, which in its cavernous parts no doubt contained great bodies of it. Here I sat down upon a log; not a breath of air was stirring, and it was still too close and warm to walk with comfort. A Georgian, however, whom I found there, told me that he found it cool at this place compared with his residence in the low country. On my return to the village, I observed that almost every store in the place was a dram shop, and the evening's amusement of a great part of the population seemed to consist in going about from one to the other; and when they got what they call in this part of the country "high," which means red-hot drunk with whisky, they would go to the tavern and bully the people they found there. Several times in the course of the evening, the landlord had great trouble in turning them out of his house.   Two incidents occurred before I went to bed very characteristic of the habits of the country.

A young white fellow came to the tavern with a frightful wound in his leg, and so drunk that all we could get from him, amidst a torrent of the most audacious blasphemies, was that " his horse had fixed it for him."   Next came a half-breed youth, about twenty years old, with his wife, a pretty Cherokee creature, about seventeen, each on horseback, on their way to the council.   This young fellow's head was bound up, and when they removed the handkerchief, his eye was so dreadfully bruised, that it appeared to me he would lose the use of it.   He had got beastly drunk on the road, and tumbling from his horse the animal had struck him with his hoof.   The young wife seemed to take it as a matter of course, being probably accustomed to see him drunk every day.

July 30.—At 4 A.M. I got into the stage, the air being cool and agreeable, and for a long distance kept crossing alternate beds of limestone, strongly veined with white spar and shale.   This continued to the Coosawattie River, or Coosa Wāhtay, as the Indians call it.   (*Coosa* is the Indian name of the Creek nation, and *Wāhtay* means old.)   This stream runs at the foot of a ridge of micaceous slate bearing N.N.E., being a continuation of the Unáykay chain. Here we stopped at an Indian tavern kept by a half-breed Cherokee of the name of Bell, one of the Indians opposed to John Ross and the majority of the nation.   They had nothing but some filthy pieces of bad cake to give me made of Indian corn.   Upon my asking a Cherokee woman who spoke English why they did not provide themselves with milk and butter, she said " it was too much trouble to keep cows."   Everything about their house was dirty and disgusting, and I was glad to see the horses brought out.

Just before I started, I learnt that from two to three hundred Creek Indians were hid away in the mountains, and were at this time suffering extremely for want of food. Their nation having been compelled to emigrate, these unfortunate beings had escaped and taken refuge in these hills.   A Creek interpreter, accompanied by an United States officer, rode up to acquire information respecting them, with the intention of bringing a party to surround them and force them away to Arkansa.

We had now before us an arduous journey of fifteen miles over the mountains and streams, every foot of which I had to walk over the talcose slate in a burning sun, for the horses were such wretched animals they had enough to do to drag the vehicle.   At 4 P.M. we reached a poor settlement, near a place called Carmel, where I got a drink of water, and our animals having rested awhile, we pursued our dreary and fatiguing journey, occasionally enlivened by bands of Cherokees on horseback and on foot going with their women and children to Red Clay.   After a very hot and exhausting journey of forty-five miles, thirty of which I had to walk, we arrived at 8 P.M. in a valley where there was a tolerable tavern kept by one Tate; and having refreshed myself with some food and got a bath for my feet, I was most glad to lie down.

July 31.—Having slept comfortably, we resumed our journey at 4 A.M.   I was informed that gold-dust was found near this place, and gold-veins worked a few miles off; so that, as I suspected from the prevalence of the talcose slate, I was now in the Gold Region.   We passed a tolerable good-looking house belonging to a half-breed named Robert Daniel, whose drunken son, the driver told me, it was whom I saw at Spring Place with his eye almost stamped out by his horse.   I got a miserable breakfast at one Field's, a Georgian. The people about were tall, thin, cadaverous-looking animals, looking as melancholy and lazy as boiled cod-fish, and when they dragged themselves about, formed a striking contrast to some of the swarthy, athletic-looking Cherokees. This, no doubt, is to be attributed to their wretched diet and manner of life; for the better class of Georgians, who lead more generous lives, contains many fine-looking individuals. What these long parsnip-looking country fellows seem to enjoy most is political disputation in the bar-room of their filthy taverns, exhibiting much bitterness against each other in supporting the respective candidates of the Union and State-rights parties which divide the State, and this without seeming to have the slightest information respecting the principles of either. Execration and vociferation, and " Well, I'm for Jackson, by —— !" were the nearest approach to logic ever made in my presence. Their miserable attempts at farming, when compared with the energy, foresight, and neatness of the people of the Northern States, are as absurd as they are ridiculous; indeed, it is quite distressing to see the most numerous class in the community condemned by their ignorance to be the slaves of those demagogues, who with their eternal elections encourage them in these tavern-haunting habits, which bring nothing but misery and ruin upon themselves and their families, generation after generation.

The road to the Chatahoochie River was tolerably good at this season, running the whole way over micaceous sandstone and talcose slates, with occasional hornblende rocks, which are the prevailing rocks in the Gold Region. The country was well wooded, and from the summit level, descended rapidly to that pretty stream. At half-past

4 P.M., we reached the town of Gainsville, a small collection of houses, with a square and a large brick Court-house in the centre. Here I was dropped at a humble sort of tavern, kept by a very unprepossessing person, called Widow Holland. I ingratiated myself, however, so far with her that she gave me a large, airy room ; but I could get nothing to eat until 8 P.M., when I was summoned to a public table to partake of the humblest fare in the company of the driver and persons of his caliber. This was another exhibition of dirt, ignorance, and indolence. The mistress of the house left every thing to some ignorant slaves she had, and gave no directions whatever ; her energies being exerted in another line, that of scolding at anything and everything. I was glad to leave the table, and was in bed before 9 P.M.

August 1.—Mrs. Holland's dirt did not prevent my having a capital night's rest, and I rose refreshed at 6 A.M. Having been fortunate enough to find some letters here, I walked about a mile and a half to see a very fine public spring, which they had had the good sense to clean out and surround with benches for the general accommodation. It was in a low piece of ground, prettily cleared, and there were trees enough left to form an agreeable shade. The water was very clear and pure, but appeared to have no mineral properties, and came bubbling up through veined and party-coloured limestone, in an area of about eighteen feet square. Many of the Georgia planters escape from the extreme heat of the low country to Gainsville which is comparatively cool ; and some of them supposing this spring to have curative properties, drink freely of it. I met a person there, looking emaciated and pale, who said he drank as much as six or eight quarts a-day, and that he thought he was worse since he came to

Gainsville, for he was unable to sleep at night. His complaint, he said, was dyspepsia. I explained to him that it was nothing but common limestone spring-water, and advised him to drink no more of it, but to rise early and go to bed early, and take as much exercise as he could when it was cool enough to walk, avoiding tobacco and ardent spirits altogether. The man was evidently killing himself with chewing tobacco. About three miles from the place there is a similar spring, but I did not visit it.

August 2.—I was awoke about midnight by Mr. M—, of Georgetown, in the district of Columbia, who being on his way to the Cherokee Council in the character of Special Agent from the United States Government, and hearing of my being in the house, came and proposed that I should accompany him there. I willingly consented to relinquish my night's rest, and rose to prepare for the journey. We got away some time before day-break; and shuffling along with horses so lame as to be scarcely able to stand up we reached Tate's where I had slept on the 30th of July, in time for me to visit a deposit of white marble I had been informed of. It was of a very fine quality, and the quantity immense, there being a ridge of at least six miles long, entirely consisting of this mineral, of which I brought several specimens away.

August 3.—We were on the road again at half-past 3 A.M., one of our horses so lame that we could never get him off a walk. The day was burning hot, and to make thirty miles it took us twelve hours. We reached Spring Place at half-past 8 P.M., and were fortunate enough to get a small garret, with two beds to lie down on, to ourselves.

CHAPTER LIV.

MODERN CONDOTTIERI.—REACH RED CLAY, THE PLACE OF MEETING OF THE
CHEROKEE NATION.—GREAT ASSEMBLAGE OF INDIANS.—CHEROKEE CHRIS-
TIAN WORSHIP AND CIVILIZATION.—THE GOING SNAKE AND WHITE PATH,
TWO ANCIENT CHIEFS.—A CHEROKEE DINNER.—A CHEROKEE PREACHER,
BUSHY HEAD.—A WHITE PREACHER, NICKNAMED THE "DEVIL'S HORN" BY
THE INDIAN WOMEN.

August 4.—This morning, whilst we were at breakfast,
a company of Georgia Mounted Volunteers rode through
the place on their way to the Cherokee Council. All had
their coats off with their muskets and cartouch-boxes
strung across their shoulders. Some of the men had straw
hats, some of them white felt hats, others had old black
hats on with the rim torn off, and all of them were as
unshaven and as dirty as they could well be. The officers
were only distinguished by having Cherokee fringed
hunting shirts on. Many of the men were stout young
fellows, and they rode on, talking, and cursing and
swearing, without any kind of discipline. Upon the whole
it was a picturesque sight, and brought to my recollection
the descriptions of the condottieri of ancient times.

Having engaged the stage to take us to Red Clay, we
left Spring Place at 8 A.M., passing for twenty-five miles
through a wild country with a rolling surface, pleasingly
wooded, and sufficiently open to admit of the growth of
various beautiful flowers. We crossed the Connesawga,
which is a beautiful mountain stream, and were frequently
gratified with the sight of fine fat deer bounding across the
narrow wood road with their magnificent antlers. The

quail, too, were numerous, and the young birds large.
The soil being derived from the lower Silurian limestone is
very fertile, and certainly I never saw heavier Indian corn
than in two or three settlements that we passed, especially
at one Young's, about fifteen miles from Spring Place.

Towards the close of our journey we called upon
Colonel Lindsay, who commanded the United States
troops in this district, a detachment of which was here for
the purpose of preserving order. His accommodations
were rather humble, and every body seemed to be aware of
it but himself, who appeared too intent upon the delicate
duty he had to discharge to think of indulgences. The
Colonel's quarters were upon the edge of an extensive rich,
dry, bottom of land, thickly covered with young trees,
most of them not more than from twenty to thirty years
old, through which a graceful little stream, called Cóoayhállay, ran meandering. Advancing through the grove,
we began to perceive symptoms of an assemblage of
Indians. Straggling horses, booths, and log tenements
were seen at a distance through the trees, young Indian
boys began to appear running in the woods, and the noise
of men and animals was heard in the distance.

Hearing that a half-breed Cherokee named Hicks, whom
I had formerly known, had put up some huts for the
accommodation of strangers, we found him out, and he
assigned us a hut to ourselves, the floor of which was
strewed with nice dry pine leaves. It contained also two
rude bedsteads, with pine branches as a substitute for
beds, and some bed-clothes of a strange fashion, but
which were tolerably clean. Chairs we had none; and
our first care was to get a sort of table carpentered up,
and to place it in such a position that we could use our
bedsteads for chairs when we wrote. Our log hut had
been so hastily run up that it had neither a door, nor

bore evidence of an intention to add one to it, and its walls were formed of logs with interstices of at least six inches between them, so that we not only had the advantage of seeing every thing that was going on out of doors, but of gratifying every body outside who was desirous of seeing what was done within our hut, especially the Indians, who appeared extremely curious.

Having refreshed ourselves with a cup of tea, we walked out with General Smith, the Indian agent for the United States, to see the Council-house. Crossing the Cóoayhállay, we soon found ourselves in an irregular sort of street consisting of huts, booths and stores hastily constructed from the trees of the forest, for the accommodation of Cherokee families, and for the cooking establishments necessary to the subsistence of several thousand Indians. This street was at the foot of some hilly ground upon which the Council-room was built, which was a simple parallelogram formed of logs with open sides, and benches inside for the councillors. The situation was exceedingly well chosen in every respect, for there was a copious limestone spring on the bank of the stream, which gave out a delicious cool water in sufficient quantities for this great multitude. What contributed to make the situation extremely picturesque, was the great number of beautiful trees growing in every direction, the underwood having been most judiciously cut away to enable the Indians to move freely through the forest, and to tie their horses to the trees. Nothing more Arcadian could be conceived than the picture which was presented; but the most impressive feature, and that which imparted life to the whole, was an unceasing current of Cherokee Indians, men, women, youths, and children, moving about in every direction, and in the greatest order; and all, except the younger ones, preserving a grave and

thoughtful demeanour imposed upon them by the singular
position in which they were placed, and by the trying alternative now presented to them of delivering up their native
country to their oppressors, or perishing in a vain resistance.

An observer could not but sympathize deeply with
them ; they were not to be confounded with the wild
savages of the West, being decently dressed after the
manner of white people, with shirts, trousers, shoes and
stockings, whilst the half-breeds and their descendants
conformed in every thing to the custom of the whites,
spoke as good English as them, and differed from them
only in a browner complexión, and in being less vicious and
more sober.   The pure bloods had red and blue cotton
handkerchiefs folded on their heads in the manner of
turbans, and some of these, who were mountaineers from
the elevated districts of North Carolina wore also deer-skin
leggings and embroidered hunting shirts; whilst their
turbans, their dark coarse, lank hair, their listless savage
gait, and their swarthy Tartar countenances, reminded me
of the Arabs from Barbary.   Many of these men were
athletic and good-looking ; but the women who had passed
from the maidenly age, had, owing to the hard labour
imposed upon them by Indian usages, lost as usual every
feminine attraction, so that in my walk I did not see one
upon whom I had any desire to look a second time.   In
the course of the evening, I attended at the Council-house
to hear some of their resolutions read by an English missionary, named Jones, who adhered to the Cherokees ; a
man of talent, it was said, and of great activity, but who was
detested by the Georgians.   These were afterwards translated, *vivâ voce*, into Cherokee by Bushy-head, one of the
principal half-breed Cherokees.   A most refreshing rain
fell in the evening, and about 8 P.M., somewhat fatigued

with the adventures of the day, I retired to our hut, from whence, through the interstices of the logs, I saw the fires of the Cherokees, who bivouacked in the woods, gleaming in every direction; and long after I laid down, the voices of hundreds of the most pious amongst them who had assembled at the Council-house to perform their evening worship, came pealing in hymns through the now quiet forest, and insensibly and gratefully lulled me to sleep.

August 5.—The voices of the Cherokees already at morning worship awoke me at the dawn of day, and dressing myself hastily, I went to the Council-house. Great numbers of them were assembled, and Mr. Jones, the Missionary, read out verses in the English language from the New Testament, which Bushy-head, with a singularly stentorial voice and sonorous accent, immediately rendered to the people in the Cherokee tongue, emitting a deep grunting sound at the end of every verse, resembling the hard breathing of a man chopping trees down, the meaning of which I was given to understand was to call their attention to the proposition conveyed by the passage. This I was told is an universal practice also in Cherokee oratory. When they sang, a line or two of a hymn printed in the Cherokee language was given out, each one having a hymn book in his hand, and I certainly never saw any congregation engaged more apparently in sincere devotion. This spectacle insensibly led me into reflection upon the opinion which is so generally entertained of its being impossible to civilize the Indians in our sense of the word. Here is a remarkable instance which seems to furnish a conclusive answer to scepticism on this point. A whole Indian nation abandons the pagan practices of their ancestors, adopts the Christian religion, uses books printed in their own language, submits to the government of their elders, builds houses and temples of worship, relies upon agriculture for their support, and produces men of great ability to rule over them, and to whom they give a willing obedience.   Are not these the great principles of civilization ?   They are driven from their religious and social state then, not because they cannot be civilized, but because a pseudo set of civilized beings, who are too strong for them, want their possessions !   What a bitter reflection it will be to the religiously disposed portion of the people, who shall hereafter live here, that the country they will be so proud of and so blest in was torn from the Aboriginals in this wrongful manner.   God be thanked, that in acquiring the dominion of India, Great Britain protects and blesses the people whose country owns her sway !

After breakfast I made myself acquainted with Mr. Jones, the Missionary, whom I found to be a man of sense and experience, and who must have received a tolerable education, for he was not even ignorant of Hebrew. He was exceedingly devoted to this nation, having resided a long time amongst them in the mountainous region of North Carolina.   The Georgians, and I found most of the other white settlers had a decided antipathy to him on account of the advice he gave to the Cherokees, which had frequently enabled them to baffle the machinations of the persons who were plotting to get their lands. Conscious that he was watched by his enemies, he had become so suspicious of all white men, that from habit he had got a peculiar sinister look.   We had a great deal of conversation together, and when he found I was an Englishman, and deeply interested for the welfare of the Indians, and extremely anxious to acquire the Cherokee language, he became less reserved, and I obtained a great deal of information from him. I also formed an acquaintance with several intelligent Cherokees and half-breeds, for the purpose of collecting vocabularies and acquiring the pronunciation of their language.

About 10 A.M., a deputation, consisting of members of the Cherokee Council, and some aged persons, formerly chiefs of some celebrity, came in procession to our hut, to pay a visit of ceremony to my companion, the United States special agent; but he being at Colonel Lindsay's, I received them in his stead, gave them seats on our bedsteads, and immediately sent a messenger for him, who soon after arrived with Colonel Lindsay and a military escort. An ancient chief, named Innatáhoolósah, or the Going Snake, addressed him, and complimented him upon his arrival. This old warrior had led a large body of his people in former times to assist General Jackson against the Creeks, and contributed much to the victory he obtained over them at the battle of the Horse Shoe, where he received a wound in the arm. He was a fine old man, with a good deal of Indian dignity. Nothing appears to have stung the Cherokees more deeply than the reflection, that after serving General Jackson so effectually, it should have been under his administration of the Government, from which they had so much right to expect protection, that their independence had been broken down, and their territories appropriated without their consent. There was also another old chief remarkably cheerful and light of step, although seventy-six years old, called Nennenóh Oonáykay, or White Path. After an interchange of compliments they retired. This day we dined by invitation with Mrs. Walker, a fine old Cherokee lady, who spoke a little English; and met John Ross, the principal chief of the Cherokees. Our hostess received us in a very polite and friendly manner. The dinner was good, we had boiled beef, chickens and bacon, with excellent vegetables. Coffee was served with the dinner, and we retired as soon as it was over, according to the custom. Large wooden bowls of *connaháyny*, or Indian corn boiled almost to a *purée*, with a small quantity of ley in it, were placed on the table. This is a favourite dish with the Cherokees, and I observed the young people ate it with great avidity ; indeed, when mixed up with the broth of the boiled beef, it makes a capital soup; something like peas-soup.

The expense of feeding this multitude, which was defrayed by the council, was very great. Fifteen beeves were said to be killed every day, and a proportionate quantity of Indian corn used. Twenty-four native families were employed in cooking the provisions and serving the tables which were set out three times a-day. The beef was cut up into small pieces of three or four inches square, and kept stewing for several hours in large pots. The broth of this mess, without the meat, was the first dish offered to us at the excellent Mrs. Walker's, but when it was handed to me I found it was nothing but a mass of melted fat, the surface of which was oscillating about like quicksilver, and I had to send it away at the risk of giving offence. It was a most amusing scene to walk from table to table and see the Cherokees eat ; every one was permitted to eat as much as he pleased, just as at the Bodas of Camacho ; it really appeared to me as if they never would be satisfied, and as if their real business was not to refresh themselves, but to gormandize every thing up that was set before them. Upon making further inquiries, I learnt that Mr. John Ross was the sole director of every thing, that he paid about three hundred dollars a day to the persons who contracted to furnish the provisions, the beef being paid for at the rate of four cents a pound. The expense was ultimately to be carried to account of the Cherokee fund. Mr. Ross invited us to dine with him at his house to-morrow.

In the evening the same scene of gormandizing was again exhibited, the woods gleaming with fires in every direction ; several thousand Indians being scattered about in small groups, each with its fire, near to which a few sticks were set up, and a blanket or two laid over them to screen the women and children from the wind. The greatest tranquillity prevailed, and I walked about among them to a late hour, observing them, and asking the men the names of things with a view to catch the pronunciation.

August 6.—Rising at day-break, and taking a cup of tea, I went to the Council-house to attend divine service. From a rostrum erected near it, a native Cherokee preacher delivered a very long sermon to a very numerous assemblage of Indians and white people who had assembled from various parts. The discourse came from him with great vehemence both of action and voice, gesticulating and grunting at every instant, and never stopping to take breath, as it appeared to me, in half an hour. It was like a continual stream of falling water. All the Cherokees paid great attention to the sermon, and the most perfect decorum prevailed. After the sermon we had a psalm, led by Bushy-head, the whole congregation uniting in it. Mr. Jones then preached in English, and Bushy-head, with his stentorian voice, translated the passages as they came from the preacher, into Cherokee. During all this time, the ardent beams of the sun were pouring upon our bare heads. I felt at length as if I could not bear it much longer, and therefore went away before we were dismissed, rather than by covering my head to appear to offer any irreverence.

At noon Colonel Lindsay called at our hut with an escort of cavalry ; he had been kind enough to provide a horse for myself and we proceeded to a place called Red Hill, the residence of Mr. John Ross ; here, on our arrival, we were shewn into a room and remained there two hours before dinner was announced, when we were taken to a room, upon the table of which a very plentiful dinner, singularly ill-cooked, was placed.   Neither our host nor his wife sat down to eat with us, the dinner, according to Cherokee custom, being considered to be provided for the guests ; a custom evidently derived from their old savage state.   I was helped to some meat, but could not tell what it was, or whether it passed for roast or boiled.   It was afterwards explained to me that it was pork, first boiled in a pot with some beef, and then baked by itself afterwards.   Mr. Lewis Ross, the brother of our host, presided, and Mr. Gunter, a very intelligent and obliging half-breed, sat at the other end of the table. I sat on his right and obtained a great deal of information from him.

Being desirous of learning whether the Cherokees had any distinct name for the system of ridges which now goes by the name of Alleghany or Appalachian Mountains, to oblige me, he interrogated some very ancient Cherokees, but not one of them had ever heard of their having a distinct name.   The war-path, which their ancestors used in crossing them to fight the Mengwee, or five nations, had a particular name ; but they knew of no other, neither did they know anything of the words Alleghany or Appalachy.   After passing a very interesting day, and receiving the greatest attention and civility from them, we took our leave.

The rock here was a grey crystalline limestone, very

much inclined, (it is vertical at Red Clay), and contained no fossils ; in many places, there was a strong bed of red clay upon it, like that at Tuscumbia, and the soil here was quite red. From this place, I rode over to the Rev. Dr. Butler's, the head of the Cherokee Mission in this neighbourhood, who received me very politely, gave me a great deal of information, and presented me with some books and papers printed in the Cherokee language. I was happy to learn from him that the Rev. Mr. Buttrick, whom I had seen at Brainerd, was at Red Clay, and that he had taken great pains with the chiefs to prepossess them in my favour.

From hence I rode to Colonel Lindsay's quarters, and passed the evening with him, Major Payne, and some gentlemen of his family. On my return, I went to the Council-house, and heard an excellent sermon delivered to the Cherokees in English, by the Rev. Mr. Buttrick, which received great attention as it well deserved to do, being admirable both in matter and manner. The indefatigable Bushy-head, in translating this sermon, almost surpassed himself, rendered every passage into Cherokee with the most enthusiastic energy at the very top of his noble voice, and marked every sentence with one of his deep-toned, sonorous *uh-húnhgs*, that came from him like the lowest note from a bassoon. On my return to our hut, I got into a conversation with our landlord, Mr. Hicks, one of the most intelligent of the Cherokees. He told me, he had once seen some China men at Philadelphia, and that, from the strong resemblance to them in their faces and eyes, he thought it probable the Cherokees were descended from that stock. The remark is, at least, founded in fact, for the Cherokees resemble the Tartars very strikingly, both in the general expression of their faces, and in the conformation of their eyes.

August 7.—This was the day appointed for the delivery of the " Talk" or public address of Mr. Mason, the special agent, which was expected with great anxiety, and which Mr. Mason had been much occupied in the composition of. After breakfast, Foreman, the interpreter, came to the hut, and Mr. Mason gave him the "Talk" to study; he appeared to be a very intelligent man, and perfectly well acquainted with the English tongue. He told us some amusing anecdotes of an agent, named Schermerhorn, who had been appointed by the United States Government a year or two ago, as a commissioner to negotiate with the Cherokees. This man was a sort of loose Dutch Presbyterian Minister, and having taken up the calling of a political demagogue, had been rewarded with this situation by the President, Mr. Van Buren, a Dutchman also by birth. On coming amongst the Cherokees, instead of dealing fairly with them, and making an arrangement with the Council that could be sanctioned by a majority of the nation, he corrupted a few individuals to consent to emigrate, and deliver up the Cherokee territory; and reported it to the Government as if it had been a solemn contract entered into with the whole nation. The Reverend agent, also, being of amorous turn had been detected tampering with some of the young Cherokee women, so that he came to be an object of detestation to the Indians, who took every opportunity to affront him. Not more than half-a-dozen in the whole nation would speak to him at all; and whenever the rest of them met him, they made a point of turning round and presenting their backs to him. But this was not all the mortification his evils deeds brought upon him.

It is the custom of most of the Indian nations to give an Indian name to every white man who has any transactions with them of importance, or who has struck their fancy in any way. If the proper name of the individual corresponds in sound with any term in their language, they simply translate it. On the other hand, if they can find no equivalent in their own tongue, they look for words, which sound like the name they are unable to translate, and if those words are at all appropriate to the individual, whether in his appearance, his habits and customs, or character, they use them to form his Indian name. In doing this, they are remarkably skilful, and are as prompt and happy as the best *improvisatori* are in Italy. The name the Cherokees gave to me is an instance of this. It was found impossible to translate the word Featherstonhaugh, but one of their poets suggested that my Cherokee name should be Oóstanaúlee, which means "gravel or shingle brought down by floods." Having observed me frequently poking and hammering about in beds of gravel, the word which sounded something like my name, admirably answered the purpose. For the Rev. Mr. Schermerhorn, they had been so fortunate as to find a name that corresponded precisely to their estimate of him, and which was immediately adopted by the whole nation, especially the women and children, who were extremely tickled with it. It was Skáynooyáunah, or literally the "devil's horn." After I knew this story I found it was only necessary to ask the women if they knew Skáynooyáunah to set them laughing.

CHAPTER LV.

August 7.—The rain had been falling incessantly for
thirty hours, and our hut being roofed with nothing but
pine branches gave us very little protection ; the bed-
clothes were wet through, and we were thoroughly non-
plussed what to do.   It was impossible to remain long in
this state without becoming sick.   The Indians, at the
numerous bivouacs were all wet through, and apprehensions were beginning to be entertained by the Council, that
a serious sickness might fall upon them if they were detained twenty-four hours more in the uncomfortable state
they were in.   The chiefs, therefore, were desirous that
Mr. Mason should deliver his " Talk " immediately ; but that
gentleman, supposing the " Talk " would be deferred, was
gone to Colonel Lindsay's for shelter.   Mr. Ross therefore
called upon me, and drew such a picture of the consequences that might ensue, that I wrote to Mr. Mason, and
sent the note with a messenger.   In this note, I related
what Mr. Ross had said, and submitted to him, as the day
had been appointed for the purpose, the propriety of being
punctual, as want of punctuality would give the chiefs an
opportunity of dismissing the nation and laying the blame

upon him. The messenger returned about 3 P.M. with
information to Mr. Ross that he might assemble the nation.
Accordingly, horns were blown and public criers went into
the woods to summon all the males to the Council-house;
but recommending to the women and children to remain
at their fires. Every one was now in motion, notwithstanding that the rain continued to fall in torrents.

At 4 P.M., Mr. Ross conducted Mr. Mason, Colonel
Lindsay, Colonel Smith, and myself, into a stand erected
near the Council-house, open at the sides, and from whence
we could view an assemblage of about two thousand male
Cherokees standing in the rain awaiting the " Talk" that was
to be delivered. The special agent now advanced to the
front of the stand, and read his address which was translated to them by the interpreter ; after which, Mr. Gunter
addressed them, requesting them to remain until the Council
had taken the "Talk" into consideration, and informing them
that plenty of provisions would continue to be provided for
them, upon which they gave him a hearty grunt and
dispersed. The scene was an imposing one; the Cherokees
were attentive and behaved very well, but it was evident
the " Talk" made no impression upon them. If the special
agent had declared, in the name of his Government, that
the Cherokee nation should continue to enjoy their native
land, it would have been most enthusiastically received; but
anything short of that was a proof to them that there was
no hope left for justice from the whites, nor any resource
for them but in the wisdom of their National Council. The
" Talk" itself was full of friendly professions towards the
nation, and dwelt upon the advantages it would derive
from a peaceful compliance with the policy of the Government; but there was a passage in it which showed that
the United States Government were determined to enforce

the treaty which the minority had made with the Government, and even insinuated that the resistance to it was factious. This gave offence, and even Mr. Ross objected to it.

The Government now could only carry its policy out by gaining the chiefs, or by military force. From what I observed, the chiefs, if not incorruptible, were determined not to come to terms without securing great advantages, whilst it was their intention not to precipitate things, but to gain time and make another appeal to the Congress. Many of them who had heard of me through Mr. Buttrick, and who saw the interest I took in their affairs and in acquiring some knowledge of their language, spoke to me on the subject; but I invariably advised them to submit to the Government, for a successful resistance was impossible. I gave it also as my opinion that it was a very possible thing that if they procrastinated, a collision would soon take place betwixt them and the Georgians and Tennesseans, which would involve the destruction of the nation. These opinions, it was evident to me, were very unwelcome to them; and after the delivery of the "Talk," I declined saying anything on the subject. The rain continued to pour down, and on reaching my quarters, I found the hut a perfect swamp, and full of people all wet through, as many as could get there sitting on my bed. A more uncomfortable place I certainly never was in; everything was wet and smelt ill. All I could do was to lie down upon the wet bed, and keep the crowd off with my feet and arms. It was late in the night before we got rid of them: the rain still coming down in torrents.

August 8.—I rose at the dawn of day to witness a thick, close atmosphere, with the rain pouring down harder than ever. It was quite impossible that matters should remain in this state long: the low ground upon which the

Council had assembled the nation would soon be entirely covered with water as well as the floor of my hut, for it was mine now, the special agent having changed his quarters to Colonel Lindsay's : all amateurs being left to shift for themselves. I therefore wrote to Colonel Lindsay, stating my disagreeable situation, and asked if he would put me in a way to return to Spring Place. In the meantime, Mr. Bushy-head sent for me to breakfast with his family, and meet some old chiefs of whom I wished to ask some questions respecting some of their most authentic traditions, as well as to read over some of my vocabularies to them for the correction of the pronunciation From thence I had determined, in the event of Colonel Lindsay not being able to assist me, to walk in the rain to the Missionary establishment, as I began to feel a sick head-ache and pains in my limbs which would probably end in a fever. At any rate, I had determined to abandon the hut.

Whilst I was pondering over my situation, Colonel Lindsay, to my great joy, sent me a capital saddle-horse, with a well-mounted dragoon to attend me. I now bustled about, took leave of the chiefs, and giving the reins to my steed, took to the woods again. Although the rain beat furiously in my face, I could not keep my eyes off the many hundreds of poor Cherokee families cowering with their children under their little blanket tents, all wet through ; the men protecting them from the weather as well as they could, and keeping their fires alive with great difficulty. It was a very curious spectacle. I had been told on leaving the Council that it was very likely I should find the Connesauga so swollen as to render it dangerous even to attempt to swim it, and I felt a great deal of anxiety on this account whilst on the road ; but although the waters were high and the current strong, we got safely across, and reached Spring Place early in the afternoon, most thoroughly soaked.   My first care was to order the horses and dragoon to be well attended to ; and as soon as they were refreshed, I despatched them back with a letter of thanks to the worthy Colonel.   I was perfectly delighted to find my trunk with dry clothes ; and having got some warm tea, I went immediately to bed, got a refreshing nap of three or four hours, and arose free from fever and head-ache, and wrote several letters to my friends.   I had also the good fortune to learn on my arrival that the stage would leave the place the next morning at half-past 4 A.M.

August 9.—Once more I got into the old Gainsville stage at 4 A.M., and after a repetition of the scenes I had before gone through, reached that place on the next afternoon.   Finding there was a conveyance to Dahlonega in the morning, a place in the mountains which had attracted a good deal of attention from the native gold which had been found there, and having directed letters to be forwarded to me there, I immediately went and secured a place in it.

August 11.—We left Gainsville, and at day-break crossed the Chatahoochie at a good ford above its junction with the Chestatee, and pursued our way through a very pretty, wild, and well-wooded country, closely resembling the Gold Region in Virginia.   We stopped to breakfast at a place called New Bridge, on the Chestatee, where the stream had been turned from its channel by a Dr. Stevenson and other persons for the purpose of finding gold, but with not much success.   Whilst the horses were feeding I paid him a visit and found him an intelligent person. Here we entered a very pretty valley through which Cane Creek runs, the alluvial bottom of which had been entirely dug out, and the earth and gravel washed for gold with some success. The talcose slate shewed itself very strong in this valley. I reached Dahlonega amidst torrents of rain betwixt 3 and 4 P.M., having been ten hours and a half in coming twenty-nine miles. Here I got a room at a tolerably clean house kept by a person named Choice, and to my great delight found letters and newspapers waiting for me at the post-office.

Whilst I was engaged answering them, Mr. C******, the distinguished Senator of the United States for South Carolina, to my infinite satisfaction walked into the room. I had written to him some time ago to say that I proposed paying him a visit at his estate of Fort Hill in that State, expressing at the same time a desire that he would write to me at Dahlonega to say if he should be at home, and he had most obligingly crossed the mountains to meet me. Of all the men I have ever known in the United States, Mr. C— is decidedly the most remarkable for his genius; his intellect is so active and comprehensive that he is able at once to grasp the most intricate subjects without an effort. He is also one of the most perfect gentlemen I ever knew, without any vice or vicious habit, and has at all times borne the most unsullied private character.

This gentleman was a leading member of the Cabinet of Mr. Madison, when President, and his transcendent talents and fine qualities being admitted by all his countrymen, it would seem difficult to give a reason why such a man has never been able to reach the Presidency, evidently the great object of his ambition. I imagine the true reason to be that his admitted virtues and talents make him the particular object of the opposition of the northern demagogues, who not only alarm the northern manufacturing interest, by representing him as their uncompromising opponent, but seek to draw upon him, as the representative of the southern slaveholding interest, the political hostility of the free States. He has thus the north arrayed against him as a united body, in addition to the opposition, more or less powerful, which every good and eminent man is sure to meet with from demagogues. Whilst Mr. C——, evidently conscious of his own intellectual powers, relies principally upon them for his influence with the nation; he, being a man of great simplicity of character, has but an imperfect acquaintance with human nature. Thus he is continually baffled by those who are inferior to himself, and to retrieve his position, is thought to have sometimes varied too openly from an uniform line of conduct, and to have acquired the habit of being inconsistent without being aware of its being the greatest error a public man can commit. If in addition to his acknowledged merits and virtues he had practised an enduring consistency, he would have been almost as great a man, and certainly a more brilliant one than Washington.

With so agreeable a companion, I could not but pass the evening most agreeably. We conversed about the gold veins of the neighbourhood, in which he appeared to take great interest, and about the science of Government as applicable to the constitutional limits and customs of the people of his country. On this subject he was very unreserved with me, and assured me of his conviction that the form adopted for their Republican Government was perfect, and would in the end be imitated by all other countries. He would not admit that universal suffrage, which had been so successfully wielded by demagogues against himself, Mr. Clay, and other honourable men, would in the end exclude all *decent* men from power, and that there was great danger of the example of America turning out to be a salutary lesson to other Governments to avoid rather than follow it. On the structure of the Federal Government, he spoke like an enthusiast, comparing its action to the well-adjusted movements of the celestial bodies. And here I ventured to tell him that I thought he had formed too favourable an estimate of human nature; and that although the theory of the Federal Government might be a beautiful one, it required to be worked out by men whose hearts were as pure as their heads were clear, and who loved their country with the devotion that he did. He said the Federal Government had worked well until the northern demagogues had set universal suffrage and their other political contrivances in motion : to which I answered that I required him to admit nothing more, for that was the evil itself from which I apprehended the worst consequences.

On the subject of laying heavy duties upon English manufactures, Mr. C— expressed himself most decidedly; and if he is to be depended upon, he will never consent to any tariff upon English manufactures which will compel Great Britain to turn her attention to other countries for raw cotton, which is the staple of the Southern States, or which impairs her ability to pay a commercial compensating price for it. Mr. C—'s personal interest, as well as the general southern interest, is concerned here; and such is the influence he possesses, that I am of opinion the Northern States will not succeed in permanently establishing a tariff that will be injurious to the manufacturing interest of Great Britain, whilst it maintains its present advantage of capital and skill, certainly not as long as he lives. This conversation, which produced a great deal of private anecdote of the eminent men he had lived with, was a most delightful one to me, who had been compelled to associate so long with inferior persons; and I retired from it full of admiration of the patriotism, the genius, and the conversational powers of this distinguished man.

CHAPTER LVI.

DESCRIPTION OF DAHLONEGA.—GOLD DEPOSITS.—THE BEAUTY OF THE VALLEYS
DESTROYED BY THE GOLD WASHERS.—VALLEY OF NAHCÓOCHAY.—ANCIENT
CONSTRUCTIONS FOUND AT THE BOTTOM OF THE ALLUVIAL DEPOSIT.—REACH
CLARKSVILLE.—A JEWISH LANDLORD ATTEMPTS SUICIDE.

August 12.—Dahlonega is prettily situated in a mountainous country, and the great pursuit of its inhabitants is
gold mining. Having procured a horse, I accompanied
Mr. C— to Cane Creek, Pigeon Roost, and other small
streams, called " branches" here, the gravelly beds of which,
together with the low lands contiguous to them, had either
been all dug up, or were in a way to be dug up and washed.
Nothing in nature could be more picturesque than the
hills and ridges here of three hundred and four hundred
feet high composed of talcose slate and occasional hornblende,
wooded to the top, and separated by small valleys, often
not more than fifty yards wide, with streams meandering
through them ; but all the valleys being dug up and the
washed gravel thrown into heaps, their beauty was entirely
destroyed, and the scene resembled a series of brickyards.

The gold veins of this district which are most productive
appear to run N.N.E. and S.S.W. ; the cross veins run in
various directions. The talcose slate is generally in a state of
decomposition, and in various situations the side of the hills
consist of talcose slate completely rotten, and easily cut with a
knife. The order in the superposition of the soil of the valleys

is sufficiently constant to point clearly to the causes which have brought all the varieties of which it is formed into place in succession. Generally speaking, this soil in the valleys is about twenty feet thick; at the surface is a reddish soil derived from the decomposed talcose rock, mixed with fragments of rock; beneath this a bed of clay sometimes dark coloured and intermixed with hornblende, and sometimes consisting of blue aluminous earth derived from decomposed talc. Inferior to this again is a bed of gravel, with the gold lying principally towards the bottom, and lastly comes the talcose rock, forming the hard bottom of the valley.

This state of things prevails here as it does in every part of the Gold Region of North America, which extends about seven hundred miles from N.N.E. to S.S.W., and perhaps is prolonged with the talcose slate even into Canada, where, without finding gold, I have repeatedly observed that it bears a close resemblance in various mineral particulars to the talcose slate of the southern portions of the United States.

All the auriferous rocks of this continent appear to have been formed under water, and it would seem from the circumstance of the gravel always lying in these valleys next to the rock, and the lighter mineral substances lying upon it according to their specific gravity, that on the general retreat of the water from the face of the continent, of which so many proofs exist in other parts, the last waters that remained, to complete the drainage, have cut their way back by retrocession, sometimes in the direction of the gold veins, in which cases the auriferous deposit in the valleys is always found to extend to great distances, the comminuted parts being carried down along with the stream, and successively deposited according to their specific gravities; the gold and gravel at the bottom, the clays next, and the lightest soils at the top, which, as before stated, is the constant state of superposition. Although a little gold is sometimes found upon the hills where the veins or pockets come near to the surface, yet beds of gravel are never found on them, which is an additional proof that the destruction of the rocks has not been accomplished whilst they were yet beneath the ocean. In some valleys large lumps of gold have been found almost at the foot of the veins where they have been intersected, whilst their lighter particles have been found at a distance of several hundred yards. A mass of native gold was thus found in North Carolina, weighing twenty-eight pounds. On Duke's Creek in the Nahcóochay Valley, heavy pieces of gold have been found near to the veins, whilst the waters of the Chatahoochie have carried light particles of gold from the same locality, one hundred miles below the Gold Region.

In our rambles this day we were very agreeably surprized at finding a very acceptable country dinner at the cabin of a Mr. Samuel, of Virginia, who with his wife and sisters were temporarily residing upon one of these hills, isolated by small valleys, whilst he was superintending some gold washings. Even a glass of good Madeira was not wanting to enliven the cheerful hospitality we met with. In the afternoon we rode to the washing establishment of a Mr. Miller, at the head of Pigeon Roost Creek, which was all ransacked and dug up like the other streams, and here I was made acquainted with a fact which rather puzzled me, because I saw no reason whatever to doubt its accuracy. Mr. Miller showed us a log of pine-wood of large dimensions, lying upon the naked talcose slate exactly in the spot where it was found after the superincumbent soil had been removed. He assured us that he was present when it was found buried beneath the gravel, and that the gravel was covered with the usual blue clay and superficial soil, the whole deposit between the rock and the surface being twenty-one feet deep. I had no reason to entertain the least doubt of his accuracy, because he had no theory to sustain, although he was rather struck at the circumstance, having never found a tree in a similar position. I examined this log very carefully: one end of it was worn away into a crescent-like form by the trituration of other substances; the under side which laid upon the rock, was perfectly clean, and bore distinct marks of the slate impressed upon it, whilst the top had quartz gravel thickly indented into it. Part of the outside of the log was carbonized, whilst the inside was quite fresh though somewhat discoloured.

I felt very much interested in contemplating this representative of the ancient forests of this continent, of the period of which it is most difficult to form any conjecture that will be universally approved of. Nevertheless there may have been a state of things which admits of its being consistent with every thing else we observe. The interval of time betwixt the retreat of the ocean from this part of the country, and the excavation by retrocession of the valley where the log was found, may have been so long as to admit of the growth of trees, and in that case it is a very natural incident to find a tree lying upon a rock denuded by the current, and subsequently covered by detritus. It is, however, singular that no other tree is known to have been found in a similar situation, although that may have been the case, for persons engaged in washing gravel for gold are generally very incurious about anything but the gold itself. On our return to Dahlonega, after a day passed most agreeably, we found Governor Schley, of Georgia, an intelligent person, and leaving Mr. C— and him to talk American politics, I went to my room to bring up my notes.

Gratified as I had been with the geological illustrations which this day's ramble afforded me, I could not but be sorry to see the destruction which awaited all these beautiful valleys. The fine trees with which they were covered were all in a way of being rooted up; the soil, after being washed left in rude heaps, and the streams diverted from their courses; so that amidst the wildest scenes of nature, you look down from finely formed hills, gracefully covered with verdant woods, upon valleys once singularly beautiful, as well for their amenity as for the purity of the streams which flowed through them, and which were once the favourite resort of the red man when pursuing his game; but which the white man has converted into a picture of perfect desolation. To obtain a small quantity of gold for the wants of the present generation, the most fertile bottoms are rendered barren for countless generations. And this must ever be the case in countries where the Government is not intelligent and strong enough to put the mining districts under regulations. By and by, when the gravel in the valleys is all dug out and washed, they will take to the hills, which will be violated and ransacked in a similar manner, and what was once a paradise will become a desert.

August 13.—Rose at day-break, and having taken a cup of tea, Mr. C— and myself mounted our horses for a long ride. The country to the eastward was, as usual, diversified with hill and dale. Calling at a Mr. Goodram's, a store-keeper, eleven miles from Dahlonega, he presented me with a piece of auriferous quartz, and engaged to purchase some fine specimens of vein-gold for me. Pursuing our journey, we obtained several views

of an extensive chain on our left, called the Blue Ridge ;
the rock about here was uniformly micaceous, with
hornblende intermixed, and the quartz lodes rarer than
in Virginia. After riding about twenty miles, we came
to the valley of Nahcóochay, an extremely sweet place.
We stopped at one Richardson's, east of the Yónah, or
Bear Mountain, a splendid out-tier of the Blue Ridge,
about fifteen hundred feet high. It is so named from its
fancied resemblance to a crouching bear : Yónah being
the Cherokee name for a bear. The valley, as in the
neighbourhood of Dahlonega, was all dug up, and looked
desolate. The detritus which laid upon the slate was,
as usual, about twenty feet deep ; but the gravel lying
immediately upon it consisted almost entirely of pieces
of rolled quartz, many of them semi-transparent, almost
pure white, and resembling the shingles on the sea-shore.
The trituration must have been very constant and powerful to produce this effect upon the quartz, and likewise
upon the gold, which consists of large pieces, some of
them weighing three hundred and forty pennyweights,
all made perfectly flat by trituration. The quartz pebbles
of this gravel are evidently derived from a strong lode of
pure quartz, broken down by the water, and occasionally
loaded with lumps of gold. Mr. C— had obtained for me,
three years ago, a lump of flatted gold, worth about four
guineas, which every one who saw it believed to have been
made so by art : it came from this locality ; but the
moment I saw the quartz gravel, it was evident that the
gold had been brought into that form by pressure and
trituration.

At Mr. Richardson's and other places, I saw other
specimens of gold equally flat, and was informed that
all the gold found here had that character. Nothing

varies more than the manner in which gold is found in the quartz. I possess specimens in my cabinet of white quartz where not a speck of gold is visible; but which, when reduced to powder, and treated with quicksilver yields gold : in it, also, are specimens of quartz with lumps of native gold imbedded in it equal to one third of its weight. I went to a Mr. Russell's diggings, on one of the heads of the Chatahoochie, called Duke's Creek, hoping to purchase a specimen of which I had heard a good deal. Unfortunately he had parted with it; but before doing so had made a model of it in a piece of wood. It was a curious crystal, being a trihedral of pyramidal form, having a regular termination at one end, and being conical at the other. It weighed three and a half penny-weights.

About two miles from Mr. Russell's are what are called the Eaton diggings, where it is said thirty-six ancient log huts, or pens were found some time ago at the bottom of the alluvial deposit, next to the slate-rock ; and the logs are described as having been cut and notched apparently with a metallic axe: they were from two to three feet high, and had no roof when found. Some sand crucibles, almost square, were also found in the same place. I saw a trough also at Richardson's, about eighteen inches long, and six inches deep, made out of the micaceous rock, and which was so rotten, that when I attempted to handle it, a large flake peeled from off the side. Every vestige of the pens, it was said, had disappeared, for they all crumbled away on being uncovered and exposed to the air. Mr. Richardson did not see them, but gave me references to the persons who discovered them, to enable me to write to them if no opportunity presented itself of visiting the locality. This circumstance, and other notices

I had received of appearances of the labour of white men in this part of the Gold Region, of some antiquity, induced me to think that they might be attributed to De Soto and his companions, who traversed this line of country in 1539. Such pens could never be intended to live in, for I was informed there was no contrivance about them for either door or window: most probably they were intended as caches to conceal the ore they had dug, or other things they possessed, when going upon some distant excursion, and were placed at the bottom of the alluvium and upon the slate, the better to conceal them, and because the material was at hand to cover them over with.

From this place we continued our ride to Clarksville where we arrived after it was dark. Here we found an hotel (Levy's), and many families from the lower parts of Georgia who resorted here annually to enjoy the mountain air. Six or eight gay carriages were in the yard, and ladies, dressed for the evening, were promenading in the public room. We got a very good supper, and the moment it was rumoured that so eminent a person as Mr. C— had arrived, everybody flocked to see him; he soon became engaged with his friends and acquaintances, and being most heartily tired with my day's exertions, I slipped off to bed as soon as I could.

August 14.—Nothing could be more bland and agreeable than the mountain air at this place; it appeared never to be too hot, and if there was a sufficiency of respectable society, it would be the Paradise of America. Here I took leave of Mr. C—, who went to breakfast with a Mr. Mathews about eight miles off, after promising to pay him a visit at his country residence before I undertook a tour I had projected, amongst the Cherokees of Valley

River, on the head waters of the Hiwassee.   At breakfast,
I learnt from a Dr. Hawksey, one of the proprietors of
Eaton Mine, that other ancient remains had been found
near the Ocmulgee and in Stewart County, Georgia.   It
is not at all unlikely that, hereafter, the whole line of
march of De Soto may be discovered, for he was a long
time in the country before he reached the Mississippi, and
must have constructed various places of defence against
the Indians as well as huts to winter in.   I returned to
Dahlonega by a different route, east of the Yónah Mountain, and reached my old quarters about 4 P.M., after a
very agreeable ride.

August 15.—At breakfast this morning I met with
an intelligent person who appeared well acquainted with
the Gold Region, and who informed me that the most
productive line of veins that have been worked up to this
time run from Duke's Creek to the N.W. corner of
Carroll Court-house, passing by Loud's mine, Dahlonega,
the Etowah, and Blackburn's, near the Federal Road, in
Cherokee County, to Carroll County : this line runs about
N.N.E. and the points where the diggings and washings
had been carried on, which are called mines, are where the
streams have broken down the veins.   There is also a
great abundance of iron in the country.

It is to be observed that the strike of all the ridges is
in the same magnetic direction as that of the most productive veins, and the whole course of the Alleghany Mountains.   The general character of the surface of the Gold
Region, wherever I have visited it, whether in Virginia or
here, is the same ; knolls and ridges intersected and divided
by streams and valleys ; and the conclusion to which a
geologist is irresistibly brought is, that the whole of the
elevated mountain line from Georgia to Canada had been

upraised at the same period. This prevailing magnetic direction of the principal ridges, which in most countries is from N.N.E. to N.E. is a subject that deserves investigation; there must have been some potent cause in action in ancient times to have so modified the surface of the earth, and whether it is dormant or not in our times is a problem of great interest.

In the afternoon I visited some mines in the vicinity; one which was worked upon the vein, consisted of a fine lode of quartz running N.N.E. and dipped to the S.E. This vein was divided in two by the Yewhola, a stream which ran about three hundred and fifty feet below the crown of the hill, so that the lode being accessible on both sides had induced them to work upon it. I procured some very good cabinet specimens from the lode of native gold imbedded in white quartz. It was worked by a Mr. King, but his machinery was very insufficient, and I should think that from the very awkward method they had adopted of carrying the ore away and manipulating it, that they lose 50 per cent. of the gold. The vein was cut in open day in the side of the hill, just like a common quarry.

On the other side of the river, I found about three hundred tons of the ore quarried and abandoned. The proprietor had given thirty thousand dollars for this vein and forty acres of land ; but being ignorant of the art of reducing ores, became discouraged and had given it up. I had never seen a more promising vein, and it would be difficult to find one better situated for working. All the ore could be taken down the hill at a very slight expense, the water power was abundant, and the lode inexhaustible, for it was six feet wide. This is one of the very few situations where vein-mining could with their present appliances be carried on to any advantage; to sink shafts, cut adits, and bring the ore to the surface, would be beyond the skill and capital in the country at present. None of the adventurers have succeeded but those who content themselves with washing the auriferous soil. For this nothing but manual labour, which they have in their slaves, and slight machinery are necessary. A rocker is made to oscillate backwards and forwards by a slight water power, shovelsful of the earth and gravel are then thrown in, the water carries away the earth, and the motion throws out the large stones : the smaller gravel and the gold are carried through holes in the bottom of the rocker, and this last finds its way into chambers where a little quick-silver is placed, with which the finer particles of gold are amalgamated and detained.

August 16.—All my delicate specimens being packed in cotton, I arose at day-break, and having breakfasted, got into the stage for South Carolina, there being no other passenger but myself. We arrived at Clarksville between eight and nine in the evening, and found the house in the greatest confusion. The landlord, Mr. Levy, was a Jew, and unfortunately had been for some time at open war with his wife, Mrs. Levy, a not very attractive Jewess. But she had a younger sister who lived with them, and Mrs. Levy, thinking herself attractive enough for her spouse, was jealous, with or without cause, and made the house rather too hot for her lord. To add to his misfortune, Mr. Levy was exceedingly embarrassed by the proceedings of his creditors, who were also jealous as to his intentions about paying his debts; so Mr. Levy had about an hour before I reached the house attempted to liquidate all his worldly concerns by first drinking as much brandy as he could carry, and then hanging himself in a

room up-stairs.   He was found, however, in time and cut
down ; and what was exceedingly odd, instead of sending
for a doctor and keeping him out of sight, he was
brought down-stairs and exposed drunk and half dead to
the visitors and servants.   Finding I could get nobody to
give me any supper, I walked into the family room where
he was laid on a sofa, a most miserable object.   This
tragic incident had produced a regular blow up betwixt
the two sisters, who, almost exhausted with recriminations,
paid me at first no attention ; but when they found I was
the gentleman who had been there with Mr. C——, I was
told that supper would be prepared for me, and to my
great surprise, the younger Jewess came to officiate at the
tea-pot.   She was rather pretty, and apologized for my
having neither butter nor milk, adding that " Things was
a going so contrayry in the house, that she didn't know
what was a going to come of it."

CHAPTER LVII.

FALLS OF TOCOA.—A LOQUACIOUS " DRIVER."—THE EASTERN SLOPE OF THE
ALLEGHANY MOUNTAINS.—VISIT MR. C****** AT FORT HILL.—EPISCOPAL
CHURCH AT PENDLETON.—AN ODD PRESENT TO A PATRIOTIC OLD AUNT.—
AN EXCURSION TO VALLEY RIVER.—JOCASSAY VALLEY.—CATARACT OF THE
WHITE WATER.—REACH THE SUMMIT LEVEL OF DIVIDING WATERS.

August 17.—I rose at the dawn, and going down stairs,
saw the landlord pacing up and down before the house in
an idiot-like manner, and apparently much disconcerted
that his *coup d'état*, for getting rid at once of his wife and
creditors, had so signally failed. At 5 A.M. the stage came
to the door, and we drove off very rapidly for South
Carolina. Notwithstanding this very promising style of
performance of our horses, they backed at the first hill, and
after a protracted and vain attempt to get them to move,
I persuaded the driver, a very odd loquacious fellow, to take
them back and exchange them for others. On resuming
our journey, we soon got out of the Gold Region ; but the
rocks still continued to be a micaceous sandstone, and the
surface of the country to be formed of hills and dales. At
twelve miles from Clarksville, I went up a narrow ravine
to see the very pleasing waterfall of Tocoa, which is in a
semi-circular basin worn out by the water, like a similar
cascade between Fort Snelling and the Falls of St. Anthony
on the Mississippi. The height of the cascade is about two
hundred feet, and the breadth about thirty feet, falling
over micaceous sandstone, alternating with hornblende and

quartzose sandstone very incoherent.   Before the main
body reaches the ground, the sheet of water becomes as
thin as gossamer, and towards the bottom is attenuated
into a light spray.   It is one of the prettiest things I ever
saw, and is in a lovely retired place shut in by hills on
both sides, the ravine at the same time being filled with
beautiful trees in the finest verdure.   Of the Falls of
Tolulah, higher up the head waters of the River Savannah,
I had heard such a magnificent account, that I felt a strong
desire to see them.

We now proceeded for eight miles at a rapid pace down
the steep southern slope of the mountains, through beautiful woods and dales, to Jarrett's, on the Tugaloo, a main
branch of the Savannah.   Here I got an excellent breakfast of coffee, ham, chicken, good bread, butter, honey, and
plenty of good new milk for a quarter of a dollar.   The
landlord cultivated an extensive farm, and there was a fine
bottom of good land near the house; he was a quiet,
intelligent, well-behaved man, a great admirer of Mr. C—,
and seemed anxious to do what was obliging and proper,
more from good feeling than for the poor return he chose
to take for his good fare.   What a charming country this
would be to travel in, if one was sure of meeting with such
clean nice quarters once a-day !   The traveller does sometimes, but unfortunately they stand nearly in the same
proportion to the dirty ones that the known planets do to
the fixed stars.   The driver of this stage coach was a very
odd fellow, sometimes amusing, though upon the whole a
great bore, full of conceit of himself, practising the most
uncouth familiarity, and eternally making long speeches.
When I refused to listen to him he talked to himself just
with the same earnestness that he did to me.   On going
down the steepest hills, he drove so furiously as to make it

almost impossible for me to sit in the coach, talking to himself all the time, and when at the bottom he would turn round and address me after the following manner:—
"I say, stranger, do you see that are house? Last time I passed I bought a most splendid water million (they all pronounce melon thus) there for sevenpence, but it warn't ripe, that was the worst on it, and I had to throw it away jist a bit a-head here. Do you like water millions, stranger? There's a power of them in this country, it beats all. You beat all the chaps that goes this road for fixing the stones with your hammer. Do you find any thing you can sell in them? There aint no gold on this side the mountains, that's what they say, I don't know much about it. I come from the low country in North Carolina. I han't much learning though I was two quarters at school. I was a schoolmaster though one winter in Buncombe up in the mountains, but it aint no go that; I like stage driving better, if they didn't give me sich horses on this line; this unackawntabul sorrel won't back a bit going down hill, and the grey kicks like h—ll when he is going up, its next to *on*possible to git along ; but you'll have a splendid driver next stage, a reel splendid fellow that will take you twenty-nine miles to Picken's Court-house; and if I don't give it to this blasted grey when we go back and make him toe the mark, I'm no account." This was the sort of farrago I had to listen to without a possibility of avoiding it.

From Jarrett's the country was extremely wild, only here and there a settler, and abundance of small streams coming down from the mountains. The rocks were incoherent quartz, studded with small garnets, and alternating with hornblende slate, containing larger blotches of semi-crystallized hornblende. At sunset we reached Little River, where the stream falls over a bold bluff of these rocks, and would be a beautiful cascade, if it were not deformed by the shabby frame of a mill.   Half an hour afterwards, we came to Picken's Court-house, in South Carolina, a small settlement with a Court-house perched on a hill. Here I stopped at a tavern kept by a Mr. Alexander, and supped and went to bed.

August 18.—This was a beautiful morning.   I was now on the eastern slope of the chain that fronts the Atlantic, from whence the country to the north-west is an elevated table land about sixty miles broad, varied with ridges, valleys, hills and streams, and terminated by the long line of the Oonáykay, or White Mountains. This elevated country is part of the great belt that runs through the American States N.N.E. by S.S.W., and to which the Gold Region appears to be confined.   Even on the southern flank where this Court-house stands, the country is diversified with high knolls and narrow vales, after the manner of the Gold Region ; the same dynamical action having modified the country to a great distance from the belt itself. Deposits of gravel and soil of similar character to those in the Gold Region exist in the vales around, but they contain no gold, with the exception, however, of a few light particles that have been brought by the streams from a great distance.   The prevailing rocks are hornblende, micaceous sandstone, and incoherent quartzose sandstone.   Here the quartz commences to have a very transparent character ; bundles of imperfect crystals are common, and masses of fine rock crystal are occasionally found.   At this charming rural situation a pretty little river, called the Keeowee, about one hundred yards wide, runs near the village, and nothing can be more tranquil than the place and its neighbourhood.

This loveliness of the mountain scenery in the Southern

States is almost unknown in other parts of the United States, except to those gentlemen who occasionally retire to the mountains from the low country on the coast, from the scorching effects of the sun. I have travelled a great deal in the Northern States without having ever seen so attractive a country. Indeed, in what country can more attractions combine to gratify the traveller than where the last energies of an aboriginal race, the most beautiful varieties of the mineral kingdom, and the most obliging hospitalities instruct and gratify him whilst he is wandering amongst the rarest and most beautiful of nature's scenes?

About 8 A.M. two servants arrived from Mr. C— with a riding-horse for myself, and a small vehicle with a mule to carry my luggage. I now mounted and rode about fifteen miles through a pleasing country, entirely unsettled, all hill and dale, with occasional delightful pellucid streams. The road was literally strewed with semi-transparent quartz and crystallized hornblende. The same sensitive briar, the beautiful vicia, the passion flower, the convolvulus batata, and other plants I had observed in the Cherokee country, were growing here. Towards the close of the ride the country became less hilly; and passing the house of Mr. John E. Calhoun, perched on a hill, where I paid a visit last year, I at length reached Fort Hill, where Mr. C— and his family received me in the most friendly manner. A delightful room was assigned to me, and here I found myself in a charming house, amidst all the refinement and comfort that are inseparable from the condition of well-bred and honourable persons. After partaking of an excellent dinner we adjourned for the evening to the portico, where with the aid of a guitar, accompanied by a pleasing voice, and some capital curds and cream, we prolonged a most agreeable conversazione until a late hour. The air of this part of the country reminded me of that of Tuscany, in the Appenines, which is soft and salubrious at every hour of the night.

August 19.—This was a beautiful Italian-like morning, and it tempted me to stroll out before breakfast. The woods about were strewed with bunches of quartz crystals, and the most curious varieties of crystallized hornblende. Our breakfast was admirable, excellent coffee with delicious cream, and that capital, national dish of South Carolina, snow-white homminy brought hot to table like maccaroni, which ought always to be eaten, with lumps of sweet fresh butter buried in it ! this is certainly one of the best things imaginable to begin the day liberally with. How exquisitely it is prepared at Mrs. C—'s ! I passed the rest of the morning writing letters, the sun being too intensely hot to go out. At dinner we had Mr. Wayland, principal of the academy at Pendleton, a town not far distant, a sensible odd-looking Englishman. In the evening, Mr. C— and myself walked to Cold Spring, a quiet rural residence on his estate, built for his mother, but inhabited at the time by a German and his wife. I was glad to hear that he was geological, for the Germans are generally good geologists, and anticipated some satisfaction in making his acquaintance; but I perceived he was such a great smoker of tobacco, that I should not often be with him; for much as I admire volcanos, I perfectly abhor them when they come out of a man's mouth. Madame was a prettyish young woman, rather fat and very somnolent; she told me that she had fallen asleep, and let her baby fall off the bed without hearing its cries. "De boor little lamb," she said, "was lay ubbon de floor, und cry so when de nurse com to wake me." On our return to Fort Hill, the family again assembled in the portico to pass a most agreeable evening.

August 20.—This was a beautiful, but most surprizingly hot morning. After breakfast, I went in the carriage with the ladies to the Episcopal Church at Pendleton, a neat temple prettily situated in a shady grove. The congregation was numerous, and principally composed of well-dressed and very genteel people. Eight or ten nice-looking carriages were drawn up, and the scene reminded me of an English country church in a good neighbourhood. The service was very appropriately performed, and I had the greatest satisfaction in assisting at it. The Episcopal Church in Republican America, which in every essential is a copy of our national church, is a strong bond of union amongst the educated and well-bred in the United States, as it is at home. It will probably continue to receive all the opulent and intellectual classes, and eventually have a salutary influence there, not only in relation to religion, morals, and manners, but to a right sympathy and feeling towards their mother country, from which Americans have received so inestimable a blessing. Here I had the good fortune to meet my old friend Mr. Ch—, whom I had not seen since 1824, and promised to pay him a visit before I left the country. After a very pleasant dinner, Mr. C— introduced me to a Colonel Warren, a veteran of the Revolution, with a · wooden leg, who called to pay him a visit. The following anecdote was related to me of him : He left England when a youth to lend his aid to the colonists ; and his aunt, a lady upon whom he depended, finding him obstinately bent upon taking up arms against his native country, said she hoped he would get a mark fixed upon him for his rebellious conduct. At the siege of Savannah his leg was shot off by a cannon-ball, upon which he had it put up in a box, and sent it to England with his duty to his aunt.

August 21.—After breakfast I made an arrangement with a Mr. Sloane, a friend of Mr C—'s, for an excursion to the mountains to embrace the Tolula Falls, the White Mountain, and thence proceed to the Cherokee country of Valley River. This tour would enable me to see the most interesting parts of the mountainous country; and I felt exceedingly obliged to Mr. C— for having procured me an agreeable companion, who was already acquainted with many parts of it. At dinner we had Colonel Pinkney and the veteran Colonel Warren, with a great deal of interesting conversation. What an immense difference there is in the manners of the southern gentlemen, and most of those who are at the head of society in the middle and Northern States. Here the conversation was always liberal and instructive, and seldom suggested by selfish speculations of what they might gain by following particular lines of conduct. I observed a great solicitude here for the welfare of their slaves, especially on the part of the ladies, who give them a great deal of personal attendance when they are ill. The autumnal fevers are sometimes very malignant, and carry off slaves worth one thousand dollars each. This, of course, makes every one careful of their health; but, independent of that consideration, there was evidently a great deal of humanity and tenderness exercised to all who were born on the family plantation. Mr. C— cultivated both cotton and Indian corn, and was an excellent man of business. I learnt from those who knew him well, that he was a man of great punctuality in his dealings, and had never been known to run in debt, or enter into wild speculations. All looked up to him as the first man in South Carolina; and many who were embarrassed in their cir-

cumstances came to him for advice.   Whilst he declined
entering into pecuniary responsibilities for those who did
not belong to his family, he always listened to their stories,
gave them the most friendly advice, and frequently referred
them to men of business, who could assist them if their
affairs were retrievable.   By persevering in this wise conduct, he was enabled to do good to all, and keep himself
free from embarrassment.   He himself had no embarrass-
ments but those political struggles he was engaged in.
Living, however, at so great a distance from the northern
constituencies, it was impossible for them to be sufficiently
acquainted with the sterling excellence of his character.   If
the purity of his private life could be as generally known in
the State of New York as it is in South Carolina, no
demagogues could prevent him from becoming universally
popular.

August 22.—After breakfast I bade adieu to this amiable
family, and mounting my horse, proceeded with Mr. Sloane
to the head of twelve Mile Creek, where there is a fine fall
of water coming over a rock of gneiss, much mixed up with
sienite and patches of black mica.   The rock dips to the
S.E., and the waterfall would be exceedingly beautiful if it
were not defaced by a mill-dam.   The place is called Mile
Creek, being one mile from Fort George, erected in ancient
times to repress the Cherokees.   The country is broken up
into knolls and valleys as in the Gold Region, and gold in
small quantities is found in some of the mountain streams.
At half-past 5 P.M., we stopped at Major M'Kenny's,
twenty-four miles from Fort Hill, from whence we had a
fine view of the mountains we were to ascend the next
day.   The house was built in a pretty cove; the land around
was planted with corn, and produced excellent water-
melons.   Notwithstanding a bright sun, the air was balmy

and tolerably cool. Here we got a family supper and two decent beds.

August 23.—This was a cool morning, Fahrenheit at 56^0. After breakfast we pursued our journey through the coves and vales which separate the spurs of the mountains to Jocássay Valley, an oblong bottom with the river called White Water flowing on the east : from hence we ascended the Jocássay Mountain about five hundred feet to reach the ravine where the river makes its great fall. In trying to find this point, we came upon an old deserted Cherokee peach-orchard with abundance of ripe peaches, and regaled ourselves for awhile. At length we found the stream we were in search of, which certainly soon led to a very extraordinary scene.

My mind had been busy conjecturing ever since we left the Jocássay Valley as to the manner in which the White Water would fall from the mountain. There was a descent of at least five hundred feet, which would probably be expended in many interesting rapids and falls, for if it made but one plunge, it would be a cascade of so extraordinary a character, that it could not but have attracted some notice. Tracing the stream, we at length came to the edge of the ravine down which it fell. It was here about sixty feet broad, and glided at first over the gneiss rock on a smooth inclined plane at an angle of about 45^0 for twenty feet, to a coarse terrace about fifty feet wide of naked rock, extremely slippery, the water having worn the quartz and mica into a polished metallic-like face, upon which it was very difficult to stand. From hence it passed over another inclined plane at an angle of 70^0 for about eighty feet, carrying a handsome sheet of white foam to another terrace about seventy feet wide, inclining a little to the north, with a pool of water upon it. From this it passed to another plane at an angle of 45⁰ of about one hundred feet, to a broken terrace of sixty feet wide, advancing to a fourth plane at an angle of 60⁰ for one hundred and fifty feet; at the end of which it fell in a vertical cascade of thirty feet upon a fifth inclined plane at an angle of 60⁰ for one hundred feet, and from thence, by a more broken plane of one hundred and fifty feet, to where the water beginning to run off unbroken, lost itself at length to the eye in a deep and dark ravine covered with trees of the densest foliage; except on the east side, where the naked and moss-covered gneiss, with a few evergreen and deciduous trees scattered about, beetled out and added greatly to the sublimity of the scene. To the south, the ravine was closed in by a lofty spur of the Chatuga range. The perpendicular view in the plate prefixed to this volume exhibits imperfectly the character of this cataract.

I examined the whole course of the planes and terraces from the top to the bottom with much attention. The excavation of the beds of rivers, especially when they pass through mountains, is an interesting subject to a geologist, and has always engaged my attention. That the constant attrition of water upon the face of any rock will in long periods of time wear the rock away is sufficiently obvious, but the manner in which torrents proceed to effect their purpose has not been sufficiently dwelt upon; and this is one of the localities where the strongest evidence of it is presented in the great number of pot-holes which have been drilled into the face of the rock by the descending fluid.*   That the power of floods is sufficient to dislocate

* For the details of a memoir on the excavation of valleys by the retrocession of their ancient rivers, illustrated by this waterfall, and read at the meeting of the British Association at York, in 1844, by the Author, vide Chapter xxv, Vol. 1.

and remove immense masses of rock, and that the perpetual gliding of a stream over the face of a rock will gradually wear it away, is certainly true; but the construction of these pot-holes by the water is a sort of natural engineering that involves the destruction of the most obdurate strata, and is evidently the means by which rivers have, by retrocession, excavated their beds through the primary mountains. Wherever there is a slight cavity or a soft part in the strata, the water immediately effects a lodgment, and the first pebble it receives commences the work of destruction; the current incessantly whirling about the pebble, and grinding the sides of the cavity until it becomes what is called a pot-hole.

Some of these, in the terraces of this mountain stream, were four feet in diameter and six feet deep; and where they exist in great numbers and near to each other, it is evident that the resistance which the rock offers to the power of the water must become feebler every day, and that the parietes which separate them are insufficient to make the strata cohere. Sometimes the separations between them are broken down, and a great number of them coalesce into one, as in the case of the second terrace, where there is a pool of water. This process may be seen constantly going on; and on descending to the lowest level where the largest fragments of rock had fallen, I found that they had all been forced from their situs by this cause, being perforated with these pot-holes, innumerable sections of which on the fallen rocks marked the points where they had given way, and led to the fall of the rock.

But what greatly adds to the interest which these circumstances give to this locality, is a semicircular ledge of moss-clad gneiss, east of the stream, about twelve hundred feet wide, from whence it is most evident the water in ancient times made one magnificent plunge, that would have rivalled the far-famed cataract of Niagara. All the evidences of this are upon the spot ; the gneiss is worn bare for a great distance at the top, and the smooth concavity of the face of the rock that once was behind the watery screen, proves that for a very long period it had been exposed to the same influence that has modified the rocks of all existing cataracts.

This was a fatiguing and anxious day ; unceasing exertion, the danger of slipping from the rocks, in many places polished as smooth as metal, and a constant vigilance in looking out for rattle-snakes, had almost exhausted me, and I reached the top again with some difficulty. From this place our journey was constantly over mountains, following an obscure bridle-path. We entered North Carolina and crossed some hills, about four hundred feet above the table-land, of amorphous talc and talcose slate, resembling the Chatuga ridge, and at length got to the summit level of the region, in what is called Cassia Valley, where the head-waters of the River Savannah, which flows into the Atlantic, and the head-waters of the Tennessee, which flows into the Mississippi, take their rise. From this flat and swampy table-land we soon saw the crests and mountains of the surrounding region, the Blue ridge, the White-sides, the Terrapin, the Chimney-top, and other remarkable elevations. About 6 P.M., being heartily tired, we reached a house kept by one Zachary, got something to eat, and laid down to rest as soon as we could.

CHAPTER LVIII.

ASCEND WHITE SIDE MOUNTAIN.—REACH FRANKLIN.—DEGRADED STATE OF
THE POPULATION.—CROSS THE NANTAYAYHLAY CHAIN.—CHEROKEE ROAD-
MAKERS.—VALLEY RIVER MOUNTAIN.— BANDITTI LOOKING VOLUNTEERS.—
FIND COMFORT AND MOET'S CHAMPAGNE.

August 24.—At daylight, after an indifferent night's
rest, I was awoke by the daughters of the landlady coming
into the room and telling me I must get up, for they
wanted to set the breakfast; so I was fain to take my
apparatus and dressing-case to a log outside the house, and
make my toilette there.   Last night we had no meat for
supper; this morning they gave us a stewed chicken and
plenty of Indian corn bread with good milk.   Nothing
can be more awkward than these mountaineers in domestic
matters; but they were very obliging and good-tempered,
without being vicious and vulgar, like some of the people
I had lodged with in North Alabama.   What is called
the Chimney-top Mountain, is one mile distant from this
house in a N.E. direction.

At 7 A.M , having got some directions from the people
of the house, we started for White-side Mountain, the most
remarkable elevation in this country.   Our course lay over
hill and dale by an obscure path, when having made about
three miles, and advancing to the south on the sideling
path of a very steep and well-wooded hill, the Chatuga chain

on our left and a very deep ravine on our right, with the murmuring noise of a cascade on the west, the White-side Mountain suddenly appeared, distant about two miles from the ravine, with features of remarkably imposing grandeur.

WHITE SIDE MOUNTAIN.

Our first exclamation was, that it was one of the finest spectacles we had ever seen, and that we would ascend it. Having found a person, of the name of Norton, who had a cabin in the neighbourhood, he very obligingly engaged to be our guide. Proceeding through the densely wooded flank of the mountain as far as we conveniently could on horseback, and then tying up our horses, we commenced the ascent on foot, or rather on all-fours. We had to drag ourselves up several slopes at an angle of more than 60°, by laying hold of twigs of the bushes and plants that grew around, and then crawling for some distance over narrow ledges at the very edge of a perpendicular escarpment of at least five hundred feet, to recommence with other slopes almost vertical. Very fine wild raspberries were growing

almost at the top.   It took us three hours and a quarter of
unceasing exertion to reach the summit, which rises two
thousand feet above the general level.   Having gained this,
we found the rock sufficiently disintegrated to admit of the
growth of bushes and wild plants.   The crest is about a
mile long, and in many places not more than a hundred
yards wide.   From this elevated point, which is said to be
about six thousand feet above the level of the sea, I had a
very extensive view, of at least a hundred miles.   To the
north-west was the well-defined chain of the Oonáykay
Mountains ; and to the south-east, I could distinctly see the
cultivated lands about Pendleton, at least forty miles
distant ; so that we looked over the whole breadth of the
elevated belt that traverses the continent of North America.
I was exceedingly struck with the numerous pot-holes in
the rock at the very summit of the mountain, a proof that
in ancient times the mountain has been much more
extensive and lofty, and that the waters have once acted
upon this summit in the manner they have done at the
Falls of the White Water River.   Similar pot-holes exist
upon the summits of other lofty mountains, especially those
near Lake George in the State of New York.

The White-side is gneiss at the bottom, with mica
predominating, but two thirds up it becomes almost pure
white mica which, easily disintegrating, has left about
one thousand feet of the eastern face of the rock bare.
This immense escarpment being white is seen at great
distances, and hence the mountain has received the name
of White-side.   There is a vein or lode of quartz near
the top, running N.N.E. and S.S.W. and at the extreme
top of the mountain, the gneiss came in again with white
lustrous mica predominating.   Having made all our
observations, we commenced our descent at the end
opposite to that by which we ascended.   It was a difficult

and dangerous undertaking ; we had to pass down slopes of bright slippery micaceous rock at a sharp inclination, with our shoes in our hands, carefully examining the direction in which we had to go, lest it should lead us to a precipice, the return from which would be hazardous; but our guide was skilful and cautious, and conducted us safely to the dry beds of some mountain torrents, through which, after most fatiguing exertions, we reached the place where we had tied our horses seven hours before. On our return to Zachary's we found Mr. C——'s eldest son, who had left Fort Hill yesterday afternoon, but having no guide was unable to follow us. We finished the day with a hearty supper, and almost exhausted with fatigue, I gladly retired to bed.

August 25.—Having taken a cup of coffee shortly after sunrise, we mounted again and directed our course to the town of Franklin, in Macon county, North Carolina, intending from thence to proceed to the Cherokee settlements. Our way led through a succession of vales separated from each other by mountains of highly micaceous gneiss about eight hundred feet high, with innumerable streamlets flowing through them. The country was perfectly wild, without any roads but obscure Indian trails almost hidden by the shrubs and high grass. Unfortunately an obstinate and heavy rain commenced immediately after our departure, and soon drenched us thoroughly, but this was not enough, we at length came to a narrow valley, about two miles long, where the thick alders were eight feet high ; all these we had to put aside with our hands as we advanced, and certainly I never received such a continuous and perfect shower bath before or since, for what with the rain and the *rifaccimento* of it from the bushes, it was difficult to keep my eyes open. As soon as we had passed the Cowee Mountains the rain ceased, and finding a hut at Walnut Creek, we stopped and changed our clothes. From hence we pursued our ride to Sugar-loaf Creek, a pretty meandering mountain stream, flowing not unfrequently through beautiful sequestered valleys.

The country now began to descend, and the valley to widen; at length settlements began to appear, and we came to a tolerably good road for wheels, running through a country remarkable for its beauty. About 5 P.M. we reached Franklin, a small village built on a branch of the Tennessee, called Little Tennessee, and charmingly situated upon a knoll in the centre of an ample valley, flanked by lofty ranges of hills on the east and west sides, and open in front by a break in the mountains, called Rabun's Gap. This valley is probably seven hundred feet lower than the level we left in the morning. The tall maize, called flint corn, ripens here, which it will not do there, and many southern plants began to appear. Hemlock trees abounded, there we saw none, blackberries were over here and there, they were not yet ripe. On our arrival at the tavern we consulted the landlord about sleeping, and requested him to provide us a comfortable supper, which he readily engaged to do; but the moment it was known that travellers were arrived, the room we were in became filled with drunken insolent fellows, who held the authority of the landlord in contempt: he would take no step to relieve us from them, and it being evident that we should get into a quarrel if we remained below, we determined to bully the landlord a little too; without asking his permission, therefore, I went up stairs, and finding there was a tolerably good room, gave a black man some money to make a good fire there, and ordered the supper to be laid in the same place. This new plan of the guests taking the management into their own hands succeeded perfectly well; the landlord saw that we were right and submitted with good grace, and we got over the evening tolerably well.

What a dreadful state of things! Here was a village most beautifully situated, surrounded by a fertile soil capable of furnishing its inhabitants with every enjoyment, and that might become an earthly Paradise, if education, religion, and manners prevailed. But I could not learn that there was a man of education in the place disposed to set an example of the value of sobriety of life to the community. It appeared to be delivered up to political demagogues, whose only study was to debauch and mislead the people. It exhibited a perfect specimen of that kind of equality which democratic institutions too often lead to. Such is the fatal descent in the scale of human respectability, which at length brings about an equality in ignorance, depravity, vulgarity and drunkenness.

August 26.—All was quiet in the village when I arose at day-break. The landlord informed me that the place is very sickly in September and October, which surprised me considering its elevation. The fog this morning was so dense as to obscure everything; perhaps these exhalations which hang upon the surface in autumn are, in conjunction with the undrained state of the valley, the immediate causes. Having heard that there was a MSS. map of this wild part of the country at the Court-house, executed from actual survey, I went there and made a rough copy of it, as far as the mountains and streams were concerned, and found that we had another elevated chain, called *Nantayáyhlay*, to cross before we reached Valley River. At 9 A.M. we proceeded on our journey, our course laying up a narrow valley leading westwards through which ran the Warrior branch of the Nantayáyhlay River, a tributary of the Tennessee. The State of North Carolina having got possession of this part of the Cherokee country, was already making a road through it, unfinished sections of which we occasionally fell in with. We proceeded through a most pleasing country, the trail sometimes gliding through narrow vales, then rising to the summit of a lofty ridge, which looked down upon beautiful amphitheatres of low ground, surrounded by lofty hills of eight hundred feet high. At length we reached the Nantayáyhlay chain, the strike of which is about N.N.E. S.S.W. and the elevation eight hundred and fifty feet. This chain runs in the centre of the ancient Cherokee country, being about equidistant from the Oonáykay and the southern edge of the great belt of mountains, and has thus received its name of Nantayáyhlay or " in the middle." The stream called the Warrior ran at its foot. The ascent was very steep, being for a considerable way at an elevation of 50^0, and the summit was fourteen miles from the town of Franklin. The whole ridge is formed of compact gneiss, studded with small brilliant garnets. On the west side we found the descent less precipitous, being a sort of gradually descending table land, with occasional dense laurel thickets, almost impenetrable, and forming the appropriate abodes of panthers, and two or three species of wild cats. Some of these laurels were twelve inches in diameter. At the bottom of the descent we found our path full of difficulties, and had continually to cross a rocky branch of the Nantayáyhlay from one side to the other, the old trail being occupied for a great distance by the new road now constructing, and impassable for the present.

I learnt that the contracts for making the road were principally in the hands of white men, who engaged Cherokees to chop the trees down and afterwards to grub up the roots. As we advanced in the bed of the stream, we passed many groups of these Indians at work far above us on the hill side who cheered us repeatedly. It was a very picturesque and strange sight to see such swarthy Tartar countenances with turbans and striped calico hunting shirts, working in this

wild district for the men who had robbed them of their
country.   After pursuing this perplexing road down the
stream for a long time, we came to another lofty hill called
Valley River Mountain, which it was necessary to ascend,
for the bed of the stream was no longer passable.   The
descent on the other side was extremely bad, and when we
reached the bottom, we had to recommence our wanderings
in the rocky stream, advancing a few steps and then being
obliged to cross to the other side continually.   Here we
exchanged the gneiss with garnets for an amorphous
talcose rock, with the usual quartz lodes running N.N.E.,
and resembling in their mineral character those in the
Gold Region, which this part of the country may probably
be included in.

As we got clear of the mountain and entered a pleasant
valley, we met a Cherokee on horseback, named John
Welsh, whom I remembered seeing at the Council.   I
attempted to get into conversation with him about the
affairs transacted there, and the present temper of the
Indians, but he was very reserved.   I gathered sufficient
from him, however, to understand that the Cherokees were
determined not to abandon their country, whatever risk
they might run.   We were now at the north east termination of the pleasant valley through which Valley River
runs, and saw the Oonáykay chain bounding it to the north-
west.   At sunset we stopped at a very indifferent place
called Whitakers about thirty-two miles from Franklin.
Here we got a very humble supper, about which I was less
anxious than to get a mattrass to myself.   The setting in
of night always brings its anxieties on this point to me,
my travelling companions were more sympathetic, and
seemed to prefer " turning in " in pairs.

August 27.—A most beautiful morning found me at
early dawn dipping water out of the stream to make my

ablutions *aperto cielo*, preparatory to a very scrubby breakfast.
The method the Indians adopt of taking fish in this stream
is a very destructive one.   They cut a channel parallel to
the stream, and damming this last up, turn the water into
the new channel, seizing all the fish that are left in the
shallow pools of the old bed.   We continued our course
S.W. down the valley on the right bank of the stream,
the valley enlarging to a mile of rich bottom land surrounded
by lofty and picturesque hills covered with fine woods.
This was the Paradise of the Cherokees, their wigwams
being built on graceful knolls rising above the level of the
river bottom, each of them having its patch of Indian corn
with indigenous beans climbing to the top of each plant,
and squashes and pumpkins growing on the ground.   The
valley now contracted as we advanced, but contained a
great many thousand acres of the most fertile land.   Any
thing much more beautiful than this fine scene can scarcely
be imagined ; two noble lines of mountains enclosing a
fertile valley with a lovely stream running through it.   The
whole vale has formerly been a lake.   As I was riding
near the river, I perceived some appearance of limestone,
and dismounting to examine the rock, found it was statuary
marble of the same quality as that I had seen near the
Talking Rock Creek.   Its course was N.N.E. and S.S.W.,
and there is every reason to believe that it is a continuation
of the calcareous dyke which, near the Talking Rock, laid
above the surface in the form of a ridge.   The general
rock of this valley was talcose micaceous slate, and when
crossing one of the streams, I perceived the water was
turbid as it usually is below where they wash for gold ;
a person whom we met explained to me that some Cherokees
were engaged washing the mud and gravel in a rude way
at the head of that stream.

Valley River is the north branch of the Hiwassee which

is the main southern tributary of the Tennessee, and a
short distance below where it forks and forms the Hiwassee
—which was here about one hundred yards wide, but
shallow and very pellucid, as all these mountain streams
are—we crossed over to the left bank. The general rock
now became a bright lustrous talcose slate. Leaving the
river, we met in a defile, at no great distance, a company of
mounted Franklin volunteers moving to the mouth of the
Nantayáyhlay, a part of the North Carolina State troops
employed in a surveillance over the Cherokees until their
evacuation of the country should take place. They would
have been perfectly in character in the uplands beyond
Terracina, on the road to Naples, for I never saw any
fellows in my life that came so thoroughly up to the notion
entertained of banditti. With their rifles and canteens
slung over their dirty and thicket-torn clothes, they had the
easy impudent air of fellows that knew no control; and if I
had met such a set of physiognomies in the Papal States or
in Calabria, I should instantly have thought of compounding
with my purse, but several of them were civil, and I got off
with nothing worse than some awkward bumps from their
grimy camp kettles that were attached to their saddles—
a contact with which there was no escaping in the narrow
defile. My appearance, that was bad enough before, was
not materially improved by rubbing against these vessels.

About 2 P.M., we ascended a hill to Fort Butler, a
temporary camp with a block-house built for the State
troops upon this occasion: from hence we rode a mile to
Hunter's, a tavern kept by a person of that name who had
been long in the Cherokee country; it was most beautifully
situated upon an eminence commanding a view of the
Hiwassee, gracefully winding through the hills, and of the
lovely country around. There was a clever little hut in a
retired part of the garden belonging to this house, and beds

being placed in it, it was assigned to us exclusively, so that we had some prospect of comfort. Perceiving some ladies in the house, one of whom was the wife of an officer of the United States army, we made our toilette rather more carefully. The dinner was excellent, good soup, and a fine large trout from the river. We seemed restored to civilization, an idea that lost nothing by the introduction of a capital bottle of champagne, of which Hunter had brought a basket from Augusta, thinking the officers of the State troops would not sneeze at it ; but either the price or something about it did not please them, and there Monsieur Moet was likely to have remained for some time " unknowing and unknown " but for our appearance. As it is not every day that Moet's champagne, and in the finest order, can be drank on the banks of the Hiwassee, in the Cherokee country, we formed the virtuous resolution of appropriating the whole basket to ourselves, and lost no time in putting a taboo upon it.

Here I learnt that Colonel Lindsay and his staff had been here since I was at the Council at Red Clay, and that he had mentioned my intention of visiting this part of the country. Perhaps it is to this circumstance I owed the great civility I received from Mr. Hunter. In the evening I walked out, and found the hill upon which this house was built consisted of mica slate, studded with transparent garnets. At the foot of the hill, the Hiwassee, about one hundred and fifty yards wide, glided between lofty escarpments about four hundred feet high. The river was generally shallow, but at one place it deepened suddenly from the pitch of the rock, a few hundred yards below the point where Valley River empties into the Hiwassee. I found some dead valves of unios at the edges of the river, but no live shells. The same species belong to the Tennessee and Cumberland Rivers.

CHAPTER LIX.

VISIT SOME ANCIENT MINING WORKS.—TRADITIONS OF THE CHEROKEES RES-
PECTING THEM.—SKELETONS COVERED WITH PIECES OF GRANITE.—FIND AN
ANCIENT MINING SHAFT.—ITS PROBABLE REFERENCE TO FERDINAND DE
SOTO'S EXPEDITION.—RECROSS THE MOUNTAINS.—GOLD VEINS.

August 28.—After an early breakfast, I mounted my
mare and took the direction of the Mission to call upon an
old acquaintance, Squire Sterrit, whom I had seen a good
deal of at the Council at Red Clay. He had been some
time in this country, had a curious investigating turn, and
promised if I would come to this neighbourhood to take
me to some singular excavations the Indians had shown
him. I had scarce ridden five miles when I fortunately
met him on horseback on his way to Tennessee. He was
heartily glad to see me, and kindly deferred his journey on
my account. Near his house stood the Cherokee Council-
house of the district, a regular open octagon, built of logs,
with a small portal; over this, a temporary roof was
thrown upon particular occasions. In this building the
Indians of the district held their courts, performed their
dances, and other ceremonies. He gave me a curious
account of the manner in which they prepare and hold
their medicine festivals, which he promised to write out
for me. About two miles from his house, we ascended a
hill, and on the descent on the other side, found a longitudinal excavation resembling an open adit, about fifteen feet

deep at the upper end, and forty feet in length down the hill. This was made upon a vein of quartz, the parietes of which consisted of decomposed talcose slate, the course of the lode being slightly west of north. Several trees were growing at the edge of this excavation, but not apparently more than thirty years old. Numerous heaps of the ore were lying about, with mica slate containing garnets; but the slate was entirely changed in colour and fell to pieces on the slightest touch. Several smaller excavations had been made not far from this long one, and the rock at each place was in the same state, bearing evidence of having lain a very long period of time exposed to the action of the atmosphere. Mr. Sterrit informed me that gold in small quantities was found in the streams around.

It was impossible after examining these excavations not to be convinced that at some very remote period persons not ignorant of mining had made some attempts here, and had abandoned them. Mr. Sterrit informed me that he had frequently conversed with the oldest Cherokee chiefs about these excavations, but they uniformly answered that the Indians had never attempted any thing of the kind, nor had any white men made them in the memory of the oldest amongst them. They had traditions, however, of these and other excavations having been made by white men a very long time ago; and on this subject he was referred to an aged Cherokee female who had always lived in Valley River and who bore an excellent character for veracity. She told him that she had heard her grandfather say that his father remembered them when he was a boy, and that they were in the same state they are now in; and that his father also said there was a tradition amongst the Cherokees in his time, that these diggings were made by a few strangers who came into the country they did not know where from, with yellow countenances and of short stature. That they behaved very civilly, and after staying awhile and travelling about the country, they went away and returned with eight or ten more, and resumed their diggings. After remaining some time, they again left the district and returned a second time with about sixty of their companions, bringing presents with them of cloth, silk, yellow money, and other things, and began to establish themselves in the country by building huts, and digging amongst the rocks.

The Cherokees, perceiving they always returned with increased numbers, held a council, and deeming it unsafe to have so many strangers in their country, surprised and massacred them all. Mr. Sterrit assured me that the old woman repeatedly told him the same story, and that she was esteemed to be a very respectable person, and could have no motive whatever to deceive him. In fact, her story appears to confirm the conclusion I came to after seeing the decomposed state of the rocks at these excavations, that they must have been made two or three centuries ago, and very probably by some of the persons who accompanied Ferdinand de Soto. From this place, Squire Sterrit conducted me to a spring of chalybeate water, which he said the Indians resorted to for the purpose of curing eruptions of the skin by washing with the water. Not very distant from this spring was an extensive deposit of hematitic iron ore, on a ridge containing several lodes of quartz, running N.N.E. and S.S.W. Numerous excavations had been also made here apparently at about the same period.

The sky, which had been lowering for some time, now sent down such torrents of rain that we became thoroughly wet through, and the constant dismounting and mounting, and tying up our horses became very wearisome; but the Squire said he had still something more curious to show me, and indeed I had so excited his curiosity by narrating to him the expedition of De Soto that he became as eager as myself, and on we went, the rain oozing from our boots almost as fast as it fell upon our heads. We next crossed Valley River, and proceeded to a ridge where we found more excavations upon an extensive scale; and not far from them, in a place where the ground was tolerably level, was an area of about forty feet in diameter, evidently prepared for a particular purpose, for the timber was cleared away, and some very old rotten stumps remained, all evidently cut with an axe. A few trees of a much younger date were growing here and there, but by no means as old as some of those in the adjacent forest. In this area were the remains of an ancient furnace, the chimneys and floor of which were built with slabs of asbestus, which I afterwards found in place about two miles N.E. of the ridge. The face of this mineral which had been next to the fire was burnt to the depth of half an inch. Behind the furnace was a hole dug in the ground, with a throat leading from the furnace to it, evidently to convey away molten metal. In and about the furnace was a quantity of iron ore* wasted, but not fused, probably for the want of a flux. We found also a great quantity of quartz about the furnace, in a torrified state, and what was interesting to me, there was a second trough of micaceous slate, similar to that I saw at Mr. Richardson's on the 13th of August in Nahcóochay.

From these circumstances it appeared probable that

* This rock was not in place here, and must have been brought from a distance.

a band of white men, imperfectly acquainted with mining, had been here, had found native gold in the streams around, (it is still found there), had opened some of the lodes, and had attempted to roast and smelt the ore.   That they were ignorant of the method of doing it, was clear from their having tried to torrify large masses of the quartz ; for the metal, if there had been any, would not have fused under such circumstances.   Failing in this, they probably tried iron, more from curiosity than with any intention of carrying it away.   There were also several small excavations near a brook which ran at the foot of the hill, and where probably the party that had been here had encamped, for betwixt the stream and the furnace were some furrows made by the rain which appeared to have been footpaths originally.

Half a mile from this place was a lofty ridge about one hundred and fifty feet high, running N.N.E. and S.S.W. almost entirely consisting of quartz ; the ridge was very sharp and narrow at the top, and gold was still washed out of the streams that ran on each side of the ridge.   At the summit we found a transverse trench in the solid quartz to the depth of fifteen feet, and about sixty feet long.   The parietes were so altered by time, that they no longer looked like quartz, being discoloured and rather reddish.   For two inches at the surface, the quartz was decayed, but beyond that it was perfectly sound and white. The masses of quartz removed from this excavation were lying around in great quantities, and in various places were piled up in heaps rather carefully.   Observing some of these heaps at the bottom of the trench, we removed the masses of which one of them was formed, and found a skeleton beneath.   This induced us to examine the other heaps, beneath every one of which we found a skeleton. It is not very probable, that the miners who had made these excavations had put these bodies here, they would scarcely have buried their dead on the spot where they were daily working, and it is difficult to imagine a satisfactory reason why the Indians should bring their dead from a distance, and carry them to the top of a rugged hill to give them such imperfect burial, for the Cherokees have always buried their dead in the manner they do now, by digging graves in the soil. A presumption, therefore, arises that the miners had either been surprised at this place, or had retreated to it and been slain here. The ridge is so exceedingly narrow, that it would not have been difficult to hem them in and prevent their escape, and after destroying them, the Indians might have thrown these masses of quartz over them.

This conjecture is somewhat strengthened by another discovery that we made before we came away, of a rude shaft sunk upon the lode of about twenty-five feet deep. My attention was drawn to it by seeing something like a tumulus on the top of the ridge, which turned out to be the rubbish drawn from the shaft. Near the edge of the shaft was the place where the windlass and other machinery had been fixed for drawing up the mineral matter. A laurel, whose roots were struck into the side of the shaft about three feet from the top, prevented our seeing to the bottom; but, on looking into it, I saw some of the machinery resting against its sides, and could plainly distinguish the mortice and ring for the crank with other appliances. Some pieces of wood within our reach looked fresh and sound, but, upon being touched with the branch of a tree we had cut, they proved to be rotten, and crumbled away instantly. It was not improbable, if the miners had been massacred here, that the Indians had thrown these miners into the shaft. I regretted very much, that we had no means of examining the bottom of the shaft. We tried our bridles and stirrups, and endeavoured in vain to contrive some way of getting out, after we should let ourselves down. It was easy enough to get in, but *revocare gradum*, that was the point, for we were both excessively fatigued, and the day was drawing to a close. If one of us had got down, and the other had not been able to draw him out, it was very clear that he would have had to remain in the shaft all night, which would have been rather too romantic. Full of regret, that we could not examine the bottom of the shafts for any tools that might have been there, we reluctantly left the place in a deluge of rain, having first formed the determination of returning here with the means of examining the shaft in a satisfactory manner. On our return, we saw the locality from whence the asbestus had been taken for the construction of the furnace, of which there was an immense quantity in a broad vein.

It became now more probable than ever to me, that the mining localities visited to-day were links in the long line of De Soto's march. The great object of the Spanish discoverers was gold, and in all their expeditions persons accompanied them more or less versed in mining and metallurgy as they were understood in those days. The discovery of two troughs of micaceous slate at distant points, served to identify the parties who used them; and various defensive works of a similar character had been observed from the Chatahóochie in the 32^0 N. Lat., to the Towalliga Creek, which empties into the Ocmulgee; a few miles up which stream (the Towalliga) the remains of a Spanish picketted fort were found with a crucifix and a glass tube. The subject is certainly sufficiently curious to reward the industry and leisure of any one who would take up the

account of De Soto's march from Tampa Bay, and by means
of the Indian names of the districts he passed over, and the
rivers he crossed, trace his progress until he changed his
course to the west to gain the Mississippi.

August 29.—I rose rather stiff with my exertions of
yesterday, and being disinclined to ride, went out with my
hammer to look at the rocks in the neighbourhood.   The
prevailing rocks were talcose slate with quartz, and micaceous slate with garnets.   A vein of blue and brownish
primary marble, running N.N.E., crossed the country in
the neighbourhood ; but at the surface it was in lamina
not thick enough for useful purposes.   Gold in thin flakes
is washed out of many of the brooks.   Having an incipient
headache, and symptoms of sore-throat, from being too long
in wet clothes yesterday, I got some hot tea, and went to
bed early, but I had scarce composed myself to rest, when
some of my companions, accompanied by the acquaintances we had formed here, came to my room full of
concern for me to play at cards and smoke *to bear me
company*.   At my earnest entreaty they spared me the
infliction of the tobacco.   In about an hour, one of them
said, " I swar, I can't play no how if I can't smoke ;"
and all appearing to agree in that opinion, they rose, and
bade me good-night, thinking me, I have no doubt, a very
conceited and ungrateful person.

August 30.—After a good night's rest, I arose quite
well again, and my mind full of De Soto and the shaft
I had seen on the 28th, provided some ropes and tools to
explore it.   As soon as we had breakfasted, I put myself in
motion, accompanied by Mr. C——, junr., and an intelligent
young man named Dr. Isaacs, serving as assistant-surgeon
with the Tennessee State troops, in search of the excavations.   Acting as guide upon this occasion, I soon found

that on account of the rain on the previous day, I had not taken sufficient notice of the country, and we wandered about amongst the ridges a long time before we found the one we were in search of. On reaching the shaft, we let the Doctor down into it by means of our ropes, and I got down to the Laurel to hand up any thing he might find at the bottom. The first things he reported were a small grey snake, a lizard, and a fine large snail. Next he sent up the crank of the windlass, upon cutting into which and the other parts of the machinery, they were found to be made of oak, now quite rotten except at the core; all the pieces were very heavy and saturated with water, and the preservation in which we found them was probably owing to the sun's rays not penetrating into the shaft. Nothing else was found. The shaft was near twenty-five feet deep, and almost a perfect square. The rock at the bottom was quartz, decomposed into a sort of incoherent brown sandstone, on removing which the white quartz occurred again. The parietes of the shaft were also decomposed at the surface, and were of a ferruginous colour. The machinery was well but rudely made. It consisted of two stout sills into which the posts had been let, a windlass, with the mark still upon it that had been made by the rope, and a crank. The decomposition of the quartz to a brown sand, and its changed state at the transverse trench and the surface, placed the antiquity of the works beyond a doubt. I afterwards heard that an old pick-axe, almost rusted away, a crucible and a curious hatchet, with a very singular looking horse-shoe had also been found in the neighbourhood, but I did not see any of them. Before we left the ridge I visited the trench and furnace again, but observed nothing to change the opinions I had formed respecting them.

We reached our quarters again about 4 P.M., and after dinner my companions went to a ball-play of the Indians. It rained heavily, and hearing that some of the volunteers intended to go and kick up a row, I preferred to remain in my quarters and bring up my notes.   Those who went told me on their return that the Indians, fifteen on a side, were quite naked and rubbed over with slippery elm to prevent their opponents holding them fast, but the white men were so insolent to the Indians, and interfered so much with the game that everybody was disgusted.

August 31. — At 8 A.M. we left our quarters at Mr. Hunter's where we had been so comfortable, and under the guidance of a gold dealer who was going our road, shaped our course southerly by a bridle path to the mountains north of Dahlonega.   Pursuing our way over hills of talcose slate, we passed numerous promising looking lodes of quartz that had never been touched.   The face of the country was very pleasing, consisting of gracefully rounded knolls, wooded to the top, and slopes covered with ripe hazel nuts in valleys not so deep as those about Dahlonega.   When we had rode about eight miles and reached Notley River, we found three Indian women and a little boy, all squatted on their hams with their feet in the thick red clayey water washing for gold :—an old Cherokee squaw, a young married woman with her little boy of two years old, and a young girl of about sixteen.   The little fellow was sitting with his legs in the water, and amused himself by pouring dirty water on his thighs from a tin he held in his hand, whilst the shirt he had on was thoroughly wet and daubed with clay.   As soon as he saw us he began to cry out lustily.   His mother took him up and having pacified him, washed the tail of his shirt and of his little person too in the dirty water, and then clapped him down again wringing wet to get dry as well as he could. They had only collected about half-a-crown's worth of gold; and throwing them a few biscuits, we rode away leaving the little Cherokee as busy as ever with his tin. The Indians seem to be brought up from their infancy to disregard water.

From this place we rode on to Blairsville, a poor village in Union County, Georgia, near to which is a good gold vein, if one might judge from a very rich specimen which I was shown and purchased. In the course of the afternoon we crossed the Tchoiestoiéh fifteen times, which below changes its name to Notley. The country to the south, now increased in elevation, and on reaching Collins', a farmer at the foot of the mountains, which here towered to a great height before us, we stopped to refresh our horses and eat a little bread and milk. We had now ridden thirty miles, and had twelve miles further to go to our destination on the other side the mountains, with the certainty of having to ride a great part of the way in the dark. Being refreshed, we commenced the ascent of the chain which is a prolongation of the Nantayáyhlay ridge, and found it to consist as before of gneiss with garnets. The oldest rock in the series which I had examined in this elevated country appeared to be White-sides, which is composed of quartz and mica; to it succeeded gneiss with garnets, then micaceous slates with garnets, and lastly, talcose slates with gold veins. We reached the top of the ridge a little before sunset, but found the descent on the south side very bad, and our horses being jaded we had to proceed with great care. About one-third of the way down we came to a copious and beautiful spring of delicious water flowing in a great volume out of the rock. This was the head of the Tessentee River, and we were delighted to refresh ourselves at the very *punctum saliens* of a fine stream. It increased rapidly as we descended the mountain, and we crossed it various times.

Ere we reached the bottom night set in, and we had to ride six miles in the dark, repeatedly losing our way, crossing creeks and going up hill and down dale almost at random. It was 9 P.M. before we reached a place called Logan's in the Gold Region, and here we were glad to alight, tired, hungry, and sleepy. We had forded so many streams that we were thoroughly wet, and begged for a large fire to dry and warm ourselves by. The family were not at home, but the people we found in the house were obliging, and after a very humble supper, I was glad to lay down.

September 1.—I rose at 6 A.M., stiff and jaded, and after a miserable breakfast visited what is called Logan's Vein, which had been worked upon for some time; they were cutting a tunnel to the vein in order to drain the works, and had already proceeded about seven hundred feet. The vein looked curious in consequence of the decomposed pyrites, but it was very rich in some parts, and I obtained some fine specimens. From hence we rode to Loud's deposit, from whence so much gold was reported to have been taken. This was in a longitudinal valley, running N.N.E. and S.S.W. containing a deposit similar to that which is washed for gold in the small valleys near Dahlonega. A very great portion of it had not yet been dug. Considering the intrinsic value of so much fertile bottom land, and the great expense attending these diggings and washings, I imagine the profits attending them will in the end be found to be very small. Indeed I heard of no one retiring with a fortune from this golden pursuit.

Having examined this locality, we called at a Mrs.

Upton's, and got some milk, and bread, and peaches that were very acceptable, and from thence proceeded to examine the Chastell's Vein, a powerful lode, and the most promising one I had yet seen.   It ran N.N.E. and S.S.W., appeared to be all good, was of great dimensions, and laid on the brow of a hill in an admirable situation for quarrying.   The ore here was frequently agatized and abounded in ferruginous oxides, was extremely brittle, split into slices, the sides of which were thoroughly discoloured with some iron, as though it had been subjected to intense heat.   I followed the vein a mile to the south, where there has been a great deal of labour wasted in useless works.   Tunnels badly made, a furnace erected and attempts to calcine ore, many heaps of which were left about.   The vein looked very favourable, every part of the ore appearing to contain more or less gold, and was fissile and ferruginous, as I had seen it further north.   Upon opening some apparently solid masses of quartz, it was partly calcedonized in the centre, and was cellular; the cavities were also sometimes filled with pure sulphur, in quantities as large as could be heaped upon a shilling.   In many instances the quartz had a stalactitic appearance, and in some parts was so porous that water ran freely through large pieces.   All these appearances indicated a state of solution in which the quartz appears to have been at some time or other.

I had before observed another appearance in the quartz at some of the localities where it contained auriferous cubes of sulphuret of iron.   On opening masses of it, square cavities appeared into which cubes would exactly have fitted, but without any other appearance of a cube having been there, the cavity being perfectly clean and without any ferruginous taint, so that there was no stain or appearance of cubes having been there, and of having been absorbed; and it is difficult to

conceive of quartzose matter having under any circumstances a tendency to form empty cubical spaces exactly
resembling those filled by solid cubes. The talcose slate
which formed the walls of this vein was hard and black,
and looked like iron ore. Every thing here had the
appearance of having been acted upon by intense heat.
There is a fine waterfall of fifteen feet near the vein.

CHAPTER LX.

ARRIVE AT DAHLONEGA AGAIN.—A CURIOUS MARRIAGE.—THE FALLS OF
TOLULA.—RETURN TO FORT HILL.—MR. CH***'S VILLA AT PORTMAN
SHOAL.—AGREEABLE MODE OF LIVING OF SOUTHERN GENTLEMEN.—REACH
GREENVILLE.—FLAT ROCK.—ASHEVILLE.

FROM hence I rode to Dahlonega in a heavy rain, where
I was fortunate enough to get a room to myself and a fire
to dry my clothes. At the supper table we had an odd
assemblage of guests, with the usual sprinkling of dirty
stage-coach drivers; but exactly opposite to where I sat was
a rather pretty young lady, about eighteen years old, dressed
in black, and next to her a common looking man enough,
something under thirty. He had not been shaved that day,
and had certainly not been made up for company. He
looked rather grave, but she ate a very hearty supper, and
behaved with the usual *disinvoltura* of females without
refinement. I had been let into the secret of this pair, and
took my place opposite to them on purpose. She was a
young person from the low country who had lost her
parents, and had come to the mountains *three* days before
to enjoy the cool air, with the reputation of having inherited
one hundred and fifty thousand dollars. At the tavern she
had formed an acquaintance with this man who was an itinerant doctor. Nobody knew any thing more of him but that
he called himself doctor. Fortunately, or unfortunately for
him, another traveller who was a methodist preacher stopped

at the tavern in the course of the morning, and dined at the public table. They became acquainted with his character by his asking the blessing. About three in the afternoon, the doctor asked him and the landlord to walk up stairs, and having given him his instructions, in five minutes he was married to the young lady, she being nothing loth. Here was a vulgar man, probably without a dollar in the world, suddenly transformed into the husband of a reputed rich, and at any rate youthful person, who did not think it worth his while to shave himself on his marriage day. Whilst the lady, who possibly might have commanded the best connection in the country, if she had waited a little, married a fellow of a low cast, of whom she knew nothing, and took her seat unconcernedly at the public supper-table amongst stage drivers and all sorts of persons, at that peculiar moment when women of refinement shrink from the gaze of their nearest friends.

September 2.—After breakfast I rode to Cane Creek, and paid a visit to Mr. Samuel, who accompanied me to look at the Grave's vein. This was found running N.N.E. and S.S.W. in the talcose slate at the bottom of the gravel deposit, which here formed an area of perhaps five acres. It was full of pyrites, and contained a good deal of gold; but no lumps of native gold like those found when washing the gravel had yet been discovered in it; a circumstance probably owing to the surface of the areas, where the valleys now are being so much lowered; for these valleys contain the ruins of rocks which were once at a much higher level, and the veins in the rocks which have been broken up may have contained the lump-gold which is found. I had previously observed, both in Virginia, North Carolina, and in this part of the Gold Region, that as the veins descend they became more pyritiferous, the gold being disseminated in thin lamina in the cubes. Indeed, in the deepest mines the vein often becomes a mass of pyrites without any quartzose matter.

At dinner, I again sat opposite to the bride, who was not in the least degree abashed, but seemed to eat voraciously of all the coarse dishes near her. In the afternoon I walked out to take a last look at the neighbourhood. The situation of Dahlonega is a very good one, being built on a fine knoll sloping to the east, with the ground rising agreeably to the west. It possessed a rather imposing-looking granitic building, called the Mint, with a brick Court-house in the centre of the square, and a few tolerable-looking private buildings, all which gave to the town an air of pretension that was indifferently borne out by the inhabitants. There were two excellent springs of water at the village. The Court-house was built on a broad vein of hornblende slate, and the soil of the public square was impregnated with small specks of gold. Dahlonega, which the Cherokees pronounce *Tahlónekáy*, means *yellow;* al-luding to the gold found there.

September 3.—As soon as I had breakfasted, I rode out of the town, heartily tired of the vulgarity of the people, and the dirt of the tavern; and taking a bridle-path which conducted us by an agreeable shady road to Logan's, we made our way from thence to the upper part of Duke's Creek, where the huts or pens were found which are mentioned at page 257. The locality is rather a curious one, being a deposit in a circular area of about four acres, exceedingly flat, as though it had been the bottom of a lake. With the intention of draining it, some persons had cut a trench through it, of about eight feet wide and ten feet deep, and thus discovered the pens. The person we took along with us as a guide said, that four or five pens were found in this trench close to each other, forming one structure with doors cut from one to the other.   The pens were only raised three or four logs high, and the logs were notched into each other with an axe, the ends of the logs being chipped off by way of finish.   They had no roofs to them.   A part of the logs were yet sticking in the bank of the trench, having been chopped off in digging it, so that parts of the pens were yet covered up.   The lower logs were close to the slate upon which the deposit rested, and the gravel inside of the pens contained a little gold ; but whether the gravel containing gold, had fallen into the pens after they were set upon the slate, or whether it was put into them afterwards, is matter of conjecture.   Taking the facts that were related to us and what we saw together, it appeared not improbable that these pens were placed here merely as cáches to conceal something it was convenient to leave behind for awhile.   Perhaps those who made them, afterwards changed their purpose, and abandoned them, for nothing appears to have been found except a crucible and a stone trough, like that which I saw at the old furnace, and which would appear to identify the party which had been at work at both places.   The pens when found were covered with three feet of alluvial matter which might very well have been brought there by floods in the course of two or three hundred years.   I brought away a part of one of the logs with the mark of the axe, where its end was cut off, but it was so rotten, that I doubted whether I could preserve it.   From this place we rode to Richardson's, and having refreshed ourselves, continued our journey on to Clarksville.

September 4.—Having breakfasted, we mounted our horses and rode to the house of Mr. Mathews, a southern gentleman,

who had got a pretty retreat at a place called Acoa. Here we
came upon an agreeable change, a genteel well-bred family
at breakfast surrounded with every comfort, and were
received in the most hospitable manner. Mr. Mathews
shewed me some fine specimens of gold found on the
surface of his estate. Lumps of quartz with large thick
lamina of argentiferous-looking gold in them. I had never
seen such rich specimens before. He was kind enough to
present me with one, as well as with another where native
gold appears in the hornblende slate. Having informed
him of my intention of visiting the Falls of Tolula, he was
obliging enough to accompany me, and after riding a few
miles through the woods, we suddenly came upon a very
grand and wild scene, an immense chasm or ravine, one
thousand four hundred feet wide, through which the river
precipitated itself over various falls and inclined planes.
At the edge of the ravine were some bare rocks of micaceous slate, very conveniently situated for observing this
striking scene, especially from a point called the Devil's
Pulpit. The escarpment immediately below had a vertical
depth of eight hundred feet, so that great caution was
required in moving about. The top of the ravine as well
as its sides were covered with trees, and by the assistance
of the shrubs growing there we got safely to the bottom,
and examined two beautiful falls to the north.

The river here runs north and south, then inclines to
the east to be still further precipitated; but the whole
descent of the river is distributed through a course of
several miles, the most interesting points of which are the
two falls alluded to. Of these the lower one falls about
one hundred feet, the upper part of it for about sixty feet,
being at an angle of 45⁰, whilst the lower part has a
perpendicular pitch of forty feet. The upper or most

northern fall is about twenty feet high. Betwixt these two at the bottom of the ravine, which is here about two hundred feet wide, is a large pool in which a young clergyman, a Mr. Hawthorne, had been very recently drowned. Being heated and fatigued with getting down, he went into it to bathe, and disappeared almost as soon as he had entered it, having probably been carried down in an eddy, for I observed the rocks in this ravine were much worn into pot-holes, like those at the White Water, and this pool appeared to me to have been excavated in the same manner.

Every circumstance in this ravine concurred to shew that the water had worn its way through the mountain by retrocession. Many persons who observe rivers gliding tranquilly through mountains, as in the highlands on Hudson's River, jump at once to the conclusion that rivers in such cases flow through natural fissures ; but the falls of the White Water and the Tolula shew step by step the process by which a cascade,—once perhaps with a vertical height of one thousand five hundred feet,—gradually, by retrocession, wears itself a channel back into the land, forming inclined planes and vertical falls according to the mineral resistance opposed to it, over which is distributed the entire projectile force of the torrent.

Having examined every accessible point, we reached the top again greatly fatigued, and having sketched the several features around, I mounted again, and went to see a band of blue limestone running through the country about five miles off N.N.E. S.S.W. It appeared to me to be a continuation of the band which runs south of the south-west mountain in Virginia, not far from Montpelier, Mr. Madison's seat in Virginia. Here taking leave of Mr. Mathews, we made for the Tocoa falls, which I had before seen, and having taken a passing look at the misty spray, which looks like the dishevelled hair of a mountain deity, we pursued our way to Mr. Jarret's, where after riding two tedious hours in the dark we arrived.

September 5.—Having taken an early breakfast I mounted, and once more crossed the Tugaloo. Having left behind the micaceous rocks which prevail where the Chatuga range begins, we now came to the gneiss through which the Tugaloo runs, a stream which is formed by the junction of the Chatuga and the Tolula. Our route, for about twenty miles, now lay along one of those barren ridges of gneiss which abound here with the heads of tributaries of the Savannah running parallel to it. After a fatiguing ride we crossed the Seneca, another branch of the Savannah, and at length reached Fort Hill, the hospitable residence of Mr. C———, where being received in the most agreeable manner, I took possession once more of my old quarters, and having made my toilette, took my place at the dinner table with this charming family. In the evening we had music and conversation as usual on the portico.

Here I remained, partaking of the most pleasing hospitalities, and making occasional excursions until the morning of the 8th, when, having breakfasted, I took leave of the family and drove into Pendleton to take my place in the stage for Greenville; but when the stage came to the door, my luggage, which had been sent on from Fort Hill by a negro boy was missing, and the driver refusing to wait I was left behind. The exchange from a most delightful house for a filthy country tavern was not agreeable, and the suspense in which I was kept annoyed me not a little. Having waited till 3 P.M. without my luggage appearing, the landlord of the tavern expressed an opinion that the negro boy had absconded with it into Georgia.   In the course of half-an-hour I had the satisfaction of finding that the whole village was quite sure of it; persons even were found who knew the boy, and said he was a bad fellow, and had once before tried to run away.   I had no special reasons for suspecting so great a calamity had befallen me, but certainly it was true that the negro had taken five hours to come five miles, and had not yet appeared; and so as every body was quite sure the boy had gone by some other road to meet some of his accomplices, I came gradually to adopt the universal opinion that my locks had been forced before this, all my money, and what I valued still more, all my rich and curious specimens of gold and other minerals, all my vocabularies of the Cherokee and Creek languages, and all my instruments, papers, clothes and linen, had been distributed amongst various black amateurs, and that I never had been in such a fix before, having lost what I never could replace, and having been the innocent cause of depriving Mr. C—— of a valuable slave.

It being necessary to act, I procured a constable, and hastening back to Fort Hill related my "pitiful story." Inquiry was immediately made about the departure of the boy, and at once the whole mystery was cleared up, and I found myself happily relieved from the contemplation of so many inconveniences as I should have found it difficult to reconcile myself to.   It appeared that Mr. C——'s son, before we left Fort Hill in the morning, told the boy to follow me with my luggage, but without telling him where to follow me to; and as this was the negro boy who had brought my luggage from Picken's Court-house on my first visit to Fort Hill, he very naturally supposed I was going back there, and had accordingly gone in that direction. This was a solution of the mystery which had not been thought of, and a messenger was immediately despatched on horseback after the boy. In due time I had the pleasure of seeing my trunks brought back in the most approved order, and to this incident was indebted for another most happy evening with my hospitable friends.

September 9.—There being no stage-coach for some days, I determined to pay a visit to another distinguished South Carolinian, with whom I had been long acquainted, and rose early, and after breakfast again took leave, and Mr. C— being kind enough to lend me his carriage, I went in it to Mr. Ch—'s, whom I had met at church on the 20th of August. After driving eight miles through the woods I reached Mr. Ch—'s villa at Portman Shoal, where I was most kindly received by himself and his two charming daughters. The house of this distinguished gentleman was beautifully situated upon a knoll in the tranquil forest, with the Seneca River flowing in a graceful serpentine course from north to south. I had never seen a place with finer capabilities for improvement, and his house was one of the most curious and pleasing structures I had ever been in. The original intention of Mr. Ch— was merely to build a few log cabins, in two rows separated by an avenue perhaps twenty feet wide. But becoming attached to this quiet retreat, he put a general roof over them all, and added at the west end a hall or vestibule, with a parlour on the south side, and a good dining-room on the north, giving to the whole the form of a Latin cross.

The log cabins had now become spacious bed-rooms, 20 feet by 18, all of which opened into what was the former avenue, but was now become a very handsome hall, 80 feet long and 20 feet wide, through which the breezes circulated east and west from the portico. This hall was wainscoted, and the doors and ceiling were all of plain wood-work, the doors of the bed-rooms being capped with a plain gothic lanceolate ornament, so that the hall, when pacing it, resembled a cloister.

The effect of the whole was very pleasing, and nothing could be more commodious than this arrangement for a family that did not like the inconvenience of staircases. The apartments for servants, the coach-house, stables, and out-houses, were a little detached from the family mansion. At dinner we were joined by some gentlemen of the neighbourhood. The day passed very pleasantly. Mr. Ch— was what I had always known him to be, full of information and pleasantry. Once occupying a large share of the public attention as a statesman and speaker of the House of Representatives, he now appeared disposed to retire altogether from the political world. At 10 P.M. I retired to one of the nice bed-rooms, where I found everything most conveniently and comfortably arranged.

September 10.—After breakfast I accompanied Mr. and Miss Ch— to the Episcopal Church at Pendleton, where, as upon a previous occasion, I saw a most respectable congregation, and again admired the well chosen and umbrageous situation of the church. In the afternoon we dined at Colonel H—'s, who had married the daughter of a gentleman whom I knew a great many years ago. I was very much struck with the beauty of Mrs. H—'s children. It is very clear that the real gentry of America are to be found amongst the landholders. The dinner was a very handsome one, and the wines various and excellent. After passing a very pleasant evening, we returned home in the rain.

September 11.—A delightful morning, but a rather hot sun, which kept us in the house. We however got engaged in an agreeable conversation about the State of South

Carolina in old times, when the whites were contending with the Indians, the Cherokee language, and the mineralogy of the country. Mr. Ch—'s daughters were superior women, eager for information and highly intellectual. In the afternoon we drove six miles through the woods to Colonel Pinkney's to dinner. Here we met Colonel H— and other gentlemen, had a most luxurious dinner, and the greatest profusion of fine French and German wines. I was quite surprised at their excellence and variety, and could not but express my astonishment to our host. He informed me that every gentleman in the State lived in that manner, that the price of his wines never gave him any concern, being only interested in the quality ; adding, that when his crops of rice and cotton were consigned abroad, he always directed the amount of sales of ten barrels of rice, or ten bales of cotton, or some other number, to be laid out in particular wines *of the finest vintages.* These gentlemen have selected the most lovely summer retreats for themselves, and contrive to enjoy life in a very agreeable manner. You never hear the prices of things talked of at their tables, or of money being held out as the great object of human existence; they ridicule this in the northern commercial classes, but enjoy what they have without talking about it, and surprise an Englishman with their knowledge of European politics and letters, and their liberal and polite attentions to him. We returned from this agreeable visit by moonlight.

September 12.—Notwithstanding a natural inclination to indulge in such good quarters, I managed to rise early and take a walk before breakfast. The prevailing rock here is gneiss, with occasional superincumbent beds of micaceous slate. The soil is red, and has been formed by ancient decomposed talcose slate. The forest around was thickly growing up with underwood. In all the districts where I have been, which are now possessed by the Indians, the woods are open, generally with a few trees sparsely growing here and there, in consequence of the Indians firing the woods annually in order to increase the herbage, and that they may better see to pursue their game. But as soon as the Indians abandon a district, and that destructive practice ceases, the underwood begins to grow up again, as it is now doing here. After breakfast, I took leave of this kind and pleasing family, and went in Mr. Ch—'s carriage to Pendleton. At 1 P.M. got into a four-horse stage for Greenville, where I found the Rev. Mr. F—, an agreeable person and a good scholar. A little after sun-set we reached Greenville, and stopped at a low dirty tavern, a sad exchange for the comforts I had left behind me. Here I laid down until midnight, having learnt that a stage-coach would leave the place for the mountains about that time, which would give me an opportunity of crossing them once more in their extreme breadth, through Buncombe County, in North Carolina, to the Oonáykay chain, which separates that State from Tennessee.

At 1 A.M. we started on a beautiful moonlight morning, and rather cold. It took us four hours to make the first ten miles, where there was a good-looking house, called Lynch's; but I was taken to a miserable dirty breakfast at a place two miles further. The country here began to ascend rapidly, and we travelled over the gneiss again. Higher up the rock was an imperfect granite, consisting of quartz and mica, the last mineral being in seams as it is found in gneiss, and sometimes containing feldspar in a state of decomposition. I observed no regular granite. After reaching the summit of the chain called Blue Ridge, the rock changed to what is the equivalent of the Chatuga range, quartz and white mica in large bright plates.   At 2 P.M. we reached Flat Rock, where we got a tolerable dinner at a house where persons from the low country resort in the hot season.   From hence we continued on table-land to Asheville, which we reached about half-past 8 P.M., and stopped at a hotel, which appeared to be filled with southern people and their black servants.   Here I succeeded in getting something to eat and a room for myself to sleep in.

CHAPTER LXI.

BLACK LEGS AND GAMBLERS.—THE AUTHOR EXCLUDES THEM FROM HIS
ROOM WITH THE BEDSTEAD.—FRENCH BROAD RIVER.—WARM SPRINGS.—
A FILTHY HOTEL.—THERMAL MINERAL WATERS.—ROCKS OF THE OONAYKAY
CHAIN.

September 14.—What a merry race of people the
negroes are.   The house was overrun with black servants
belonging to southern families, all well dressed and well
fed, and more merry, and noisy, and impudent than any
servants I had ever seen.   At the gentlemen's at whose
houses I had lately been staying, every thing announced
order, cleanliness, and cheerful refinement ; here boisterous
disorder, dirt, and coarse vulgarity prevailed. Many of the
white *gentlemen* I met in the breakfast-room seemed to
know a little of every thing except genteel society and
manners ; spitting, smoking, cursing and swearing in the
most frightful manner, gave them a bad pre-eminence even
over the negroes.   By the gold chains about their necks,
and the thorough swell manner they put on, it was obvious
they were gamblers and blacklegs by profession, which I
found out in the course of the day was really the case,
being favoured by one of them with an invitation to join
them at cards.   After a so-and-so breakfast, with a
thorough-bass accompaniment of spitting and hawking by
those around me, I sallied out and joyfully got into the
open air.

This was a pretty place, a table-land of irregular surface, hemmed in by lofty mountains wooded to the summit, with occasional spots of great fertility. The strata of the table-land were on their edges, some of them a fine-grained gneiss, others micaceous and talcose slates and quartzose sandstones, running N.N.E. and S.S.W. All were decomposed to some depth, cohering very little together, and admitting of a sharp iron being thrust down into them. Immediately at the surface, the mica was altogether decomposed, and the soil in consequence had become red for an inch or two, and sometimes to greater depths. A great profusion of pieces of mica slate with garnets was strewed about in a high state of decomposition ; the garnets also were decomposed, and nothing left of them occasionally but thin plates, as the gold is sometimes left in auriferous pyrites. The surface of this table-land appeared to have been greatly lowered, and it is probable that the slate with garnets had once been in place here.

From an eminence called Mount Pisgah, which terminated the spur of a ridge running north and south across this table-land to the Oonáykay chain, there was a very fine view of the country to be obtained. In many parts, the surface of the table-land was modified just as that of the Gold Region is, into small valleys separating round hills, with a deposit of clay and gravel in the depressions through which the streams flow. I passed a very pleasant day out of doors, but my miseries began when I returned to my lodgings at night. The house seemed to be crammed full of noisy, spitting, smoking, swearing, Georgia planters and gamblers of the worst class. I, therefore, determined to defer my examination of the mountains in this vicinity to another opportunity, and took my place in a stage-coach, that was to go a little after midnight to the Warm Springs close to

the Oonáykay chain.   The next step was to secure myself
from any interruption during the short time I should
remain ; so giving a dirty male negro waiter who made the
beds a quarter of a dollar to bring me a couple of candles
and some supper to my room, and promising him a further
fee if he would call me at one in the morning, I retired to
my room, and finding there was no lock to the door, I
fortified myself there by putting my trunks against it, and
drawing my bedstead, which was a low wooden one, to the
same place.

As soon as I had supped I laid down, flattering myself
that I had nothing to apprehend from intruders.   It was
well I took these precautions, for about ten I was awoke
by somebody pushing against the door from the other side ;
and calling out to know what was the matter, a voice,
which I recognised to be that of the swell who had asked
me to play at cards, answered, " Stranger, what in h—l
have you got agin the door ?"   Upon which I said : " You
had better not push any harder, for there is a loaded rifle
nigh the door and it may go off."   He muttered something
to another fellow who was with him, and said, " I wish I
may be   *   *   *   *   if I ever seed a man cut sich
bl—d shines as this afore."   This incomprehensible
opposition which they met to the opening of the door
completely *stumped* these worthies, and they went
away.

September 15.—The negro called me up faithfully and
was as much puzzled as my visitors of last night were
when he tried to open the door ; but I got up and let him
in, and explained my tactics to him, at which he laughed
immoderately.   " By goly, Massa," said he, " dat beats all
de patent locks I nebber seed before.   Dems two sharp
fellers, dem two gemmen, I tell you, Massa, dey comes here

ebery year, and got a big room at de toder end of de house, and dey gives de gemmen what comes from Georgy and Sout Caroliny cegars and brandy, and by goly dey takes it out of em wit de cards. Dey plays all night long and all day too, and dey want you Massa to play, but by goly you lock em out wit de bedstead. If dat don't beat all!" And then he laughed and turned up the whites of his eyes, and diverted me so exceedingly, that I gave him half a dollar.

I now got into the stage-coach again for the Warm Springs, and found a family in it with two young children and three negro women: the morning was cold. The negresses were tolerably well dressed as far as their backs were concerned, but one of them being ordered to get some water at a place where the coach stopped, I observed she had neither shoes, nor stockings, nor hat. This appeared to be the custom, and probably in the low country, where it is so hot, they prefer to be so lightly clad, but the poor creature shivered and evidently suffered very much from the cold air of the mountains.

After leaving Asheville a few miles, we struck the French Broad River, a tributary of the Tennessee, and followed it on the right bank for thirty miles down the channel it had made in the mountains. This was a remarkably interesting part of the country. The gneiss rocks were on their edges dipping S.E. and running from N.N.E. to S.S.E., and the river which is very shallow, and varies in breadth from one hundred and fifty to six hundred feet, crossed them nearly at right angles, so that it was one continuous rapid, the water breaking against the edges of the gneiss and foaming and clamouring during the whole of its descent, which was at least six hundred feet, the fall being more or less about seventeen feet to the mile. The road along the bank was in many places very narrow, scarcely admitting of two carriages to pass. The channel of the river had evidently been worn by the usual agency of pot-holes, numerous vestiges of which appeared.

For the first twenty-nine miles from Asheville, the rock was gneiss, to this succeeded clay slate, and on approaching the Warm Springs a striped sort of quartzose rock appeared. At these springs, which are prettily situated in a valley excavated by the river, a strong bed of inorganic limestone came in, blue with seams of white carbonate. We were near sixteen hours in driving thirty-eight miles, so that I had ample opportunities of walking as much as I pleased, and making observations, and have seldom been more gratified with a day's work. This road through the mountains is the avenue of a great commerce betwixt the Western and Northern States. I met this day no less than six droves of horses and mules in high condition, going from Kentucky to a southern market, and was told that last year seven thousand horses and mules passed through this avenue alone, and about eighty thousand fat hogs.

Kentucky is a fertile country, inhabited by a manly and industrious community, and the immense crops of bread stuffs that they produce exhibit their effects in the shape of horses, mules, and fat hogs. The public attention also was beginning to be turned in that State to breeding the short-horned Durham cattle, introduced by Mr. Clay, who preeminent as a statesman, and the intelligent patron of every branch of agriculture, had seen in what direction the great resources of the State could be profitably turned, and did not confine himself to encouraging the farming interest with precepts embodied in eloquent speeches, but went practically to work, selecting the finest animals from the most celebrated English breeders, and preserving under his own discriminating eye, their fine qualities with great judgment and care. The State was thus annually reaping great benefits from his spirited efforts to advance its interests, and certainly nothing could surpass the affectionate devotion which the Kentuckians seemed to bear to this distinguished man.

This water of the Warm Springs, as the name imported, was thermal, about 95^0 Fahr. The taste was agreeable, and its properties nearly the same as the other thermal waters in this elevated Belt. The situation had great natural beauties, and in proper hands it would be a very attractive place to retire to during the hot months. But all these places seemed to have fallen into the hands of low ignorant persons, who had neither capital nor even a decent taste in the promotion of human comfort. Certainly, at this hotel, nothing like comfort was to be obtained for money; yet gentlemen of some distinction were here who at home probably live amidst much refinement. I found Judge G—, of North Carolina and his family, and other persons of great merit, submitting to the most abominable filth and dirt, and all sorts of discomfort, without saying one word about it. Probably they had discovered that it was useless to complain. In fact they were very few in number to the overpowering quantity of sheer blackguards and gamblers with whom they were obliged to eat and to mingle pêle-mêle. A room was assigned to me, and the very sight of the walls, covered with tobacco spittle and worse filth, turned my stomach; but it was the only one to be obtained, and I owed this privilege to the interference of a gentleman who had some influence with the landlord, and who conceded it to me with a sort of gracious manner that indicated the intrinsic value of the privilege.

As this was to be my citadel, it was my first care to make as much of it as I could, and having given the dirty negro, with a ragged hat on his head without any brim to it, who shewed me up to the room, half-a-dollar to get me clean sheets and towels, I stood over him directing him how to make the bed. Smelling some tobacco, I asked him who was in the next room, and he answered : " Some gemmilmen, massa." " I suppose they are playing at cards ?" said I. " Yes, massa," said he grinning, " De gemmilmen play cards all day, play cards all night sometime." So that I found I had got a room adjoining to that of the professional gamblers. I saw with great satisfaction, however, that there was a lock to my door, so having got my bed made, and water and towels, and a small rickety table and one chair, and my luggage around me, I entered into a close alliance with my black friend with the brimless hat, locked the door, put the key in my pocket, and went down stairs. I was delighted to meet with a gentleman of the respectability and intelligence of Judge G—, and we walked out together on the hills. The rocks alternated a good deal, quartz and decomposing feldspar, and talcose slate were the principal minerals. The view down upon the valleys and river was beautiful, with a very mountainous country all around. The supper-table was better provided than I expected it would be ; some ladies were there, and for an hour afterwards we got up a pleasant conversation. As I found the respectable families retired early to their rooms, I followed their example, and getting blacky to give me a couple of candles and a pair of snuffers with one handle, I proceeded to write some letters and bring up my notes, after which feeling sleepy, I got into my bed and soon fell asleep.

September 16.—About day-light I was awoke by shrieks of laughter and loud shouting in the next room. The gamblers were evidently most of them half-drunk, and after listening awhile to their execrations and their bawling, I looked around, but withdrew my eyes as quickly as possible from the bedaubed walls. I could willingly have laid longer in bed, but all my senses were so offended, that I hastened to make my toilette and sallied out to the hills, forgetting as soon as I could, in the balmy air of the morning and in the fine natural scenery, the disgusting objects I had escaped from.

The lime stone here appeared to be a broad vein running N.N E. across the river. Some of the hills consisted of immense masses of coarse quartz ; others had feldspar in them, in which grains of quartz seemed to be imbedded. Varieties of slate alternated with these minerals. On returning to the hotel, I took a bath, the thermometer standing in the water at 95^0. It resembled very much the water at the Warm Springs, Virginia. After breakfasted, I sallied out again and had a good stroll in the mountains. The rocks which rise from the eastward appeared to conform to the ordinary succession of the primary beds, gneiss, mica, slate, clay-slate, clouded quartz rocks and huge masses of quartz stained with iron. The feldspar here had the peculiarity of containing grains of quartz imbedded in it, as though the quartz had been exposed to attrition before it was enveloped. The limestone which I had before observed crossing the river N.N.E. and S.S.W. appeared to me to be a continuation of the same limestone dyke I saw near the Hiwassee and in other places. It observed the same course and maintained about the same distance from the Oonáykay chain. Huge bluffs of it stood out near the river, and a voluminous spring issued from it on the left bank of the French Broad ; an immense quantity of air came up with the water, which I took to be atmospheric, as it was not sensibly present in the water after dipping it up. The weather was charming, and I returned exceedingly pleased with the country, and quite hungry.

As I approached the house, all the disgusting objects I had fled from in the morning rose to my view, and if I could have found something to eat, I should have been tempted to lay down in the woods all night, for the company of wild beasts is to be preferred to that of human beings when so depraved and filthy. However, I made rather better out than I expected at the tea-table. At this place, tea appeared to be considered as the ladies' meal; the table was spruced up a little, there was less dirt and noise, and the tea and sugar were tolerably good, with plenty of good milk. As I did not trouble them at dinner, my ally with the brimless hat brought me something substantial. In fact, it was the only meal where comfort was to be had, for the worst blackguards appeared to be awed by the presence of females. How much society is influenced by them, and how immeasurably superior they are in this country to the men !

September 17.—As usual, I rose early in the morning, and after breakfast, having procured a horse, rode to the outward edge of Oonáykay chain, below the Paint Rock and the Chimney-top. On leaving the western edge of the limestone, a glossy shale came in, then sandstone with loose shale beneath. What they called the Paint Rock, was a huge bluff of sandstone overlying shale, which beetled over the narrow road that was closely hemmed in by the river. The Indians had left some figures on it, as they have done on the sandstone bluffs of the Upper Mississippi. The Chimney-top is another bluff of sandstone with shales intervening, which give it a striped appearance. Limestones appeared now frequently in the hills; but sandstones and shales were the prevailing strata. These beds divide the fossiliferous beds of East Tennessee from the primary rocks, and are the representatives in this country of the Cambrian Rocks of Professor Sedgwick. Having ascertained that the Oonáykay chain was composed of these beds, I returned towards evening to the hotel; but before coming to an anchor, went about two miles up a very pretty but narrow ravine, with a stream coming brawling down it which contained red trout. It was by this ravine, only from twenty to thirty yards broad, that the celebrated Daniel Boon is said to have passed through the mountains for the first time into Kentucky. It was well fitted for his purpose, as it avoids the usual gap through the mountains, and would afford him shelter, wood, and water, and concealment from the Indians. It was perhaps an important consideration too for him, that the smoke of his fire could not be visible to those out of the ravine, who were not very near to him. In the evening, I shook hands with the few pleasant acquaintances I had formed, and retired early to my room to pack my specimens, and bring up my notes preparatory to my departure in the morning.

September 18.—Having got an early breakfast, I walked out to look around me for the last time. The thermal waters here could be traced continuously on a line for about one hundred and fifty yards, coming through the limestone in a N.N.E. direction. On my return in the stage to Asheville, I had an opportunity of again tracing the primary rocks in the descending order. Limestone, quartzose rocks, slates, imperfect gneiss to compact gneiss at Asheville. On reaching the hotel there, I found the same vulgar crowd ; but, as I had a friend at Court in the merry negro, who had been so amused with my patent lock, I got a room to myself, and something to eat alone. The stage was to start for Rutherfordton, in North Carolina, a little after midnight, so securing my place in it, I laid down for two or three hours.

CHAPTER LXII.

DEPART FOR RUTHERFORDTON.—BRUTALITY OF STAGE-COACH PASSENGERS.—
MAGNIFICENT SCENERY OF THE MOUNTAIN DEFILE.—REACH RUTHERFORD-
TON. — VISIT BECHLER, A GERMAN COINER.—MAJOR FORNEY'S MINING
ESTABLISHMENT.—GOLD VEINS AND DEPOSITS.

September 19.—On taking my place in a corner of the
stage-coach at 1 A.M., I found three male passengers
besides myself, and certainly they turned out to be three of
the most consummate blackguards I ever had the misfortune to be in company with. Their language was infamous;
I had not conceived it possible for human beings to make
themselves so detestably odious, or to express themselves in
such a horribly profane manner as they did. They had
been drinking and gambling up to the moment they got
into the stage, and when they got tired with screaming and shouting, they began the most beastly practices,
and made the stage-coach so offensive, that the instant the
dawn began to appear I stopped the coach, just as we
entered the defile, or " gap," as it is called, and apprized
the driver of my intention to proceed the rest of the way
down the mountain on foot. As the descent through the
defile was precipitous, the stage-coach was obliged to
proceed very slowly, so that I had sufficient leisure to look
at the rocks, and enjoy the magnificent scenery for eight
miles from the summit of the mountain to Harris's, where

we were to breakfast. I had a charming cool walk, free from the offensive noise of those execrable villains, and wished from the bottom of my heart, that this noble defile with its magnificent escarpments, instead of being only eight miles long, had extended all the way to Ruther-fordton, where I proposed stopping. The rocks towards the upper part of the " gap" were gneiss, with an imperfect sort of granite at the bottom.

The breakfast-house, which I reached some time before the stage-coach, turned out to be a clean place, and the landlord and landlady consequently respectable people, so true it is that cleanliness is allied to Godliness. My first care was to let them know what sort of wretches were coming on in the stage, and what their conduct had been. I had gathered from their infamous colloquies, that one of them was named Ruff, another Alston, and the third they called Doctor. The landlord knew who they were, and said, " There wasn't one of them was fit to carry guts to a bar." To understand this estimate of their manners, it is necessary to understand that the country people, when they take a bear cub, frequently tame it, and chain it in the yard, where it is the business of some negro-boy to carry the entrails of any other animal to it for its food. I gave the landlord a sketch of the long journey I had performed, and told him that I had not met with such consummate scoundrels on the whole route. This procured me the satisfaction of eating my breakfast alone, and of learning that it was the intention of the landlady (who was a South Carolina woman, and a countrywoman of these worthies, who, I was told, came from Winnsborough, in Fairfield County, of that State) to give them a little of her mind on the subject of their conduct, and to make the lesson more impressive, she began by giving them a very bad breakfast, which calling forth remonstrances, she entered upon the subject, *con amore.*

On re-entering the stage, I was surprised with an unexpected abatement of their insolence: the most offensive of the three, Ruff, (who was very much in want of three additional letters to his name) got to the top of the stage, and I saw no more of him until we arrived at Rutherfordton. The Doctor and the other fellow, having found out that I was a friend of Mr. C —, in South Carolina, and that I knew who they were, and had it in my power to expose them, were submissive and civil. I was happy to be relieved from their odious society by reaching Rutherfordton at half-past 1 P.M., where, to my great pleasure, I got a good room to myself at Mr. Twitty's, a very intelligent and obliging landlord. Here I made a clean and comfortable repast, during which Twitty crowned my satisfaction by producing a bottle of excellent London brown stout, of which he had received a hamper. Such a long period had elapsed since I had met with such a treat, that this noble bottle, of which I took every drop, made me forget all past annoyances; and after taking a very pleasant walk in the environs of this pleasing village, I retired to a nice clean bed.

September 20.—The morning was beautiful, but cool enough to make a nice wood fire agrceable in my bedroom, which was not too well protected against the wind. After breakfast, I walked a few miles to visit a German, of the name of Bechler, who issued a gold coinage of which I had seen several pieces. He received me very civilly, and I passed a great part of the day with him at his cottage in the woods. Bechler emigrated with a very clever young man, his son, from the Grand Duchy of

Baden, where he had been a gunmaker and goldsmith of
some reputation, and had acquired a considerable knowledge in the management of metals. He had resided
seven years in this country, and had established for himself a character for integrity, as well as skill in his
profession. I found him rather mystical and imaginative,
as many Germans are; and certainly if he had lived when
alchemy flourished, he would have been a conspicuous
operator in that inviting art. It was probably this bias
that induced him to settle in the Gold Region of North
Carolina, where his career had been a rather singular one,
but hitherto distinguished for much good sense.

The greater part of the small streams in this part of the
Gold Region, have more or less gold in them, so that
all the settlers upon the streams were engaged, more
or less, in washing for gold. Each of them possessing but
a small quantity, and there being no general purchaser,
it was an article not easily disposed of without taking the
trouble to go great distances. Bechler had also obtained
some in the usual manner, and having made a die, coined
his gold into five-dollar pieces, of the same intrinsic value
as the half-eagles of the United States, which are worth
five dollars each. He also coined pieces of the value of
two dollars and a half, and stamped the value, as well
as his own name, upon every piece that he coined. These,
after awhile, found their way to the Mint of the United
States, were assayed, and found to be correct. This
becoming known, all the gold-finders in his vicinity—and,
indeed, from greater distances—began to bring their gold
to his mint to be coined. At the period of my visit,
his gold coinage circulated more freely than that of the
United States, which was very scarce. He told me that
his books shewed that he had coined about two millions of

dollars from the gold found by the settlers; putting his name, with its weight and quality to every piece. On receiving the gold from the country people—which in this part of the Gold Region is alloyed with silver—he first reduced it to a common standard, then made the five-dollar pieces equal to those of the United States in value, and when coined, delivered it to the respective proprietors, deducting two per cent. for the seignorage. It would be in his power to take improper advantage of the confidence placed in him; but I heard of no instance of his having attempted this. Some of the gold of this region is alloyed with platina, the specific gravity of which, compared with that of gold, is as 21 to 19. He might, therefore, have made the difference in weight up with platina, which would have put fourteen per cent. into his pocket. As a metallurgist, he had all the skill necessary to do this; but when I mentioned the possibility of this, as an argument against its being received into general circulation, he answered that it was what an honest man would not do, and that if any man were to do it, he would soon be found out, for the gold did not remain long in circulation, since it found its way very soon to the United States Mint, where it was necessary for him to keep a good character.

Bechler's maxim was, that honesty is the best policy; and that maxim appeared to govern his conduct. I never was so pleased with observing transactions of business as those I saw at his house during the time I was there. Several country-people came with rough gold to be left for coinage: he weighed it before them and entered it in his book, where there was marginal room for noting the subsequent assay. To others he delivered the coin he had struck.

The most perfect confidence prevailed betwixt them, and the transactions were conducted with quite as much simplicity as those at a country grist-mill, where the miller deducts the toll for the grist he has manufactured. As gunsmiths, he and his son were pre-eminent for their ingenuity; they had invented various ingenious modes of firing rifles eight times in a minute. One with a chain for sixty caps, revolving by a catch of the trigger, was very neatly constructed, and was exceedingly curious. Young Bechler fired it off several times at a target placed at a distance of one hundred and sixty-five yards, and with great success. Having partaken of Mr. Bechler's frugal dinner, I walked over his farm with him, which consisted of four hundred acres, with several mineral veins running through it N.N.E. and S.S.W.; some of which were auriferous, but, as I thought, not at all promising. This was not Mr. Bechler's opinion, who was a great enthusiast about gold-mining, and entertained extraordinary mystical notions about mineral veins. Some of the specimens of auriferous rock were associated with arsenic; and in a tunnel which he had driven upon a vein, I observed talcose slate loaded with fine garnets. It appeared to me that he was in some danger of wasting the fair profits of his industry upon impracticable schemes, many of which his son did not approve of.

Highly gratified with my visit, I returned to my quarters at sunset, got a comfortable supper, and, by the side of a cheerful wood fire, wrote my letters and brought up my notes in peace and tranquillity in my bed-room.

September 21.—Having breakfasted early, I left my luggage under the care of my worthy host, Mr. Twitty, and mounted a horse he had procured for me, for an excursion into the mountains, directing my course to Major Forney's at Minersville. On my way I called at Bechler's, and directed him to have my name inlaid with the gold found on his own farm, on the barrel of one of his pistol rifles that kills at one hundred yards. From thence I rode to Jamestown, a straggling place in a valley something like the Nahcóochay Valley, in Georgia, but all turned topsy-turvy by the gold-diggers, who had utterly ruined these beautiful valleys for agricultural purposes. Continuing from hence, I reached the beautiful situation where Major Forney had established himself, and where he had made another desolation. His buildings were situated on a knoll in a lovely valley surrounded with lofty hills, which was defaced in every direction with piles of washed earth and gravel eight and ten feet high. Here I saw the first attempt to restore some fertility to the soil by paring the best part of the alluvial earth from the top, and throwing it on one side to be afterwards replaced when the subjacent gravel had been washed.

The general formation here was gneiss ; hornblende slate also abounded. Major Forney was a country-merchant and store-keeper as well as a gold-washer, and politely asked me to stay at his house, offering to accompany me in any excursions I was desirous of making. These kindnesses I gratefully accepted ; and after dinner we went to look at a vein called the Nichol's vein, running on the side of a hill east and west, and dipping to the north. The older veins, running N.N.E. and S.S.W., appeared to have been swept away from where the valley now is when it was excavated, but can be yet traced. The Nichol's vein is composed of a brittle, glossy, and fissile quartz, con-taining a good deal of galena, with copper pyrites, malachite, and blue carbonate of copper.   Specks of native gold are occasionally found in it.

On our return in the evening, I went to see the closing of the day's work at the gold-washing.   Twelve men were employed.   Major Forney had dug a trench through the alluvial deposits, about nine feet wide, and with a view to prevent the rich bottom-land from being utterly destroyed, had very laudably adopted the following process.   A small portion of the trench was dug until they came to the gravel containing the gold ; the metal being taken out of this by means of the rockers, the gravel was then thrown to the left of the trench, and covered with sand and loose soil at hand ; as fast as this was done other labourers pared off with spades the fertile soil laying on the top of that part of the trench which remained to be dug, and placed it at the top of the sand and loose soil till it had reached its former level.   The sand being now reinstated in every thing except the gold, was ready the next spring for being levelled with hoes and harrows, and for being planted with Indian corn. As soon as one trench was dug out and the gravel washed, another was commenced.   This was an excellent piece of work, and I had the satisfaction of seeing a crop of Indian corn that would average about fifty bushels per acre growing upon land that had been trenched the previous year.

Two hundred thousand dollars worth of native gold had been already taken out of this extensive bottom, of which a great many acres remain yet untouched.   The production in gold was said to amount to about four thousand five hundred dollars annually, whilst the cost of trenching and washing one acre was about one thousand dollars, the labour being performed by both white and black men.

The first received fifty cents or half a dollar per diem, and maintained themselves. They were natives of this mountainous country, were altogether illiterate, not knowing even their letters, and with very few exceptions their children received no education whatever. I looked into many of their huts, and it would be difficult to find any thing more rude and dirty. The women seemed to be very prolific, for it was not an uncommon thing to find a woman big with child suckling an infant in her arms, and screaming to a set of brats that were crawling about like kittens in every corner of a room without either windows or doors.* And thus they crawl through life without either religious or moral instruction. Yet upon inquiring of them, they all seemed to prefer their mountain life with all its disadvantages, the greatest of which unfortunately they seem to be totally insensible of.

The black men employed in washing were slaves, and appeared to be submissive in their manners and to work very hard. They were closely watched to prevent their secreting any pieces of gold they might find. Many beautiful minerals were found in these washings, fine tourmalines, crystallized hornblende, with extremely transparent specimens of rock crystal; a few brilliant diamonds, too, although very small, had been found, and some platina, of which I collected a few grains of very small size. From the general resemblance of this mineral district to that of the Ural district in Russia, it is far from being improbable that

* In one of these places there were so many children inside and outside the house, that when I enquired of the father, who was a bit of a wag, how many children he had, he answered: " He did not know for he never could get 'em to stand still till he counted 'em."

specimens of platina of greater magnitude, as well as other minerals corresponding to those in that district, will hereafter be found in the mountains of North Carolina. Major Forney, who had had a great deal of experience in washing for gold in this valley, says, that he uniformly finds the heaviest particles of gold lying nearest to the veins, and that he is able from long practice to recognize the gold of different veins, so that when country goldfinders bring their metal to his store, he knows at once what vein it comes from.

September 22.—After breakfast, I started for an excursion with Major Forney to Huntsville. On our way, we passed some fine-looking land, and crossed a ridge of hornblende slate. The valley at Huntsville had been washed with some success, much of the gold being in rough pieces and partly crystallized into curious shapes, specimens of which I purchased according to my custom to add to my cabinet. We visited a great many auriferous veins, which although they were larger than those at Dahlonega, in Georgia, did not appear to be so numerous or so productive. After a fatiguing ride we returned to our quarters. I found the population in the course of this day's ride of a very low cast, scarce superior to Indians in any thing but the use of tools. On our arrival at Major Forney's, I again attended the closing of the gold washings, and saw that the deposit in this valley was about twelve feet deep down to the talcose slate. At the surface, there was a fertile light red-coloured loam, then a dark-coloured clay, and lastly came the auriferous gravel about two feet deep, being the order in which these substances are deposited in Georgia. A large branch of poplar had been found this day lying upon the dark-coloured clay and covered with the red loam. It looked very fresh, and on taking it up, it smelt like soaked leather. Every fibre and layer of the wood was distinctly preserved, and being saturated with water it was heavy. On applying my knife to it, it cut easily and waxily, like soap, the wood being reduced to a quasi gelatinous consistency. Lower down in the deposit, and just within the gravel, was a portion of the root of a hickory tree, just as fresh looking as the poplar, it was in the same state as the poplar and smelt exactly like it. The overseer told me he had frequently found similar pieces of wood pressed into the top part of the slate. If these facts prove that the country was wooded before the gravel was deposited, there is reason to suppose also *that it was inhabited,* for on the 6th of September, Mr. John Ewing C— shewed me an antique Indian stone pipe which one of his labourers had dug out of the slate near Dahlonega beneath the gravel. The talcose slate is often soft and decomposed for several inches below the gravel; but on applying the pickaxe to it, the dry, hard rock is soon reached, so that there is no room to doubt that it is the true talcose slate.

The soft state of the wood found under these circumstances suggests some reflections. Lignite is found in the tertiary and in some higher beds in the series which have been left dry; but these woods found in the auriferous deposits, are not in the state of lignite, but of wood saturated with water, with its structure softened down to a saponaceous consistency. The inference, therefore, presents itself, that these last specimens have been deposited at a period posterior to the tertiary beds, and that the excavation of these valleys in the Gold Region, the general modification of the surface, and the deposit of gold and gravel with wood in the valleys, may have been produced by the *historic deluge.* In this view Mr. C——'s pipe is evidence of the existence of man here at that period. Has there not been too much haste in abandoning the opinion once generally entertained, that a great portion of what geologists have called diluvium, was a result of the Noachic Deluge ?

CHAPTER LXIII.

September 23.—After breakfast we again mounted our horses and proceeded towards Rutherfordton. On our way we examined a promising looking N.N.E. vein, which cuts the valley obliquely. Forney said the gravel deposit was very rich where the vein touched the valley, and became poorer in proportion to its distance from it. The principal rock here was gneiss with occasional garnets. After looking at various veins, we came at length to Wallace's vein, which I thought the richest lode I had seen. It contained an unusual quantity of dark sulphuret of iron, and where it was above the water-level, and was affected by the atmosphere, was very much decomposed, and showed a great deal of gold in the folds of the crystallized pyrites. It was an exceedingly beautiful ore. I have seen a shaft down which the solid ore—a copper pyrites containing gold— was in a hard state, quite brilliant, and undecomposed. Two veins were here parallel to each other equally rich. At one place the ground was strewed over with pieces of massive sulphuret of iron, shewing gold, but not in the cubical form. This estate, containing three most promising

veins, belonged to Major Forney, and consisted of four
hundred acres of land with very ample and commodious
water power. The country was singularly beautiful, perfectly healthy, and if any confidence may be placed in gold
mining, I thought it one of the most promising places I
had seen. Many of these places were certainly very
productive ; but all their owners *appeared to be embarrassed in their circumstances.*

This perhaps can be explained ; they come here without
capital, buy a place on credit, apply their profits to the
purchase of slaves, and to the unavoidable expences of the
management of their undertakings ; and not contented with
waiting until they are rewarded by a patient industry that
would in the end release them from mortgage and debt,
they endeavour to monopolize every new place that
promises to be productive, purchasing them at the most
extravagant prices on credit, so that the profits they
obtain at each locality are insufficient to keep down their
debts, and they are harassed to death by their creditors.
They believe themselves to be in the possession of
unbounded wealth at the moment when every body
acquainted with their affairs believes them insolvent. If
an opportunity presents itself of selling any part of their
property, they feel as if they were parting with a mountain
of gold, and ask twenty times more than the property is
worth, and so never sell it at all, but drag on a hurried
and painful existence, the slaves of their creditors, till they
are forced to a general liquidation, and lose every thing.
This I found to be pretty much the history of all the
large undertakers in gold mining who enter upon it without
capital.

We reached Rutherfordton near sunset, loaded with fine
specimens. On the road Major Forney told me an anec-

dote about bees. He had an apiary at his place, and I had remarked that the honey was very fine. He said that was because it had been a bad season for fruit, and that he had remarked when peaches, apples, and pears were plentiful, the bees were apt to resort altogether to them to drink their juices, and to neglect the flowers; so that when the fruit season was over, they first devoured their small store of honey, then went marauding to other hives that did not belong to them, and lost many of their numbers in fighting. At such seasons, the dead bees about the hives are very numerous, many dying from their wounds and others from starvation. Steady occupation, therefore, it would seem keeps bees honest as well as men, and idle indulgences produce in the end mischief and crime.

September 24.—Having classed and labelled all my beautiful specimens; I remained after breakfast in my room writing letters, being unable to procure a horse on account of a camp meeting held in the neighbourhood for which every animal was engaged. At 2 P.M. a family arrived in the stage-coach from Asheville whom I had known at the Warm Springs. I dined in company with them when they were obliging enough to invite me to a country place they were going to. In the afternoon I took a long walk through the woods in the neighbourhood. This was certainly a very pleasing country and seemed to be quite salubrious.

September 25. — After breakfast, I walked out to Bechler's and other places in his neighbourhood. The old man was very glad to see me, and conducted me to various interesting places. I obtained some specimens of gneiss with transparent garnets from his tunnel; the arsenical rock came in at eighty feet deep from the surface. The whole of this neighbourhood was remarkable for the abundance of massive auriferous pyrites it contained, generally more or less decomposed, for about eighty feet from the surface. I observed that the rocks adjacent to the decomposed ones were sometimes tinged with a vermillion red. In many of the veins, however, the pyrites were not massive, but consisted of detached cubical crystals. These also, when they had been exposed to moisture, were partially or entirely decomposed, and the cavities in the crystals frequently contained crystals of sulphur, and then laminated gold. When the sulphuret has undergone this chemical action, the plates which form the skeleton of the cube appear in some instances to be silex, in others to be native gold. The gold appears to be perfectly covered with the sulphuret, and only exhibits itself when heat is applied. In some of the gold ores the quartz is blotched with dark purple-coloured spots, which show no gold under the most powerful microscope; but upon exposing them to heat, a small globule of gold appears surrounded by a dark stain. I suppose the gold to exist in the sulphuret in such a thin leafy state, that on application of the heat, the sulphur is driven off, and the lamina melted into a minute globule. The decomposition of the massive sulphurets beneath the surface is the effect of a spontaneous combustion produced in the manner of some shales and coal mines, and is attended with an extrication of heat sufficient to colour the rocks. These facts are deserving the attention of philosophers engaged in the discussion of "central heat." Amongst other rocks, I found one that was quartzose and brittle, containing a fine steel-grey-looking metal resembling tellurium. Mr. Bechler having inlaid my name on the rifle with native gold, I paid him for it, and took a hearty leave of him and his worthy son, and again returned to my lodgings loaded with specimens. Amongst

other practical observations, Mr. Bechler told me that the
finest gold is obtained from the streams in the winter,
because in cold weather the quicksilver only has an affinity
for the purer quality of gold, whilst in warm weather it is
more active, and takes up various metals. I saw also at
Bechler's a very sensible barometer in a tub, containing
nitrate of silver and a piece of copper, the silver floating in
fine weather, and sinking on the appearance of rain.

September 26.—This morning I walked to see a vein of
mammillary quartz, running east and west, about two
miles from Rutherfordton which was very curious. In
every direction something new was to be found in this
remarkable mineral country ; either auriferous veins, or
lodes varied with large plates of talc and other interesting
minerals. The hornblende lands appeared to be uniformly
fertile, and nothing could be more rural and picturesque
than the general surface of this salubrious country. Every
cottage had its collection of curiosities and specimens of
native gold. A more agreeable country for a mineralogist
cannot be imagined, and I prepared for my departure with
regret. Having made a last and hearty dinner at my
worthy landlord's, Mr. Twitty, and drank a bottle of his
good London porter, I got into the stage-coach once more
for Lincolnton.

We had twenty-three miles to drive to Schenck's, a house
upon the road where we were to sleep, and it would have
been an agreeable drive enough, but for the crazy conduct
of the incorrigible driver. The road went through a
pleasant woodland country, varied with gentle hills and
vales watered by the sources of the Santee River, with a few
shabby taverns here and there   The fellow had no sooner
got out of Rutherfordton, than he whipped his horses into
a gallop, which I was not sorry at, as the road was tolerably
good ; but this was only to arrive quicker at the first tavern,

where he drank rum enough to make him noisy, talkative, and obstinate. I could not prevail upon him to leave the place for near an hour, and when he got on the box, he lashed his horses again into a gallop, cursing and swearing in the most atrocious manner. Again he stopped at another tavern, and immediately flew to the rum bottle, treating all the blackguards at the place, and making the most foolish bets with them. The fellows that kept these low taverns were as bad as himself, the rum seemed to make them all supremely happy, and they cared for nothing. At last, by coaxing, I got him on the box again, but he was in such an inflamed state with the liquor he had drank, that I soon saw he had very little judgment about his reins, and on we went at full gallop, continually grazing the stumps, forty times on the point of being upset whilst at full speed. There was no remedy; once or twice I thought of knocking him off the box and taking the reins myself; but it was a perilous experiment, and, at length, I made up my mind to remain quiet and meet the chances with as much composure as I could. If he had upset us, it was very probable we should both of us had our limbs broke, and remained in the woods all night; but it was not so ordained, and we reached our destination without accident. At the supper-table I found two travelling methodist preachers, strange uncouth persons, and upon my relating the conduct of the driver to the landlord in their presence, one of them asked him, " if there was no tea-total society in the neighbourhood," upon which he answered, " No, I reckon we are all rum-total in these parts."

September 27.—The driver for the next stage, twenty-two miles to Lincolnton, came to call me at two in the morning. It was so dark when we left the place, that if this fellow had been as drunken and crazy as the last, it would have been good policy to have had our limbs broken before we left the house, as we should have been within reach of some assistance. My only hope was, that at that hour of the night the landlords at the rum cabins on the road would not think it worth their while to leave their beds to minister to his wants, and so it turned out, for although we stopped to water the horses at various places, he contrived to remain sober, and indeed conducted himself very well, for we reached Lincolnton at 7 A.M. On reaching the hotel, which was a tolerably good one, I found a note from Judge G—, informing me that he had sent a horse and servant for me, hoping that I would pay him a visit, and stating that his son would accompany me on any excursions I wished to make. I was obliged to decline this very obliging offer which would have materially interfered with my arrangements, although regretting that I deprived myself of the great pleasure of witnessing another instance of the refined hospitality which so much distinguishes southern gentlemen, and which comes so gratefully to a traveller, exposed to be rudely handled as he occasionally is in this interesting but half-civilized country. I therefore continued on to Salisbury.

About ten miles from Lincolnton there was a strong bed of iron ore, and a furnace for smelting it. It was rather a curious ore, being mixed up with a singularly unctuous talcose slate. There is a great deal of syenite here, which appears to succeed to the gneiss. We crossed the Catawba, then very low, owing to the great drought. At twenty-six miles from Lincolnton the country ceased to be hilly, and softened down into a gently undulating plane. We reached Salisbury at half-past 6 P.M., where I was so fortunate as to get a room to myself and a tolerable supper. The walls and the floors were covered with dirt as much as they were at the Warm Springs, but this is generally the case where slavery exists, for dirt is not dirty in the eyes of the negro, and the master is too lazy to give directions to have it removed. I observed to-day that the distances were marked by notches cut in the trees, or in posts by the road-side; every notch representing a mile from the principal place.

September 28.—Having engaged a horse the previous evening, I mounted soon after the dawn and rode four miles to Coughenhauer's to examine a basaltic dyke running through a bed of granite, containing large crystals of feldspar. It consisted of loose joints, almost of the shape of basaltic prisms, of various sizes, some a foot in diameter, others only an inch, and being generally well-defined pentagons. The dyke was about one hundred yards in breadth, and consisted of a vast congeries of small prisms detached from each other at the surface. Upon examin-ing the granite at some distance from the dyke, I found many prisms wedged in with it. I passed the day in investigating various localities containing different minerals. Granite and syenite, traversed by numerous lodes of different qualities, were the prevailing rocks. Iron was abundant; and I saw numerous traces of copper.

September 29.—About 10 A.M., I got into the stage-coach again, and drove to Charlotte, in the Mecklenburgh County, where I arrived between 7 and 8 P.M.; and having obtained a clean room and a tolerable supper, I retired at an early hour to rest.

September 30.—After breakfast I revisited the dyke of feldspar I had seen in 1835, the most curious and beautiful mineral I have ever seen.* The dyke is very broad, and consists of what the Germans call weisstein with dark prisms in great abundance and of various sizes. Some-

* I have deposited a large tablet of this mineral in the British Museum.

times it is in joints, and then the natural faces, presenting
sections of the prisms, look very much like the skin of the
spotted leopard. Here I passed the greater part of the
day selecting specimens of this singular mineral.

October 1.—This day I passed entirely in the house,
bringing up my correspondence and arranging my
numerous minerals to forward by a waggon that was going
to the north in a day or two. This was a quiet little
village, and seemed to be kept up principally by the
mining interest. A company works a considerable gold
mine in the neighbourhood under the direction of Mr.
Bissel, a person of great experience and intelligence, and to
whom I was indebted for many attentions.

October 2.—As soon as breakfast was over, I accompanied that gentleman to a copper mine belonging to him,
looking at two or three promising lodes on the way. The
copper vein ran east and west, and was nearly vertical.
The rock in which the vein ran was hornblende, the country
being very flat, without hills or undulations. Copper, gold,
iron, and galena, were associated in this vein. Mr. Bissel
treated it first for gold, and laid by the carbonate of copper
for smelting. The mine was a very promising one, and was
then upon trial. Being joined by another gentleman and
his daughter, Mr. Bissel took us after a severe morning's
work to a fine spring, where we found an unexpected and
most gratifying load (not lode) of cold roasted chickens,
bread and butter, Irish ale, Madeira and Champagne of an
excellent quality. Having made a patient and successful
assay of these good things, and forwarded them on their
road to our own veins, we examined on our return a
portion of Capp's gold vein, upon which they have worked
about sixty feet. It consisted of quartz with auriferous
sulphurets of iron, and its course was about N.E. and S.W.

This vein in some places was very voluminous on the surface, and its continuity had been traced for several miles. Beautiful specimens of stalactitic tarnished iron, of a shining bronze colour, were contained in the cavities.   Having selected some exceedingly fine specimens we returned to Charlotte a little after sunset.   It may be remarked here that there is a general disposition in all the rocks in this part of the country to assume the prismatic form.

October 3.—The greater part of the day I passed at the Charlotte mine, the specimens from which, and those which Mr. Bissel was so obliging as to give me, added to my other collections, weighed two hundred weight, so that I was obliged to sit up the greater part of the night to lable them to prevent confusion, intending to leave them to be forwarded to me by some conveyance or other.

October 4.—At half-past 1 A.M., I again entered the stage-coach.   It was here my bad fortune to find a party of three in the coach, two of them confirmed blackguards like those who were passengers from Asheville.   One of these wretches kept singing and screaming all the night long, and they blasphemed in such an atrocious manner that I think I never passed more painful hours.   I was, therefore, driven as soon as the day dawned to get on the box with the driver to avoid as much as I could their disgusting conversation.   At 7 A.M. we stopped at Concord, and got a wretched breakfast.   Thence I proceeded thirty-eight miles to Lexington, the scoundrels inside keeping up their disorderly conduct all the way; having, however, secured my seat with the driver and formed an alliance with him, and having the country to look at, I was less annoyed by them; but finding upon reaching Lexington that these fellows were going on all night in the stage-coach, I had my luggage taken off and abandoned the concern, having determined to take the next stage-coach, and amuse myself by examining the country; any thing appeared to me preferable to the company of such reprobates.

This is the effect of frequent elections, universal suffrage, and the doctrines of perfect equality. The first are constantly throwing all those who ought to be engaged in industrious pursuits into a frenzied agitation for or against men and measures they know nothing about; the second gives to the legionary idle, depraved, lawless scoundrels, the precious privileges that can only be safely confided to those comparatively few intelligent members of society who have a personal interest in maintaining order and good government; and the last only provoke them to offer every sort of insult and hindrance to those whom they perceive are not of their class. Over such wretches the law appears to have little or no control. If a magistrate has virtue enough to attempt to control them, they combine against him, he becomes a marked man, and is denounced as *the enemy of the sovereign people ;* and whoever is represented as that enemy, he is sure, whether he be high or low, to be turned out of his office. Under such a system, society is at length almost left without sober examples, and generations after generations are likely to be left with nothing but bad ones to follow. If the devil kept pigeon-holes with *improved* forms of government in them, as the Abbé Siéyes is said to have done, he could not have imagined anything more fatal to religion, morality, integrity and sober manners, or more sure to accomplish the ruin of a nation, than frequent elections, universal suffrage, and perfect equality.

On entering the inn, I found it full of people, and conceived a bad augury as to the accommodations I should get, but they gave me something to eat and a comfortable cup of tea. On requesting to be shewn to my room, to my great surprise I was shewn to a very comfortable bed-room, with a nice clean bed in it, as though all had been intended exclusively for my use. On looking round, however, I saw various bandboxes, and a few female garments hanging upon pegs, so that I perceived I had *déniché'd* some of the ladies of the family. The walls too were clean, and there was a carpet near the bed-side. What excellent luck, thought I, as I slipped into the clean sheets!

October 5.—I was awoke early by some giggling young girls playing on a piano in the next room, which was only separated from my bed-room by a very thin wainscot partition; and grateful for the attention that had been paid to me, I hastened to make my toilette and give up the room to the fair ladies upon whose comforts I felt conscious I had intruded. Having to pass through the parlour where the piano was, I found it occupied by an Alabama family that had arrived in the stage-coach from Washington. After having a comfortable breakfast, and taken a look at the village, which is a rural and pleasing-looking place built upon a hill with an undulating country around it, I engaged a horse and set out upon my adventures, directing my course to a gold mine of which I had heard much said, at a place called Conrad's Hill. The intervening country was flat compared with that to the north-west, but had an undulating surface, with many knolls and small valleys. In these features, all the parts of the Gold Region where I have been resemble each other remarkably, and the fact warrants the inference that all the formations in the Gold Region have come into place and been modified at the same time and by the same causes.

Conrad's Hill is a knoll consisting entirely of auriferous veins. The main lode runs N.N.E. is a very stout one, and is intersected by cross veins. They were at this time working upon a productive vein of auriferous oxide of copper, and here I found some pretty specimens of fibrous malachite. The mine abounded in micaceous iron. Dr. Austin, the superintendent, was very attentive to me, and politely insisted upon my dining at his house where some agreeable ladies were on a visit. How much it would be to be lamented if the United States with a magnificent territory, comprehending all the elements of national respectability, and containing so many estimable and accomplished persons, were permanently to be abandoned to the rule of demagogues and their turbulent sovereign people !

Having passed the day very agreeably, I returned in the evening to Lexington, with the intention of intruding again upon those benevolent ladies whose comfortable room I had occupied; but I found that a court of justice was sitting in the town, that some fresh travellers with ladies had arrived, and that difficulties existed about lodging them. It looked exceedingly probable, therefore, that I should be asked to give up my comfortable quarters, and go to some poly-bedded room with the judge and the grand jury perhaps. How could I have refused ? The dilemma pressed upon me very painfully, so considering how it was to be met, it struck me that if I took possession of the room and got into the bed before they had the pain of proposing and I of deciding, that I should promote a salutary economy of feeling on both sides; so at nine o'clock without saying a word, I very quietly transferred myself from the parlour into the bed-room. About half-an-hour afterwards the door was opened and closed, and I heard a gentle, squeaking voice say, " Well, I declare if he ain't got into the bed!" Never was anything more true spoken!

October 6.—Having engaged a carriage, I went in it twenty-five miles to a Mr. Roswell King's copper mine, about three miles south of Jamestown. The vein, which appeared to be a very rich one, runs N.N.E, is from two to four feet thick, and has been penetrated upwards of one hundred feet by blasting through a rock composed of quartz and mica, but not a regularly constituted gneiss. The ore is very beautiful, and I collected some handsome specimens containing native gold. Gold, more or less, seemed to be a constituent mineral in all the veins in this part of the country; but this place could not be properly considered as in the Gold Region, the copper having supplanted it. When this part of the country shall receive a more minute investigation, I should not be surprised to learn that many valuable veins of other metals are discovered, for the general appearance of the country, and that of various lodes at the surface, none of which had been worked, indicated decisively a metalliferous district. At night, I returned to Jamestown to sleep, to take the stage-coach in the morning.

October 7.—At daybreak I got into the stage and drove to Greensborough to breakfast, and from thence continued to Hillsborough, the principal rocks being a prismatic greenstone with a gneissoid granite. The land appeared good on approaching Hillsborough, being a red decomposed greenstone resembling that of the south-west mountain in Virginia, upon which the finest tobacco is produced.

October 8.—At a very early hour I continued my route to Raleigh, the capital of North Carolina, crossing a belt of slates about ten miles before we reached Raleigh; this is probably the belt of auriferous slate which constitutes the eastern edge of the Gold Region, and of which I had seen many fine specimens. At Raleigh I took a look at the new capitol which is a handsome building, not quite finished; and is built of a very beautiful species of granite drawn from a quarry in the vicinity. About half-past 3 P.M. I was in motion again in the stage-coach for Gaston, on the Roanoke. We supped at Louisburgh at half-past 10 P.M., and travelled all night.

October 9.—Passing through a little village called Warrenton, we reached Gaston on the Virginia side of the Roanoke, at the station of the Petersburgh railroad. At 3 P.M., I got into the train for Petersburgh, and accomplished the sixty-four miles in six hours. Having refreshed myself at the Petersburgh hotel, I entered into the stage-coach once more at 11 P.M. and reached Richmond (twenty-four miles) at 3 A.M., and an hour afterwards got into the train for Fredericsburgh, where we arrived at 9 A.M. From this place I drove in an hour to the steamer on the Potomac, on board of which I dressed and shaved, and at half-past 5 P.M. reached Washington, having happily accomplished a journey of about five thousand miles.

THE END.

INDEX

ABERT, LT. COL. JOHN J., directs
geological surveys, 1:xxxii–xxxvii,
xli, 4; role in Mather feud,
1:xxxviii–xli
Abolitionists, 2:151. *See also* Slavery
Adam, Negro servant, 2:188, 191,
194
Agriculture, F's interest in, 1:xxviii,
xxxii, 205, 319, 328. *See also*
Corn, various crops
Alabama, 2:171; F's travels, 1:xxiv,
2:179, 182–203; railroad, 2:186–
188
Albany, Ill., 2:134
Albany, N.Y., 1:xxviii
Alexander, ———, tavernkeeper,
2:266
Algonquin Indians, 1:107
Allegheny Mtns., 1:3, 17, 44; geology, 1:9, 13, 16, 18, 20–22, 29,
30, 31, 2:211, 259; coal seams,
1:20–22, 32; names, 2:238
Allegheny River, 1:33, 34, 35, 38,
42, 43, 61, 62
Alliquippa, Indian queen, 1:42
Alston. *See* Alton, Ill.
Alton, Ill., described, 2:45
American Fur Co., Mendota, 1:259,
260; cart trail, 1:328, 329; accounts, 1:408. *See also* Fur trade,
individual traders
American Geological Society, 1:
xxxii
Amherst, Sir Jeffery, 1:116, 117, 120
Amherstburg, Ont., 1:95
Amhurst. *See* Amherst, Sir Jeffery

Ansley (John D.) South Copper
Diggings, 2:116
Appalachian Mtns., 2:238; described, 2:251–255, 266
Arikara Indians, 2:57
Arkansas, 2:225; Ozark survey,
1:xxxiv, xlv; lead deposits, 2:35
Aroostook War, 1:xliii
Asheville, N.C., 2:339; F visits,
1:xxvi, 2:313–317, 323
Ashley, William H., fur trader,
1:xxiii; 2:52
Assiniboin Indians, 1:307, 351;
chief, 1:387
Assiniboine River, 1:351, 416, 2:13
Atkinson, Gen. Henry, 2:55
Audubon, John James, artist, 1:xxx
Austin, Dr. ———, miner, 2:349
Aztalan, 2:103

B———, COL. *See* Bomford, Col.
George
B———, Gen. *See* Brady, Gen.
Hugh S.
B———, Jacob. *See* Barker, Jacob
B———, Lt. *See* Bomford, Lt.
James V.
B———, Mrs. *See* Biddle, Mrs.
Thomas
Baby, François, trader, 1:117n, 119
Baby, Jacques D., trader, 1:117n,
119
Bad Axe River, 1:222, 223, 2:20, 21
Badin, Fr. Stephen T., curé, 1:101
Bagby, Edmund P., political speech,
2:192–194
Bagsby. *See* Bagby, Edmund P.

Baker, Benjamin F., trader, 2:9, 12
Baker, Romelius L., at Economy, 1:65, 66, 68, 80
Bank of the U.S., 2:108n, 112
Baraboo Hills, 1:192
Baratz, Detun de. *See* Detandebaratz, Martial
Barker (?), Jacob, 2:98n
Bath Springs. *See* Berkeley Springs, W. Va.
Bears, 1:387, 2:154, 204, 326; Sioux name, 1:325
Beaupré, Louis, voyageur, 1:158, 160, 163, 168, 169, 170, 216, 229, 235, 249, 250, 2:2, 29, 37
Beaver Creek, Sioux name, 1:323
Beaver River, 1:91, 92
Bechler. *See* Bechtler, Christopher
Bechtler, Augustus, 2:327, 330
Bechtler, Christopher, goldsmith, 2:327–330, 331, 339–341
Bedford, Pa., 1:xviii; springs described, 1:30–32
Bell, John A., Cherokee Indian, 2:224
Belland, Mrs. Henry (Mary Jeffries), 1:364
Bellefonte, Ala., 2:203
Belmont, Wis., 1:xxiii, 2:67
Bentley, Richard, publisher, 1:xvii, xxii n, xlvi–xlix
Bentley, Samuel, printer, 1:xlvi
Berkeley Springs, W. Va., described, 1:16
Berry, ———, tavernkeeper, 2:220
Bethlehem, Pa., 1:65n
Biddle, Edward, 1:144
Biddle, Mrs. Thomas, widow, 2:58, 59, 60
Big Beaver. *See* Beaver River
Big Leg, Sioux chief, 1:298
Big Stone Lake, 1:xxi, 319, 373, 378, 383, 388, 395, 411, 2:7, 8; Sioux band, 1:366, 399, 400; described, 1:398; name, 1:401
Birbeck, Morris. *See* Birkbeck, Morris
Bird's Point, Ill., described, 2:163
Birkbeck, Morris, 1:61, 2:66

Bissell, J. Humphrey, miner, 2:345, 346
Black Dog, Sioux village, 1:284
Black Hawk, Sauk chief, 1:222
Black River, 1:124, 126
Blacksmith, Winnebago Indian, 1:163
Blairsville, Ga., 2:297
Bliss, Maj. John, commandant, 1:xxvii, 258, 260, 263, 265–267, 278, 288, 2:5, 9, 10, 12, 14, 15, 149
Bliss, Mrs. John, 1:260, 265, 266, 267, 278, 282; 2:5, 9, 10, 12, 14, 15
Bliss, John H., comments on F, 1:xvi n, lxi; at Fort Snelling, 1:266, 267, 281, 282, 283, 2:9; accompanies F, 2:12, 15–18, 30, 32, 35, 39, 49
Bloody Bridge, 1:103, 119, 120
Bloomington. *See* Muscatine, Ia.
Blue Earth River, 2:1, 13, 35, 42, 129; Le Sueur's mine, 1:2, 279–281, 301–304; Sioux name, 1:301; described, 1:301, 303, 304, 306
Blue Mounds, 2:105, 124; described, 2:87
Blue Ridge Mtns., 1:9; described, 2:256, 264, 272, 275–280, 322, 323
Blue River, 2:119; described, 1:201; lead diggings, 2:120
Bluff in the Water. *See* Trempeauleau
Blunt, Ainsworth E., mission farmer, 2:213, 216
Bogy, Joseph, Sr., "judge," 2:139
Boice. *See* Boyce, John
Bois Franc River. *See* Robert Creek
Bolivar, Tenn., 2:182
Bomford, Col. George, 1:125
Bomford, Lt. James V., 1:125, 129
Bonibou. *See* Baraboo Hills
Boone, Daniel, 2:323
Boyce, John, tavernkeeper, 2:139, 155, 156
Braddock, Gen. Edward, defeat, 1:xviii, 56–59, 111; in French and Indian War, 1:36, 44–54

Jacques River. *See* James River
James River, 1:384, 415
Jamestown, N.C., 2:331, 350
Jamet, Lt. John, 1:115n
Jarrett, Devereaux, landlord, 2:264, 307
Jarvis, Dr. Nathan S., 1:264, 267
Jasper, Tenn., 2:190
Jefferson Barracks, 2:55
Jeffrey. *See* Jeffries, Joseph
Jeffries, Joseph, trader, 1:364
Jeffries, Mary (Mrs. Henry Belland), 1:364
Jocássay. *See* Jocassee
Jocassee River, 2:272
Johnston, George (?), 1:254
Jolliet, Louis, route, 1:xxi
Joncaire, Chevalier François Chabert de, 1:39
Jones, Evan, missionary, 2:232, 233, 234, 237
Jones, George W., Wisconsin congressman, 2:122

KAHKAHINHAHAH. *See* Credit River
Kearney, Col. *See* Kearny, Lt. Col. Stephen W.
Kearney, Lt. Col. Stephen W., 1:xxiii, 2:42
Keating, William H., 1:xxxvii
Keeowee. *See* Keowee River
Kendall's (James) Diggings, copper, 2:114
Kennedy, Allen, tavernkeeper, 2:210, 216, 218
Kentucky, 1:206n, 2:323; F's travels, 2:163–170, 172, 318
Keokuk, Ia., 2:42
Keowee River, 2:266
King, ——, gold miner, 2:260
King, Roswell, copper mine owner, 2:350
Kinnikinnick, 1:265, 325
Kittle, ——, steamboat captain, 2:170–172, 174–176
Kittle, Mrs. ——, 2:174–176
Knoxville, Tenn., 2:188, 189, 190

L——, MAJ. *See* Loomis, Maj. Gustavus
La Butte, Pierre, 1:119

Lac le Boeuf. *See* Buffalo Lake
Lac qui Parle Mission, Sioux, 1:xxii, liv, lx, 307, 309, 323, 336, 339–343, 349–351, 370; missionaries, 1:348, 355–357, 358, 370, 409
Lac qui Parle River, Sioux name, 1:339
La Crosse, Wis., 2:20; name, 1:228
"Lady Marshall," steamboat, 2:166
Lafayette, Marquis de, at St. Louis, 2:59–61
La Guerre, ——, 2:142
Lahontan, Louis A., 1:2, 108, 280
Lake Calhoun, Sioux village, 2:10
Lake Erie, 1:38, 48; geology, 1:92, 205, 274; steamboats, 1:93–95; as commercial artery, 1:206, 207, 212
Lake Michigan, 2:90; steamboat travel, 1:148–150; water action, 1:151–153, 156
Lake Monona, 2:94, 99, 101, 102
Lake of the Rushes. *See* Puckaway Lake
Lake of the Spirit. *See* Devils Lake
Lake Ontario, 1:156, 274
Lake Pepin, 1:237, 241n, 288, 2:18; trading post, 1:247–249; Sioux name, 1:248; described, 1:249–251, 271–273; French post, 1:250
Lake St. Clair, described, 1:123
Lake Traverse, 1:343, 373; lignite, 1:319, 2:13; described, 1:382–385, 388, 396, 415; name, 1:383; Sioux at, 1:383, 385, 402
Lake Winnebago, Indian village, 1:170–174, 239; geology, 1:204
Lake Winnipeg, 1:1, 415, 2:13
L'Amirant, Louis, voyageur, 1:158, 169, 197, 216, 218, 242, 297, 334, 366, 397, 412, 2:2, 37; Sioux interpreter, 1:235–237, 241
La Montagne de Trombalo. *See* Trempealeau
Lancaster, Wis., 2:121
Land speculation, 2:167, 182, 221; Missouri, 2:74–77, 149; Wisconsin, 2:77–79, 89, 97–99, 105–109; Iowa, 2:134–136
La Rocque, Augustin, Jr., Indian

Stephenson, Matthew F., gold seeker, 2:246

Sterrit (?), Squire Preston, 2:287–290

Stevens, Rev. Jedediah D., missionary, 2:11

Stevenson. See Stephenson, Charles

Stevenson, Dr. See Stephenson, Matthew F.

Stewart, Sir William D., 1:xxiii, 2:56, 62

Stitt, William, 2:12

Stout's Creek, 2:143, 146

Sturgeon, Winnebago chief, 1:182

Sugar River, 2:87

Sugarloaf Creek, 2:280

Swan Lake, Sioux name, 1:309

T, JOHN SMITH, 2:158

T———, R. C. See Taylor, Richard C.

Tagliaferro. See Taliaferro, Lawrence

Taliaferro, Lawrence, comments on F, 1:lx; Indian agent, 1:278, 281, 2:10

Taliaferro, Mrs. Lawrence (Elizabeth), 1:278, 282, 2:10

Talking Rock Creek, 2:284

Tall Island. See High Island Creek

Tallulah Falls, 2:264, 270, 307; described, 2:272, 305

Tate, ———, tavernkeeper, 2:225, 228

Taylor, Richard C., F's companion, 1:xxiii, lvii, 2:64, 70, 94, 95

Taylor, Sarah. See Davis, Mrs. Jefferson

Taylor, Col. Zachary, commandant, 1:xxi, xxiii, xxvi, 213–215, 222, 2:24, 28, 128, 130

Tchaypehamonee. See Little Crow

Tchoiestoiéh River. See Nottley River

Temperance societies, 1:28

Tennessee, 2:204; F's travels, 1:xxiv, 2:177–182, 188–190, 210–221, 229; militia, 2:201, 206, 212, 294; gold, 2:225, 226. See also Cherokee Indians

Tennessee River, 1:xxiv, 2:163, 166, 285; described, 2:170, 172–174, 177, 179–184, 197–199, 203–205, 207–210; headwaters, 2:275. See also Steamboats and steamboating

Terrapin Mtn., 2:275

Terre Bleu. See Blue Earth River

Terribaux. See Faribault, Jean B.

Terribaux Island. See Pike Island

Tesnattee Creek, 2:297

Tessentee River. See Tesnattee Creek

Tetrao cupido. See Grouse

Texas, 1:xxxiv

Thompson, Stephen (?), guide, 2:206–210

Tobacco, smoking, 1:liii, 136, 260, 263, 265, 344, 346, 2:5, 22–25, 30, 45, 61, 128, 294; as crop, 2:178

Toccoa Falls, described, 2:263, 306

Tolula, Tolulah Falls. See Tallulah Falls

Towaliga Creek, Spanish fort, 2:293

Tracy, ———, trader, 1:115

Traverse des Sioux, 1:409; traders, 1:lvi, 298, 316, 317, 2:3

Trempealeau, Wis., bluff described, 1:230, 235, 236; Sioux name, 1:231, 2:20

Triana, Ala., 2:198

Trollope, Frances, author, 1:xv, xvii

Trombalo. See Trempealeau

Tugaloo River, 2:264, 307

Turkey River, 2:29

Turkeys, sold, 2:53, 138; wild, 2:156, 204

Tuscumbia, Ala., 1:xxiv, 2:194, 211; described, 2:184–186, 191, 239

Tuscumbia, Courtland & Decatur Railway Co., 2:184, 186–188

Twelve Mile Creek, 2:271

Twitty, William L., landlord, 2:327, 330, 341

Tychoberah. See Four Lakes

UNAYKAY MTNS. See Unicoi Mtns.

Unicoi Mtns., 2:270, 282, 312, 315, 316, 322; Indian name, 2:221;